IMAGES
of America

BEDFORD

On the cover: The Heitger brothers, who owned the Heitger Hardware Store on the east side of the public square in Bedford, are showing a big catch of fish. This picture was taken in 1910, and the fish were caught in White River, which runs through the southern part of Lawrence County.

IMAGES
of America

BEDFORD

Maxine Kruse

ARCADIA
PUBLISHING

ISBN 978-0-7385-4055-9

Published by Arcadia Publishing
Charleston, South Carolina

Printed in the United States of America

Library of Congress Catalog Card Number: 2006920844

For all general information contact Arcadia Publishing at:
Telephone 843-853-2070
Fax 843-853-0044
E-mail sales@arcadiapublishing.com
For customer service and orders:
Toll-Free 1-888-313-2665

Visit us on the Internet at www.arcadiapublishing.com

This book is dedicated to all the people who have had a love for history and genealogy. These dedicated researchers are preserving the past for future generations.

Contents

Acknowledgments

Without the help of special people, this book could not have been written. Thanks must be given to Larry King, president of Lawrence County Historical and Genealogical Society, and Joyce Shepherd who works diligently to preserve and save our history. The early historian and author, Jim Guthrie, and the correspondents Zora Askew and Bernice Martin, must also be recognized for their contributions to future generations. These predecessors have preserved the history of "The Land of Limestone." Most of the photographs herein are the compliments of the Lawrence County Historical and Genealogical Society, while others are from the author's collection. I am indebted to my good friends Mary Margaret Stipp and Mary Johnson for their expertise in proofreading.

I also wish to thank my editor at Arcadia Publishing, Anna Wilson, for helping me with the task, as well as friends who provided some photographs.

INTRODUCTION

Situated about 75 miles from two well-known attractions—the Indianapolis 500 Race and the Kentucky Derby—is the city of Bedford. The Piankashaws, Delawares, Shawnees, and Potawatomis once held claim to this area before the first white settlers came and purchased land along the east fork of White River and named the town Palestine. Sickness from either milk fever or malaria caused people to move the county seat from Palestine to the hill above the river in 1825, thus naming the new county seat Bedford. This was a thriving community with mercantile businesses, groceries, a woolen mill, liquor stores, general stores, banks, and doctors' offices. When Winthrop Foote, the father of Bedford Limestone, opened the Blue Hole Quarry, the limestone industry began. By 1858, the stone industry grew as a result of the railroads, a more economical means for transporting the heavy stone. From the time that limestone was recognized as a very good building material and that the fine quality in this area was excellent for artistic statuary and carvings, stone workers and master carvers came from such places as Italy, Germany, Wales, Scotland, England, and other countries. Our cemeteries are filled with the bodies of early carvers, some of the epitaphs written in their native languages. Our Green Hill Cemetery is a popular tourist attraction, known throughout the country for its stone artistic carvings.

The city is nestled among the rolling hills and the beauty in the spring and fall is beyond compare. Redbud and Dogwood trees in bloom dot the hillsides with pink and white. The fall is an artist's pallet of color. The summer is a time for recreation and our parks and golf courses are a treat to behold. Spring Mill State Park is just minutes away and it boasts an old 1800s village, a gristmill, and several caves. Otis Park has an 18-hole golf course, which is considered the finest in southern Indiana. Other parks and golf courses are located in the county.

Take a mystic boat ride in Bluespring Caverns and see the formations inside the cave as well as the blind fish that live there. There are over 300 caves in the area, but only a few are commercialized.

There is a lot of history behind the solid stone houses, which once were the homes of the limestone owners and executives. Many of the homes have stone porches, the result of the work of stonecutters who worked in the mills. Stone birdbaths, benches, and other pieces of art can be found in many yards in Bedford. Because most of our churches are made of stone, the town is sometime known as "the City of Stone Churches."

Many famous people have called Bedford home. County records show that on March 15, 1893, Joseph and Enola Lee Gardner deeded 782 acres, located south of Bedford on State Road 37, to Clara Barton, founder and president of the American National Red Cross, "for the sum of One Dollar, and the hereafter consideration . . . for a National Headquarters of the American National Red Cross." Later, headquarters were located in Washington, D.C. Barton visited

Bedford many times as a friend of Joseph and Enola Lee Gardner. They had met during the Civil War. Just south of Bedford is the Red Cross Cemetery, which takes its name from the failed attempt to establish national headquarters here.

Three astronauts are from this area: Virgil "Gus" Grissom, Charlie Walker, and Ken Bowersox. At least two major league baseball players are from Bedford: Bill Rariden and Yank Terry. Claude Akins, the actor, was a graduate of Bedford High School, and very successful in both the movies and television. Several well-known musicians, including Bobby Brooks and Robert Fortner, were from Bedford. They went on to perform with such notables as Louis Armstrong, Eddie Rabbit and Kris Kristofferson.

The new location of the Lawrence County Museum of History and Edward L. Hutton Research Library is an attraction for researchers. It is located in a remodeled historic building on the public square, and its grand opening was in 2005.

Bedford has become a tourist attraction in the last few years and is well known as the home of one of the best building materials. The people here are friendly and welcome visitors. Make an escape to the Hoosier Heartland and enjoy the Hoosier Hospitality.

One

Early Settlers and Other People

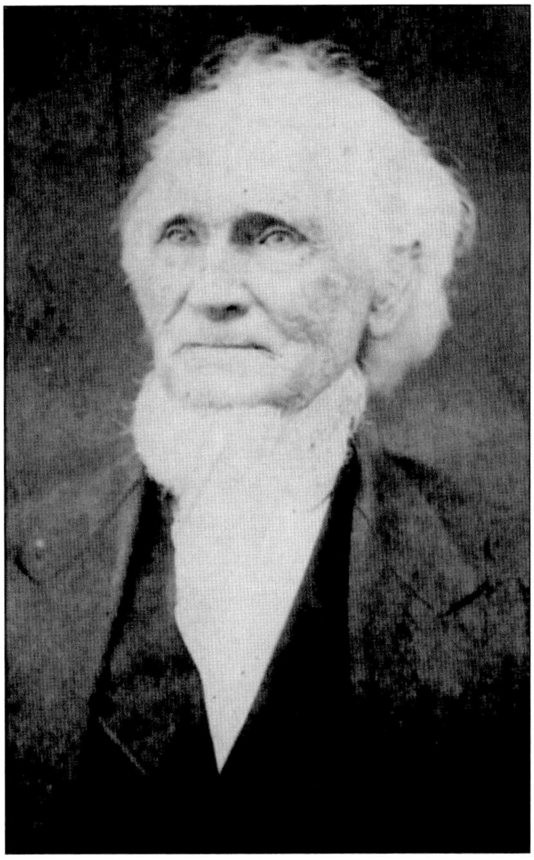

Joseph Rawlins was born in 1796 in Danville, Kentucky. He and his brother Charles and his uncle Roderick and their families came to early Indiana before 1818. Joseph fought against the Native Americans on the northwest frontier and received a pension for his service. He was a flatboat man and piloted produce to New Orleans during the 1820s and 1830s. He was in the merchandise business and also the first county assessor. Joseph Rawlins named the town of Bedford. Legend has it that the name came from his earlier home of Bedford County, Tennessee.

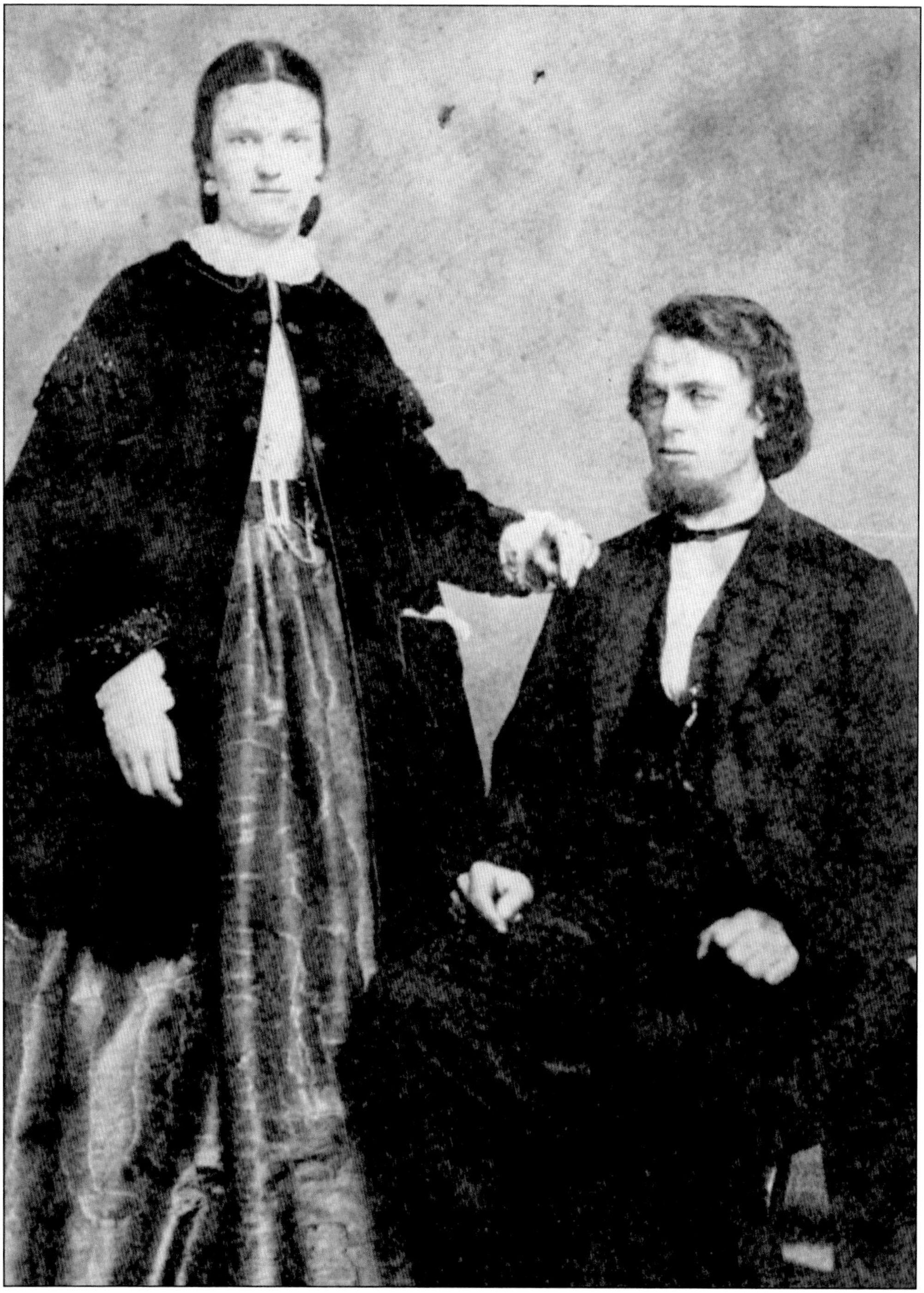

Dr. Joseph and Enola Lee Gardner were close friends of Clara Barton, founder of the American National Red Cross. Barton visited their home many times. They had met during the Civil War, taking care of the dead and wounded. The Gardner family deeded their farm, just south of Bedford, to Barton to be used as the national headquarters, but it was soon decided it should be moved to Washington, D.C.

Mary I. Rariden (née Howland) was the wife of Dr. Samuel A. Rariden who was a popular doctor in Bedford during the early 1900s.

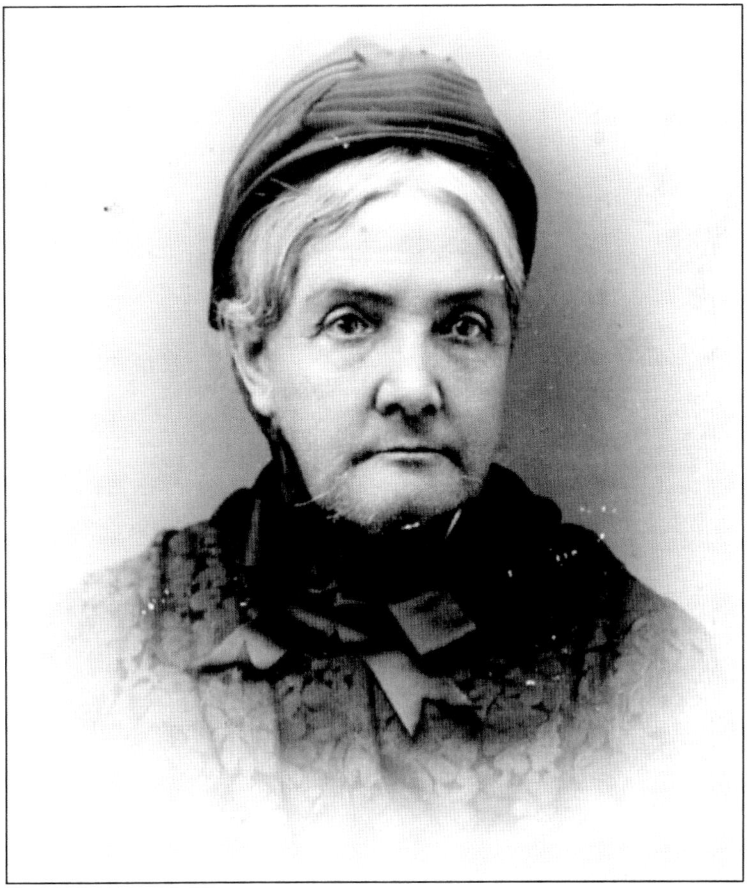

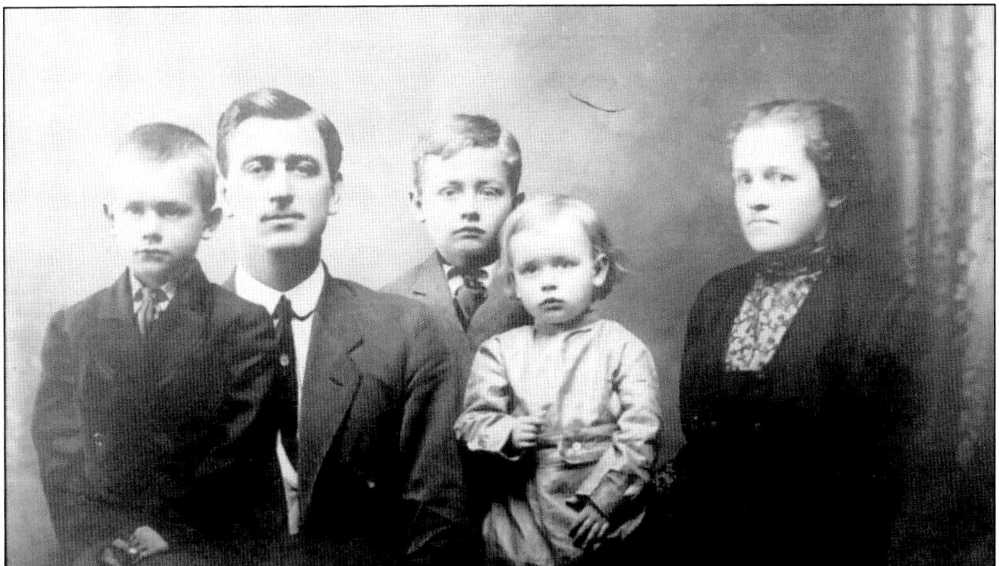

The Tom Chapman family is pictured here. His wife was Della Chapman (née Bass) and his sons were Wayne, Lewis, and Oran. Tom was an early Lawrence County treasurer.

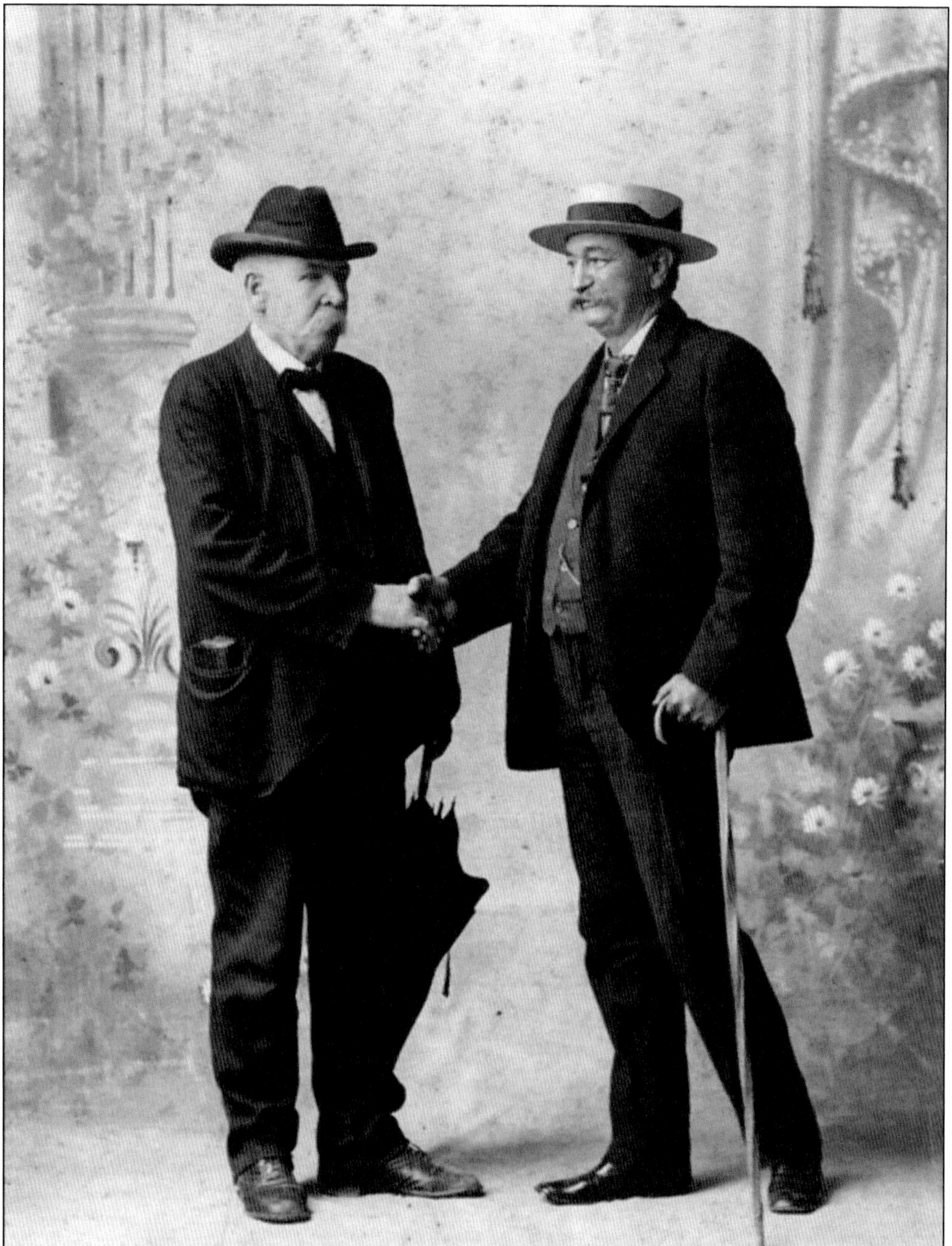

Dr. T. Ellison and the Honorable judge Moses Fell Dunn were close friends and early leaders of Bedford. Judge Dunn was a lawyer and a well-known politician. He traveled throughout Europe, was quite an orator, spoke several languages, and was a collector of first editions and very rare books. He was a generous man and gave much to the community. The local county hospital bears his name; he donated money along with his exceptional library to the Bedford Masonic lodge and funded the *Soldiers, Sailors and Pioneers Monument* statue on the courthouse lawn. This photograph was taken in 1900.

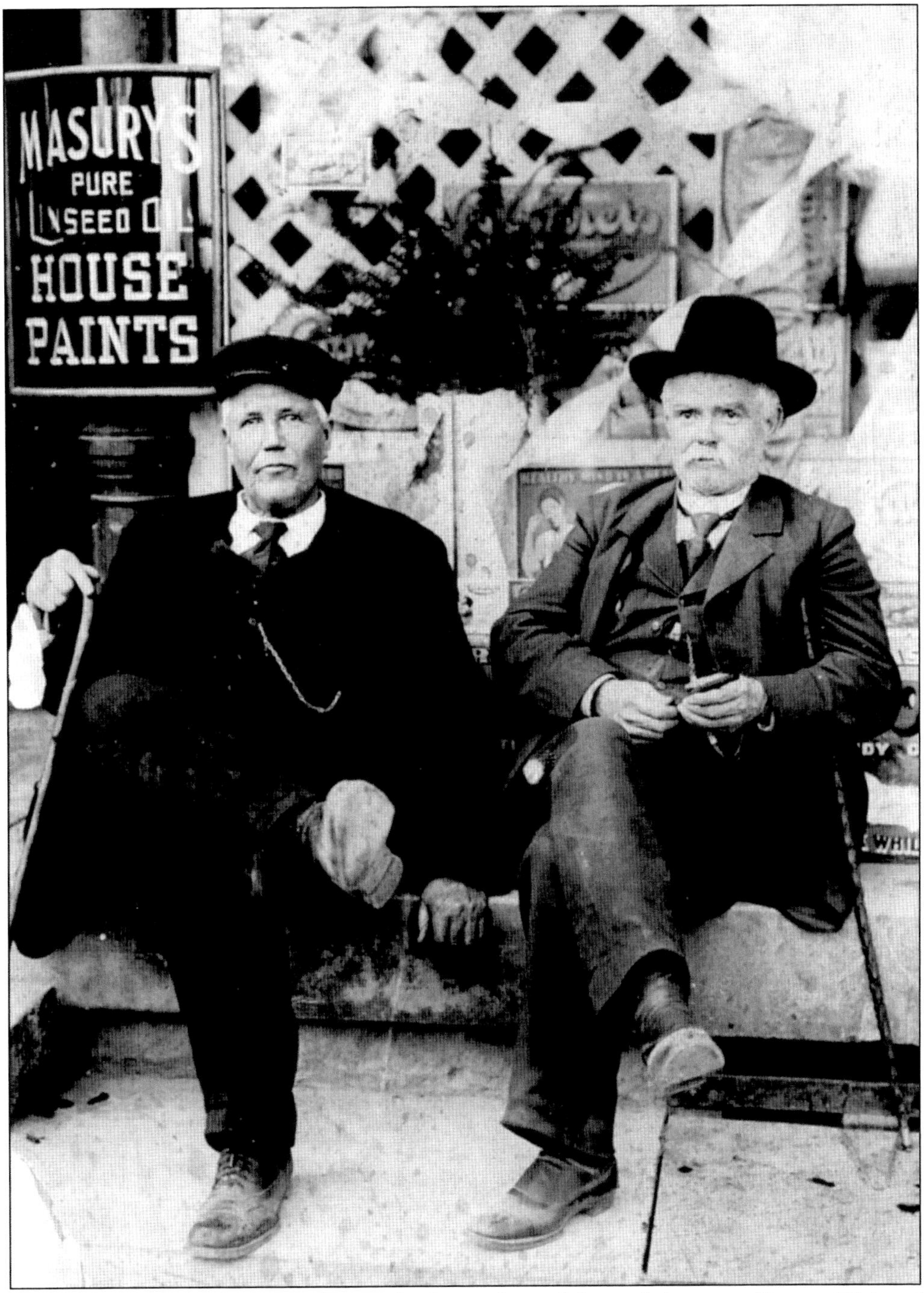

David Newkirk and Robert N. Palmer sit loafing in front of this early business, House of Paints. It is not known just where this business was located in Bedford. Newkirk was the son of Benjamin Newkirk and Eupha Newkirk (née White). Palmer's parents were James W. Palmer and Laura Palmer (née Newland) who came to Lawrence County from Fauquier County, Virginia, and settled early in the county. Palmer became a well-known attorney in Bedford. This picture was taken around 1890.

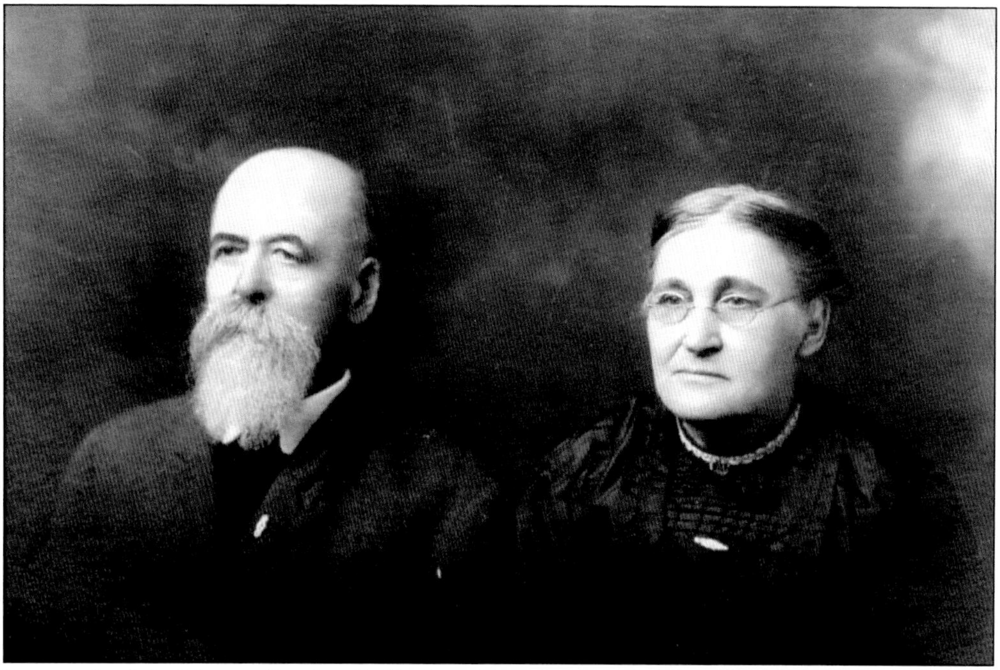

Joe and Sarah L. Johnson lived in Bedford in the early 1900s at Thirteenth and K Streets. There were several unrelated branches of the Johnson family living in this area.

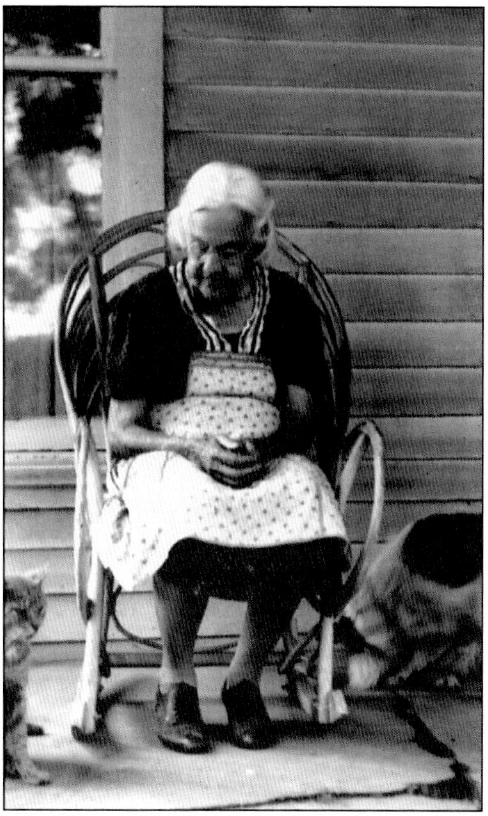

Hester Ann Crane sits in her hickory wicker rocker on her front porch with her two well-loved pets, Scamper the dog and Figero the yellow stripped cat. Crane was quite the storyteller in the 1930s, remembering when her mother and father came to Indiana around 1855 from Tuscarawas County, Ohio, by covered wagon.

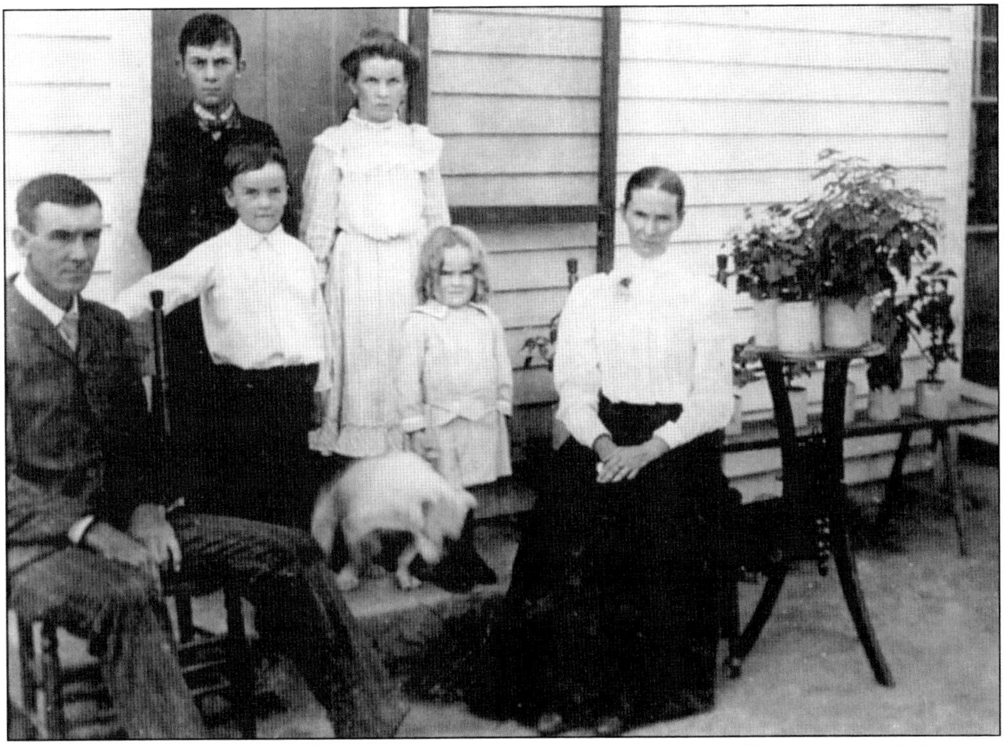

The Frank Smith family is shown outside their home. In the early 1900s, this kind of family portrait was quite popular.

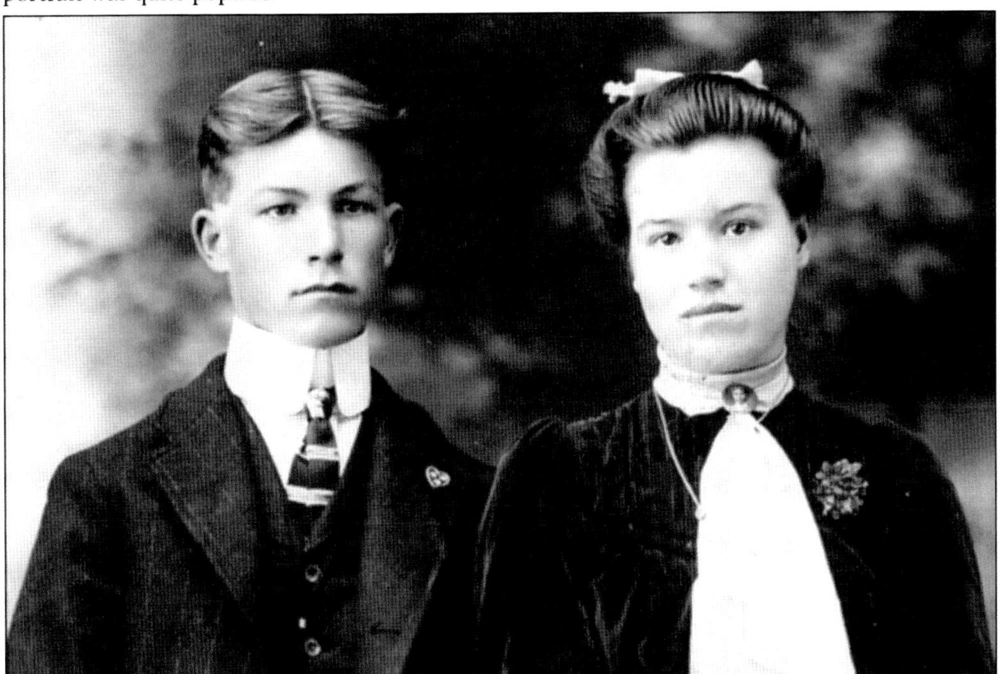

Arthur and Effie Crane, brother and sister, posed for this photograph in the 1920s. The early Crane family of this area is said to have come from Calvert County, Maryland.

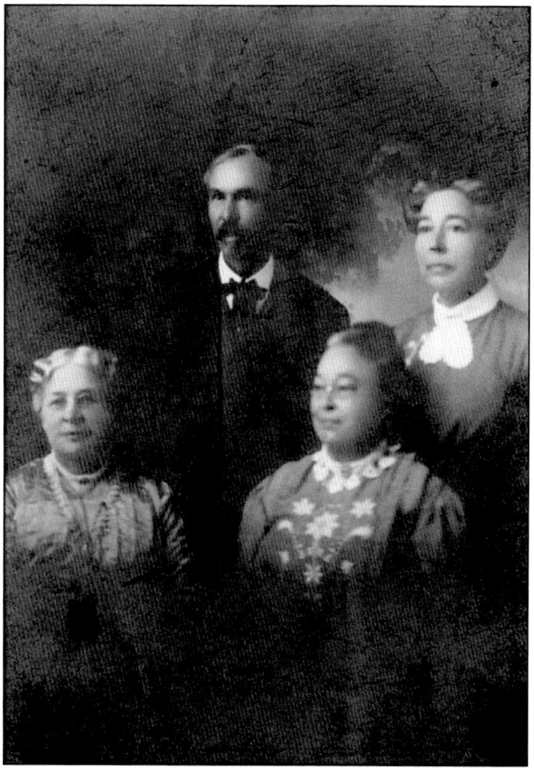

Fred Bishop Otis and his sisters lived in Bedford. The three sisters are, from left to right, Frances, Hattie, and Fannie. Fred was a newspaperman who never married. He was born on February 28, 1863, and died at the age of 81. Otis Park is named after him.

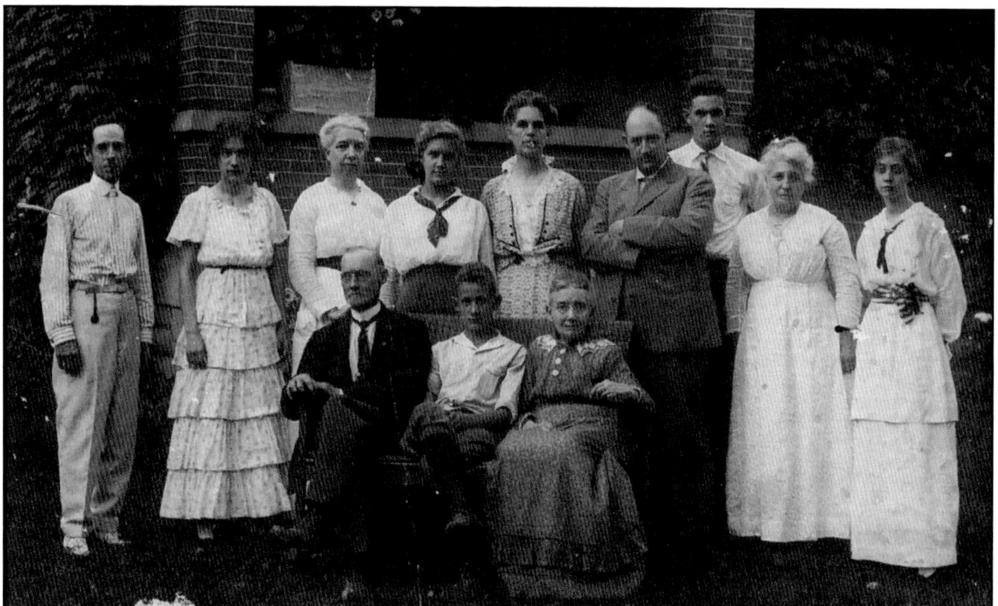

This vintage photograph is of the Emery family. Those family members pictured are, from left to right, (first row) John G. Emery (grandfather), Charles H. Emery, and Mary Emery (grandmother); (second row) Dr. Trainer, Florence Emery, Mrs. Trainer, Mary Alice Emery (wife of George Rowe), Rose E. Emery (wife of Charles Emery), Dr. Charles H. Emery, John Howard Emery, Cora Ferris, and Dorothy Trainer.

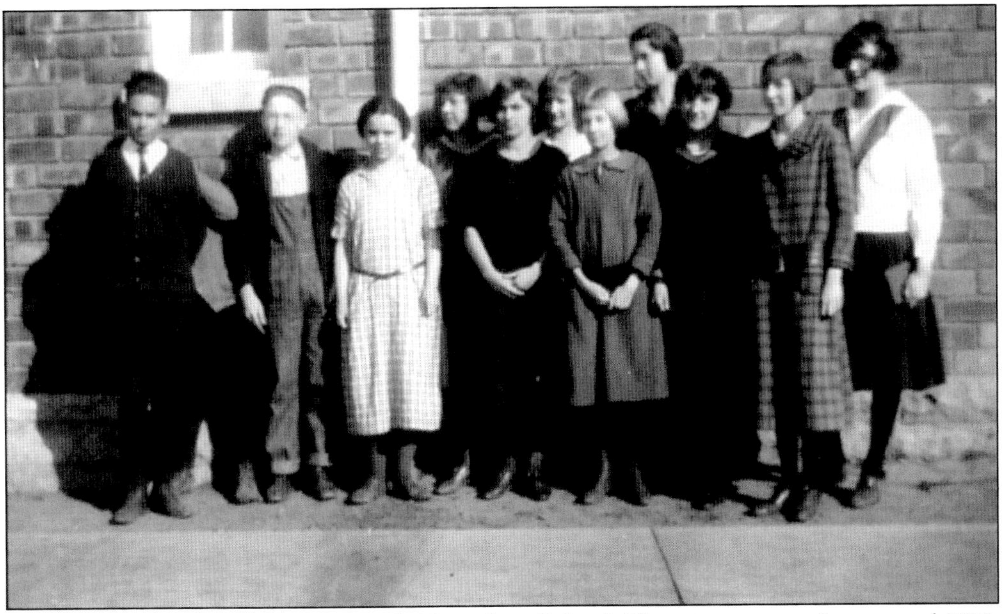

A group of students is standing outside Tunnelton School. The picture was taken around 1928, and the students are probably seniors. Consolidation in the 1970s caused many of the smaller schools to close.

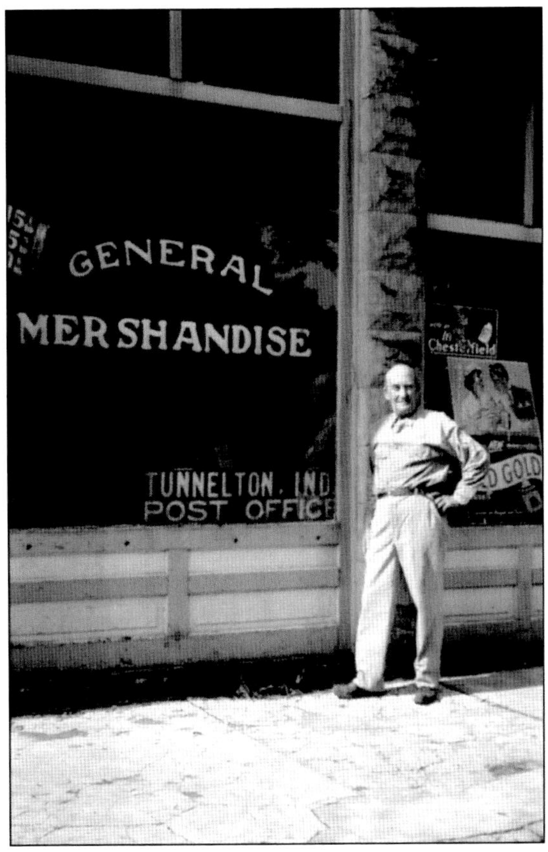

Homer Ingle was the proprietor of the general store and post office in the small community of Tunnelton. During the early days of the railroad, this community was thriving. The town got its name because it was situated between two tunnels, a big one and a little one.

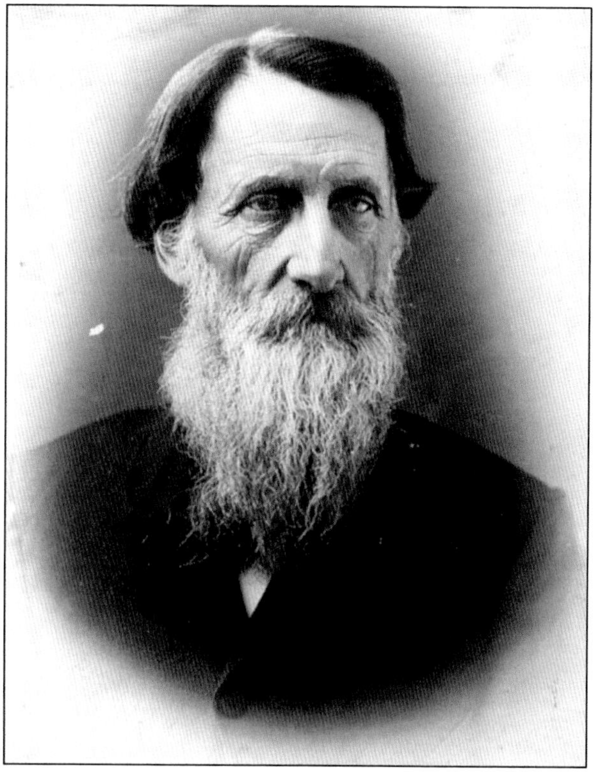

This photograph is of J. A. Rogers and was taken by the Rogers East and South Side Galleries around 1890.

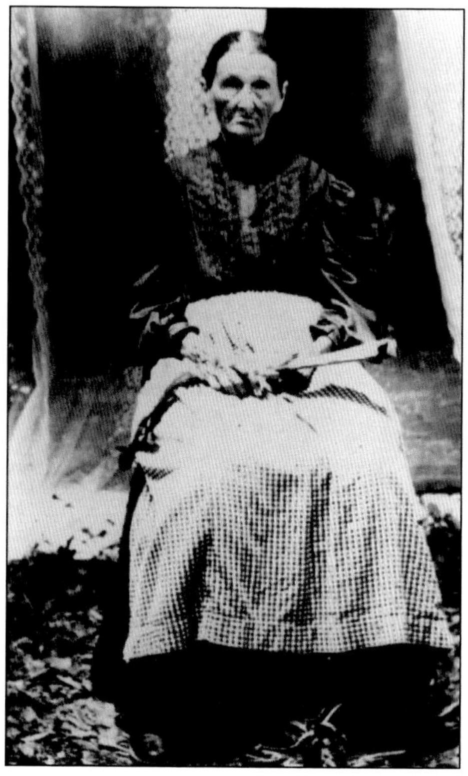

Sylvania Stogdill Kinworthy had two daughters who lived in Bedford where she visited quite often. Those daughters were Sally Martin (née Kinworthy), wife of Tom Martin, and Minnie Baker (née Kinworthy), who married Daniel Baker.

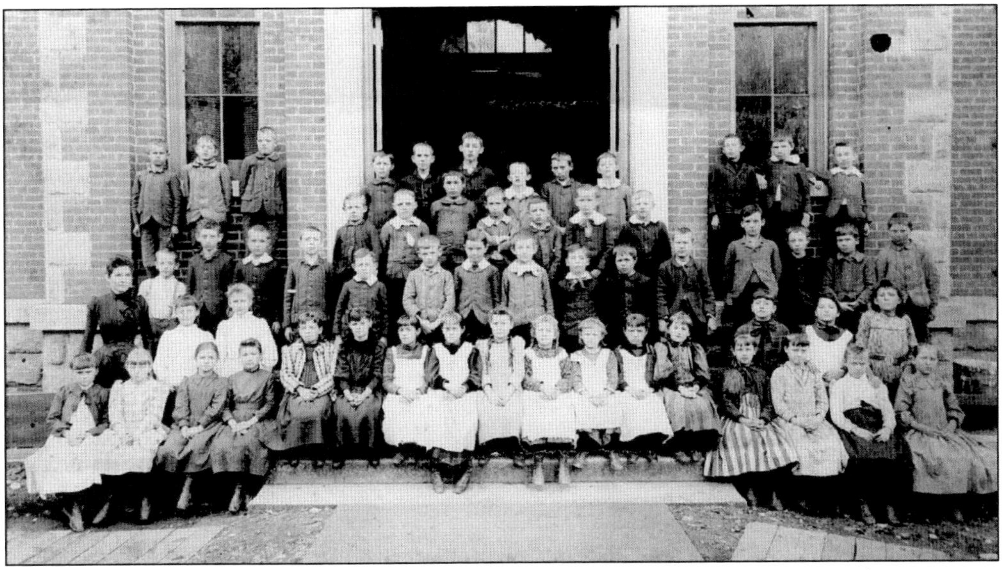

Shown here are students in the old Central School during the 1890s. This is Mary O'Connel's class.

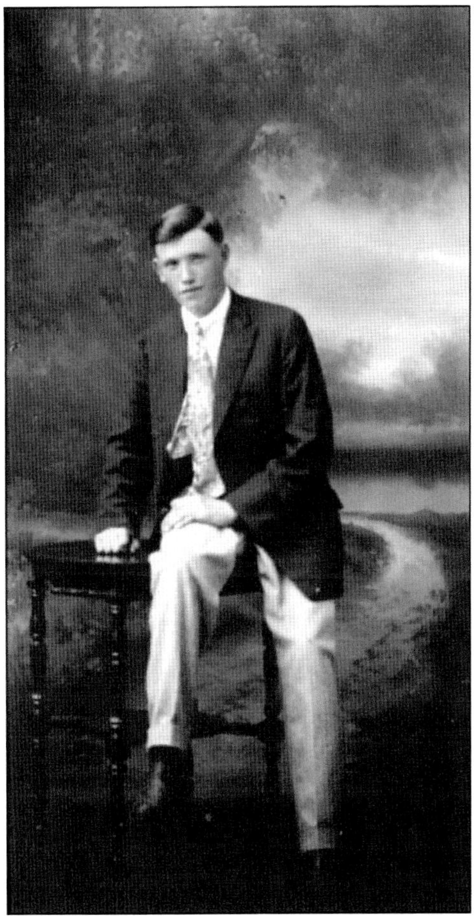

George Hitchcock was a young man when this photograph was taken, around 1926. In later years, he became a master stone carver and much of his work can be seen today. Hitchcock was the son of Jacob Mancel Hitchcock and Charlotte Hitchcock (née Crane).

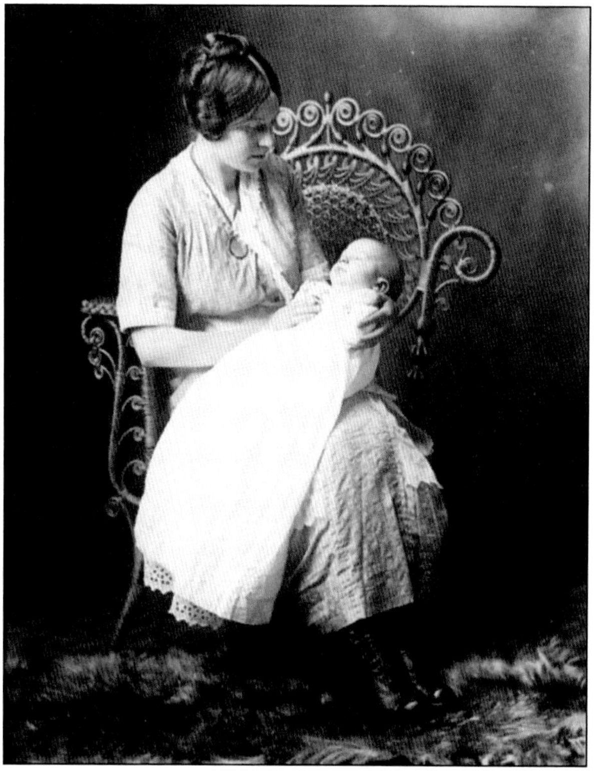

This 1925 picture of an unidentified mother and baby was taken by one of the local photographers. The wicker chair prop can be found in many of the photographs taken in the Lawrence County area.

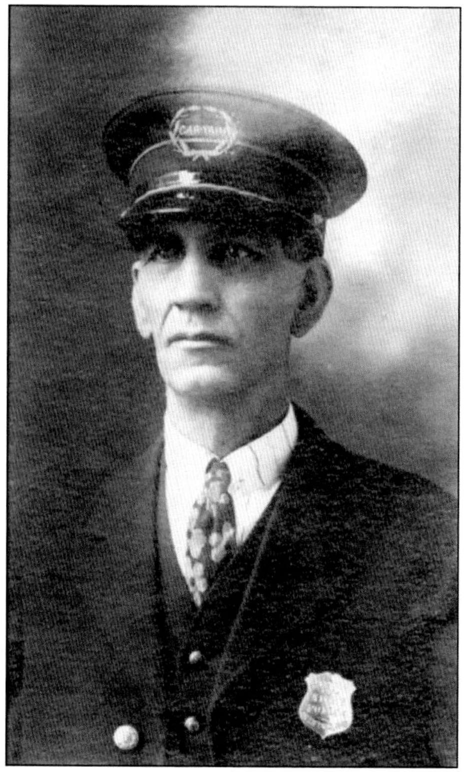

Bedford Police Department uniforms have changed through the years as shown by this captain who wears a white shirt and tie of choice.

This is the photograph of the Lewis family who lived in Bedford. Ellsworth Lewis owned and operated the Lewis Lumber Company in the Englewood neighborhood. After his retirement, one of his sons, Ermel, continued the business. Ermel and his wife Kathleen Lewis (née Sexton) owned and operated a skating rink during the mid-1900s. Another son of Ellsworth, Gladys, was a school teacher.

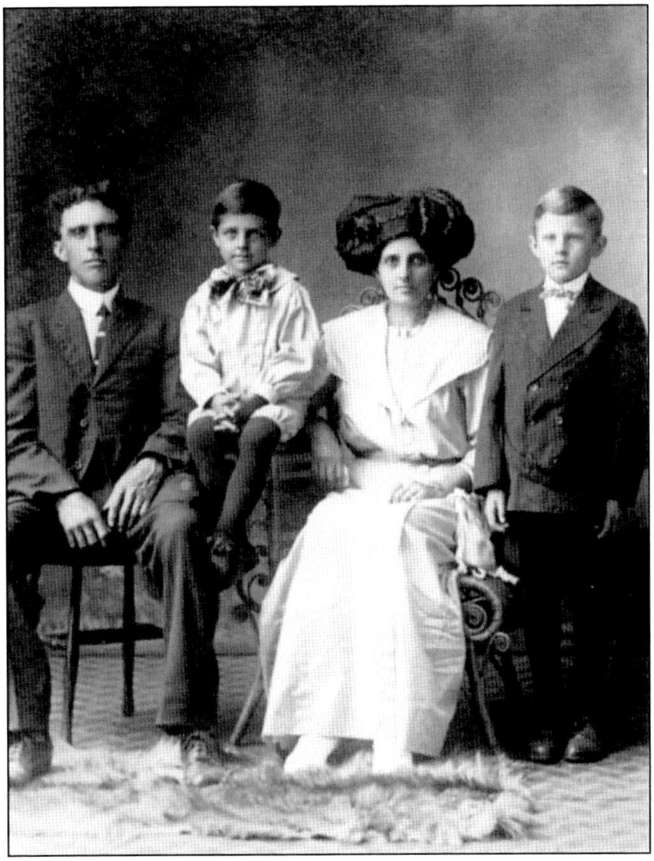

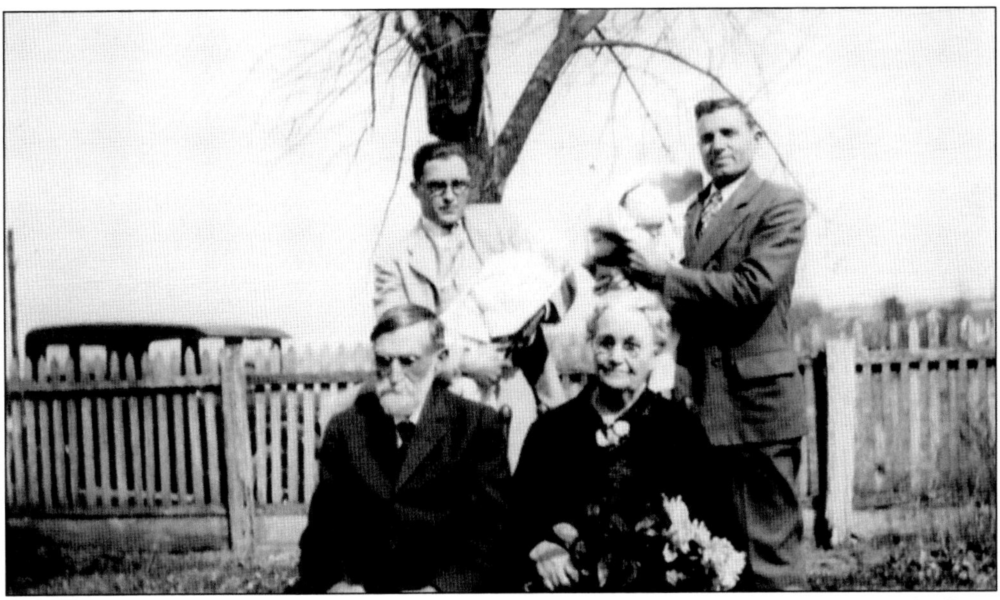

The Burch family lived on South I Street in Bedford during the 1930s. Charles Burch (front row, left) was a teacher in Monroe County before retiring. His wife Louisa sits beside him. Other family members are unknown.

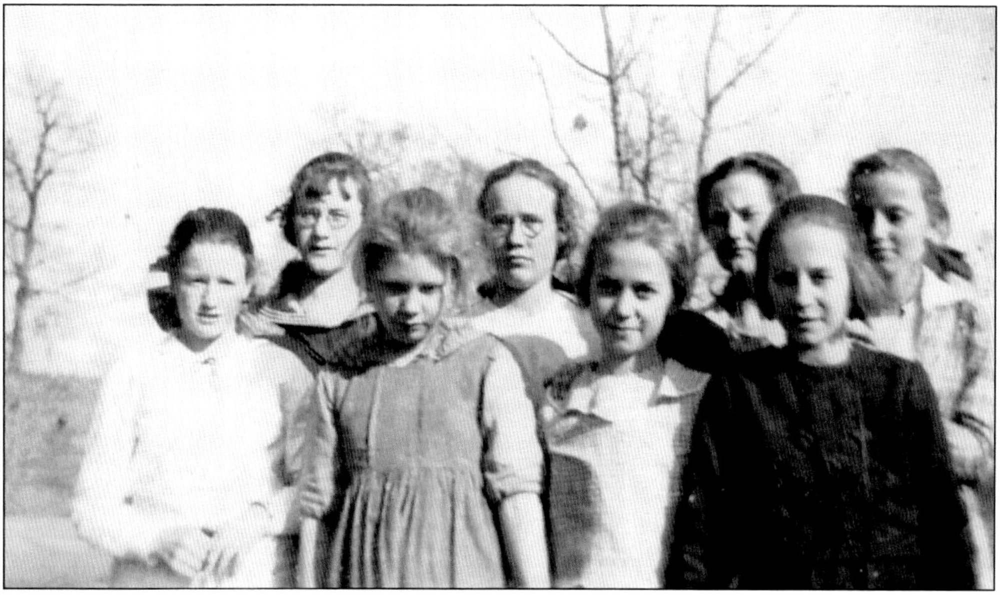

This is the eighth grade domestic science class at Tunnelton School. This photograph was taken during the 1921–1922 semester.

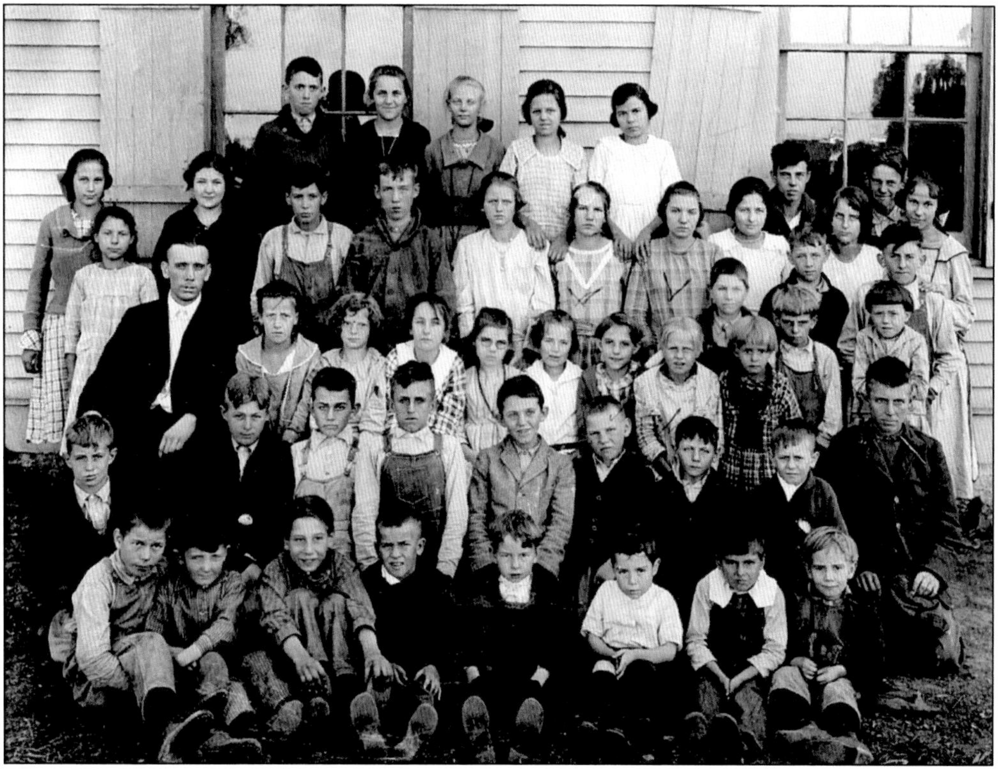

One of the early schools in Bedford was the Cross Lanes School located on South I Street. The school no longer exists. This photograph was taken around 1920, and includes children of such families as; Baker, Bright, Dodd, Woodward, Lambrecht, and others. The teacher is believed to be Henry Fortner.

Bedford once had a Bowen and Long Studio. This unidentified little boy posed for this photograph at that studio. The chair is called an "ice-cream" chair because this type of chair was used in ice-cream parlors. Notice the style for boys in the 1890s.

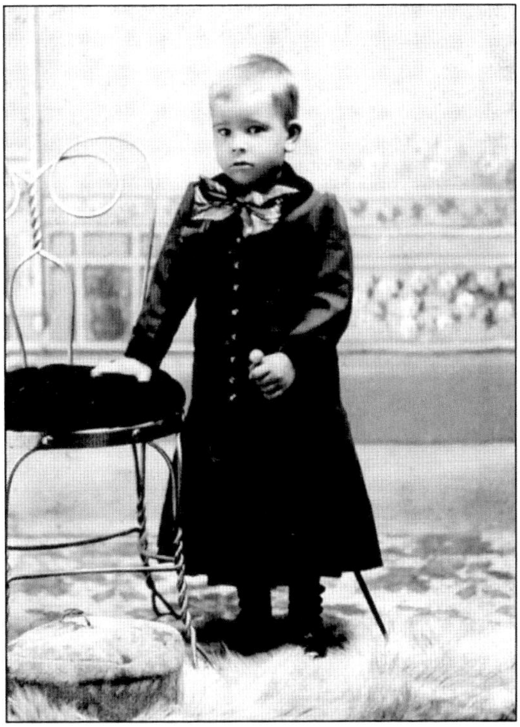

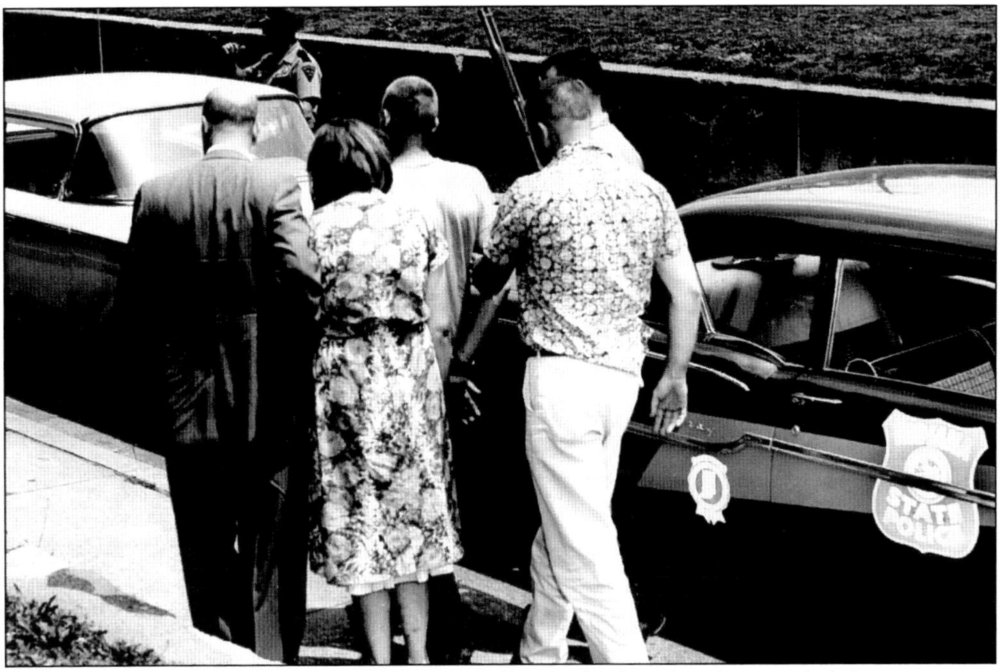

In 1960, state police trooper Bob Gillespie was shot in the leg after this couple left a gas station without paying for gas. The man shown with his hands handcuffed behind his back had pulled a gun on Gillespie when the trooper tried to arrest them. The husband and wife went into the hills around Avoca, a short distance from Bedford. Here they have been caught and are being escorted to the waiting police car.

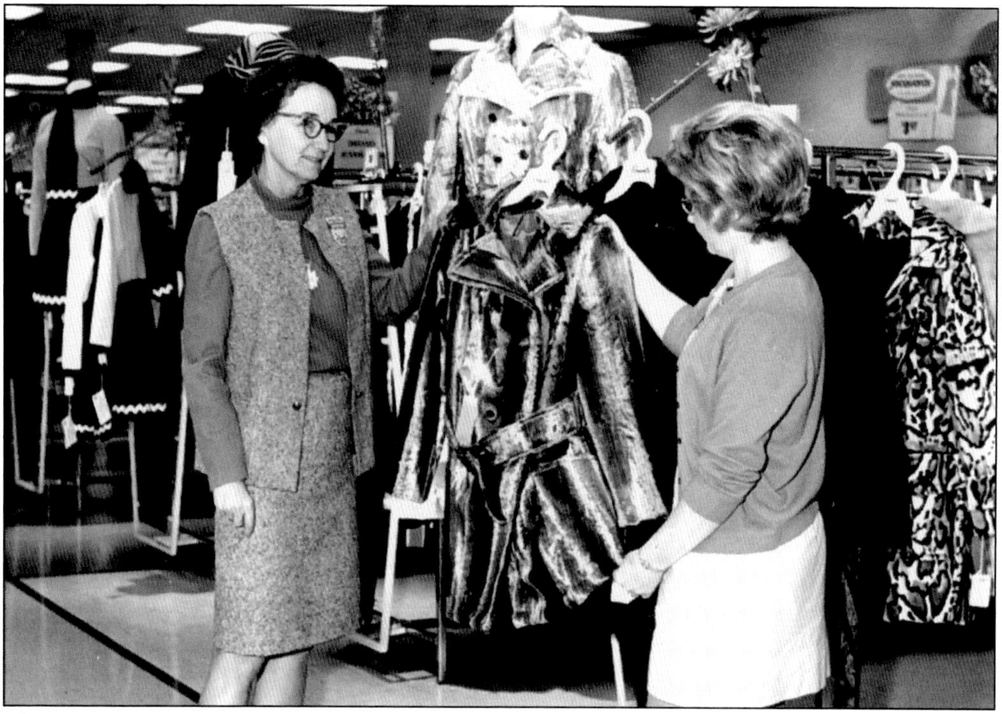

This picture was taken inside the old W. T. Grant Store, which was located in Bedford until 1975. The sales person in the ready-to-wear department is Rose Robertson (left) and the customer is Mary Bridges.

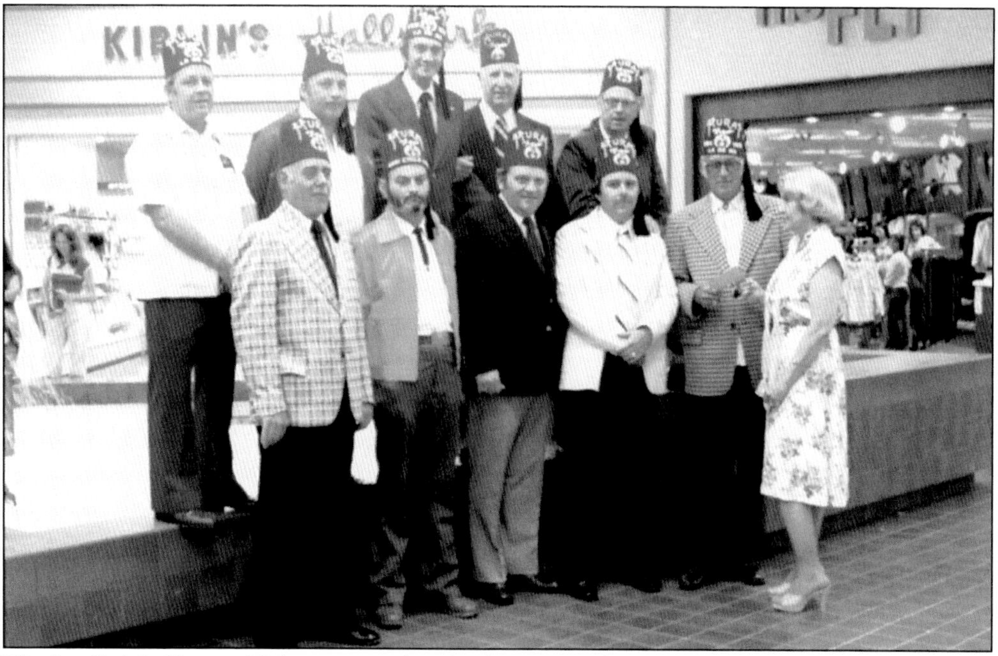

The La-Or-Ma Shrine Club is posing beside the quarry fountain at Stone City Mall in 1985. The clubhouse is located just south of Bedford on Old Indiana Highway 37. The mall has been replaced with another business.

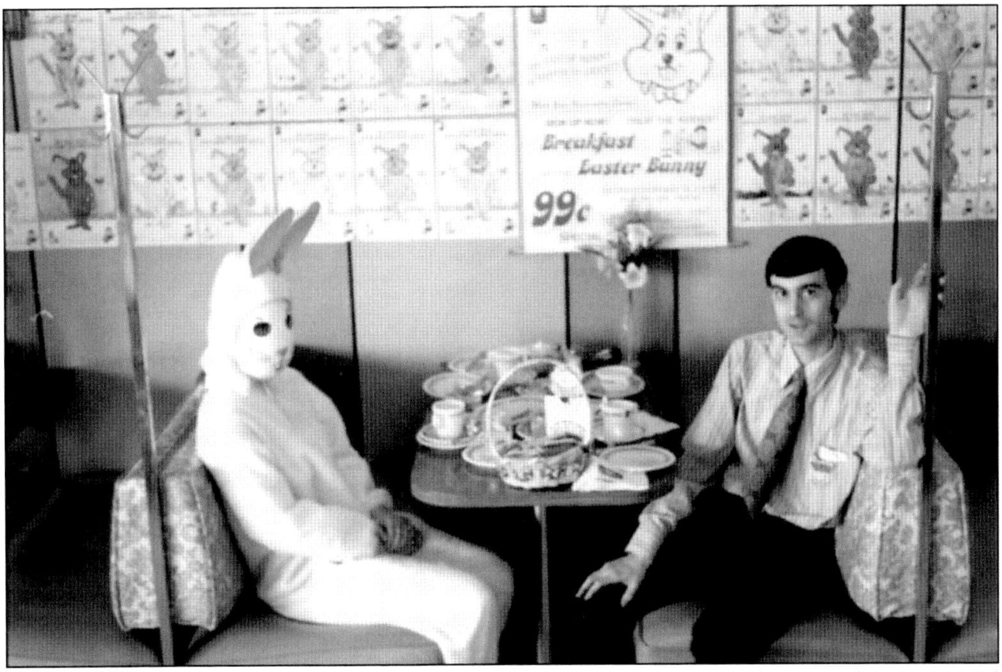

Norm Dalby, manager of the restaurant in W. T. Grant's, is entertaining the Easter bunny around 1974. He later owned his own restaurant south of town until he moved to Florida. Norm had many friends and was well liked.

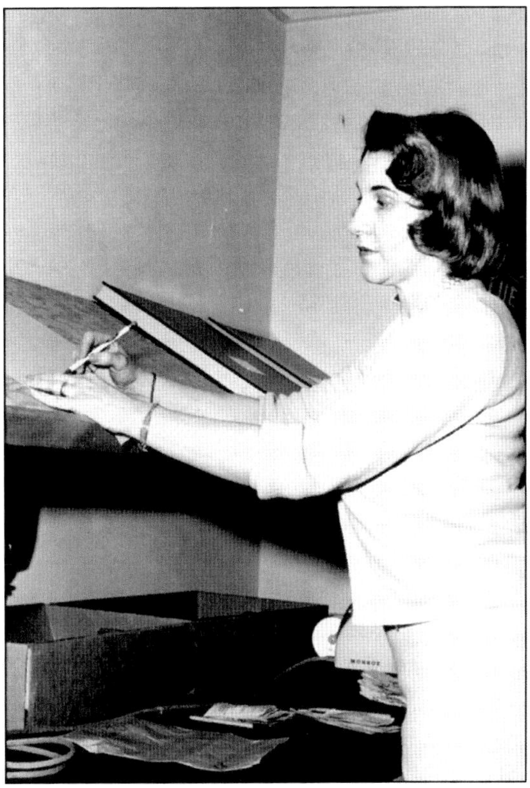

In 1965, a new W. F. Woolworth was built on the south side of the public square. Maxine Kruse, the author, was hired as the first advertising and display manager for the company. The building is now used as a government building with several offices.

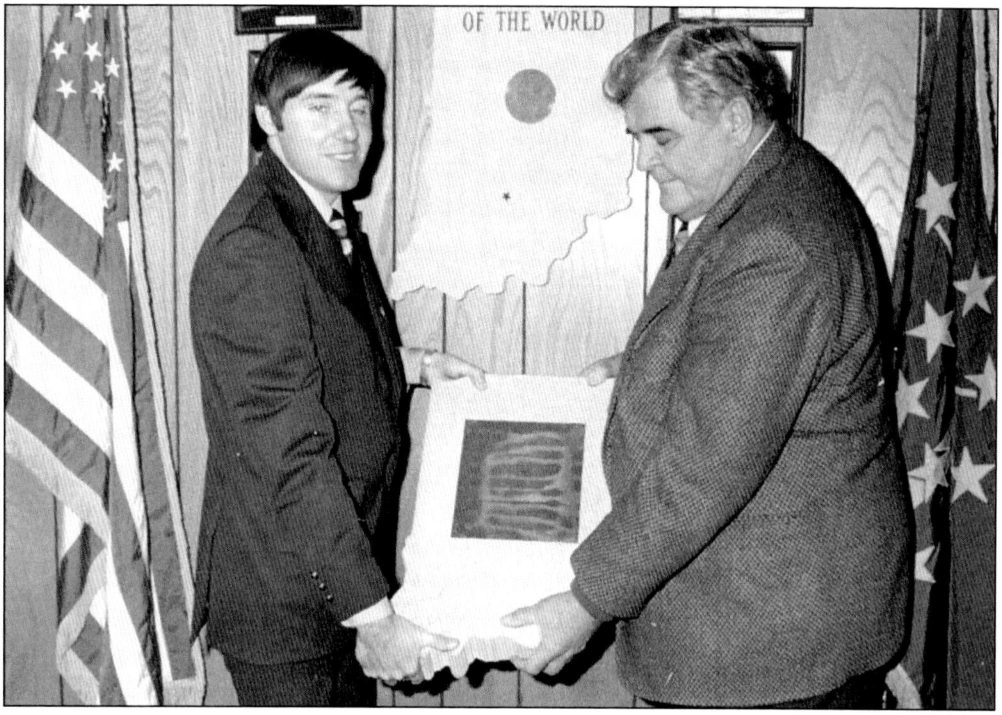

Merle Edington (right) was executive director of the Bedford Area Chamber of Commerce in the 1970s. He is presenting a limestone plaque in the shape of Indiana to an unidentified person. The Edington family was in the limestone business.

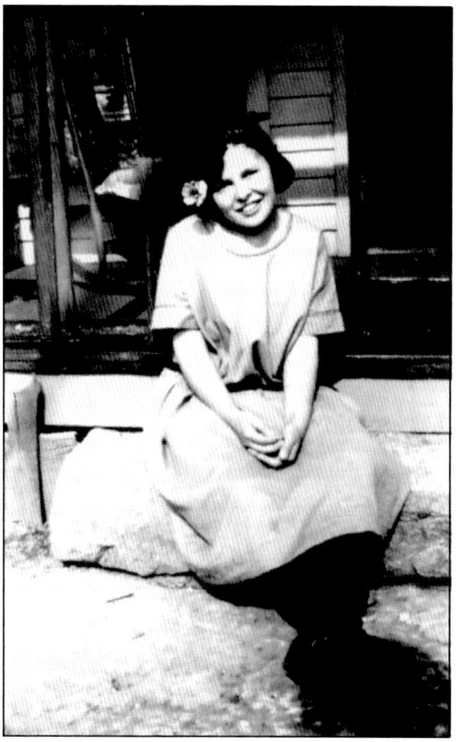

Ina Wright of Tunnelton was the daughter of Robert "Bert" and Ella Wright. She sits on the steps of the Wright home.

This young man, Wesley Crane, is pictured in 1916. In later years, he married Melinda Bough and lived in the Englewood community with his family of seven children.

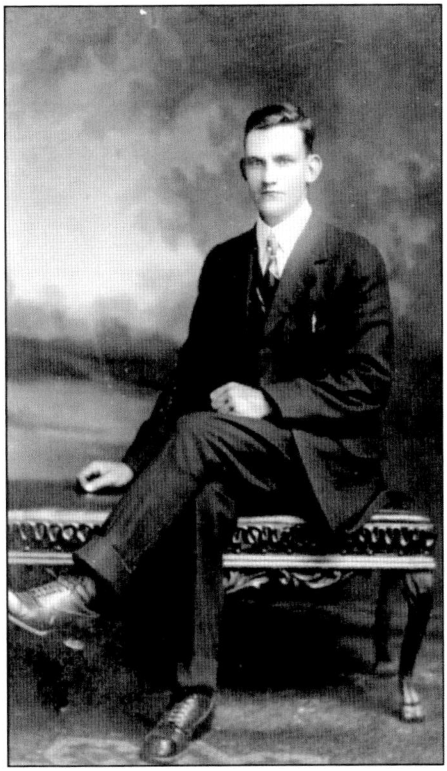

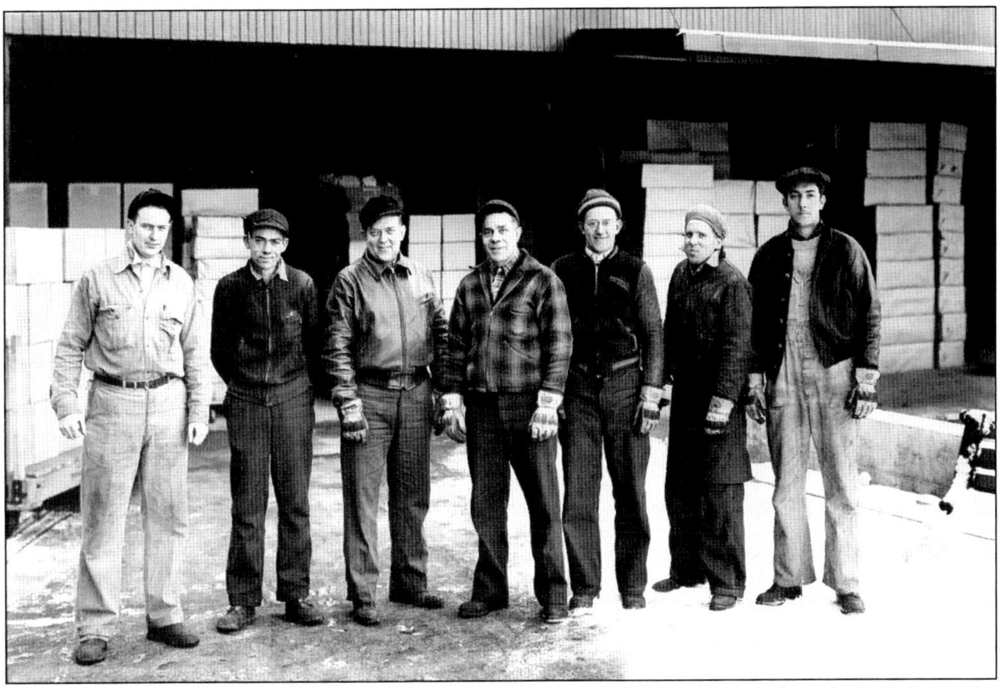

This group of men is working in a warehouse. Only one man can be identified in the photograph. Milton Myer, second from right, retired years later and lived with his wife Mae on Q Street in Bedford.

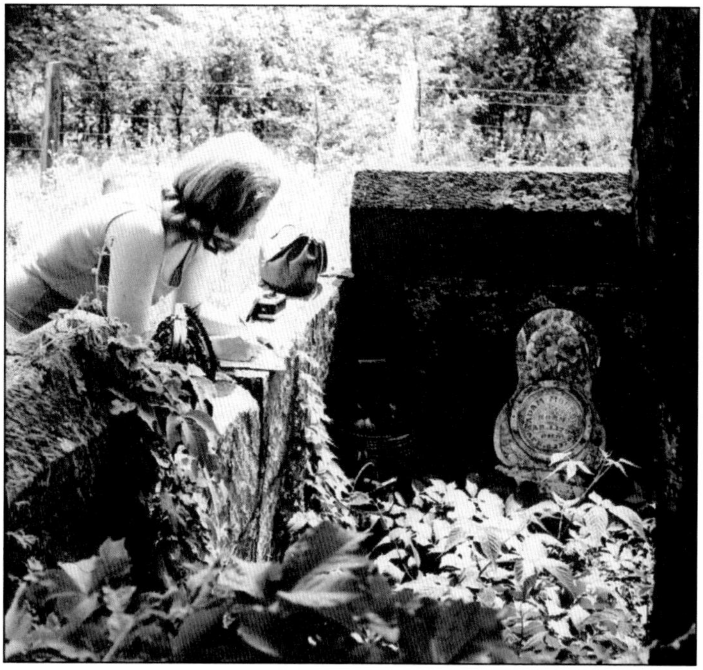

This local Daughters of the American Revolution member is researching old cemeteries, preparing to record information on the various burial grounds. The stone states that Mr. Morrow was born March 1, 1794.

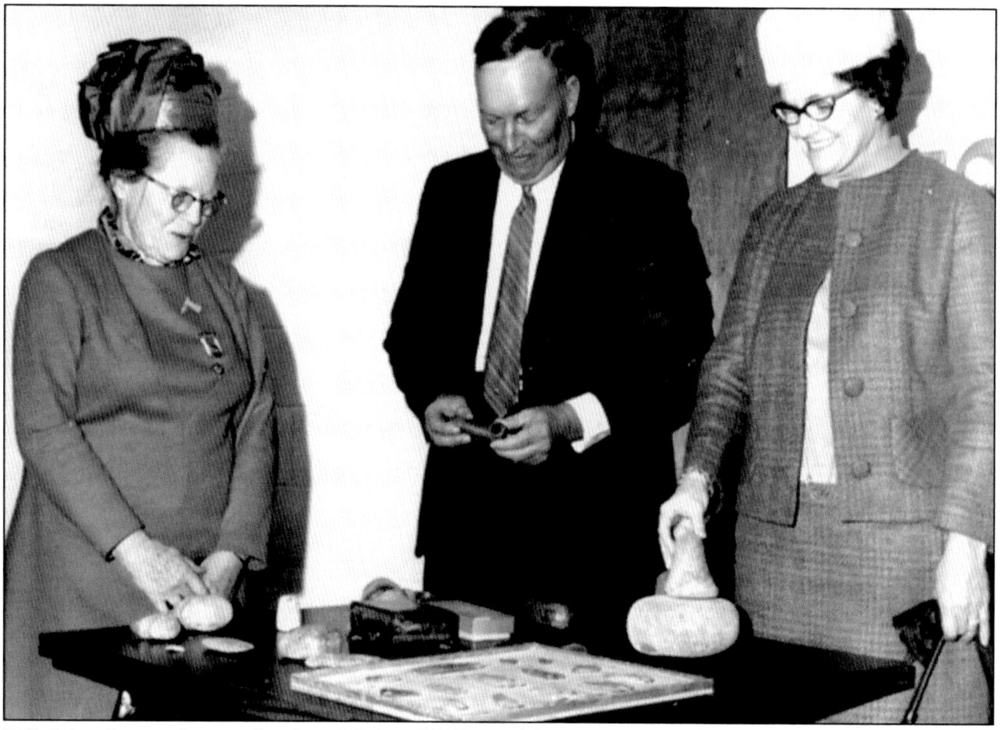

Bill Murphy spoke to the local John Wallace Chapter National Society Daughters of the American Revolution about his huge collection of American Indian artifacts that he discovered on his farm south of White River. This photograph was taken in the 1970s. At one time there had been an American Indian camp and burial ground on his property. He recalled that his grandmother played with some of the American Indian children when she was a child.

Madge Crane was a well-known correspondent for *The Times Mail* newspaper. She was also a teacher for many years until her eyesight failed and she had to retire from the vocation she loved. This picture was taken in 1928.

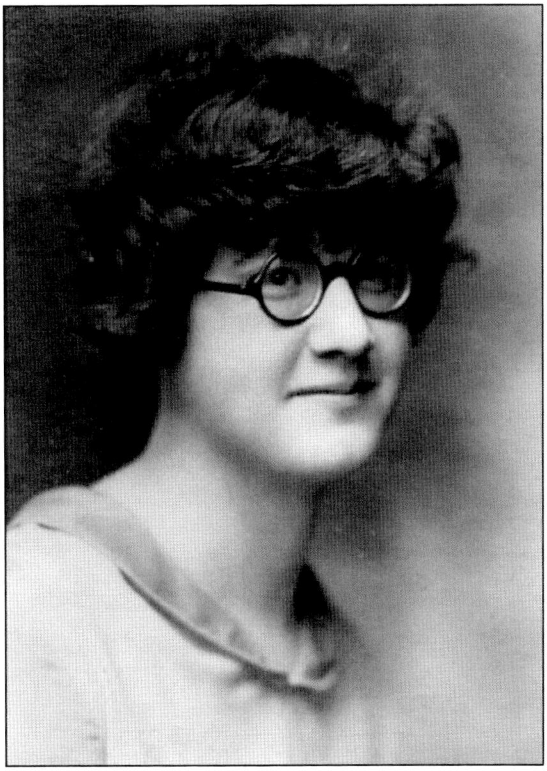

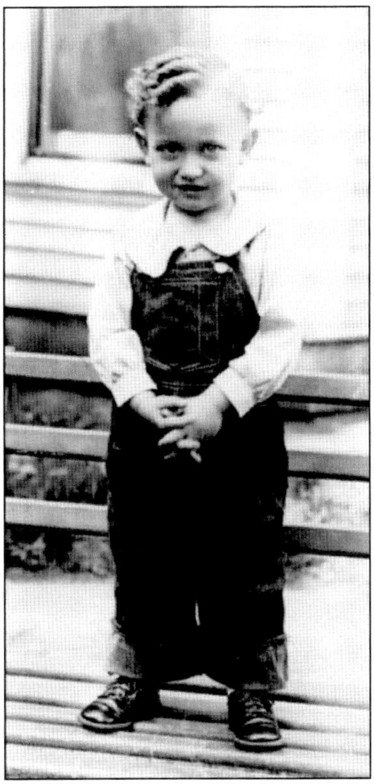

An unidentified little boy poses for this snapshot in 1928. He is standing on a bench in front of photographer Grant Wright's home.

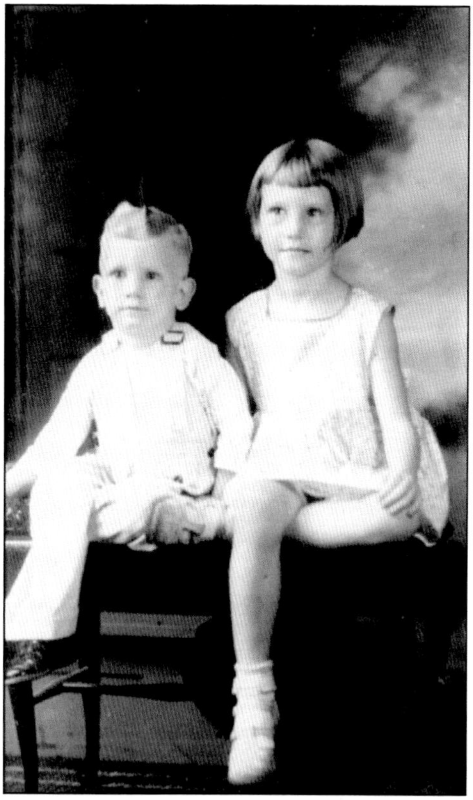

This is a photograph of a brother and sister taken at Jackson's Studio in Bedford in 1935. This studio was located on North I Street.

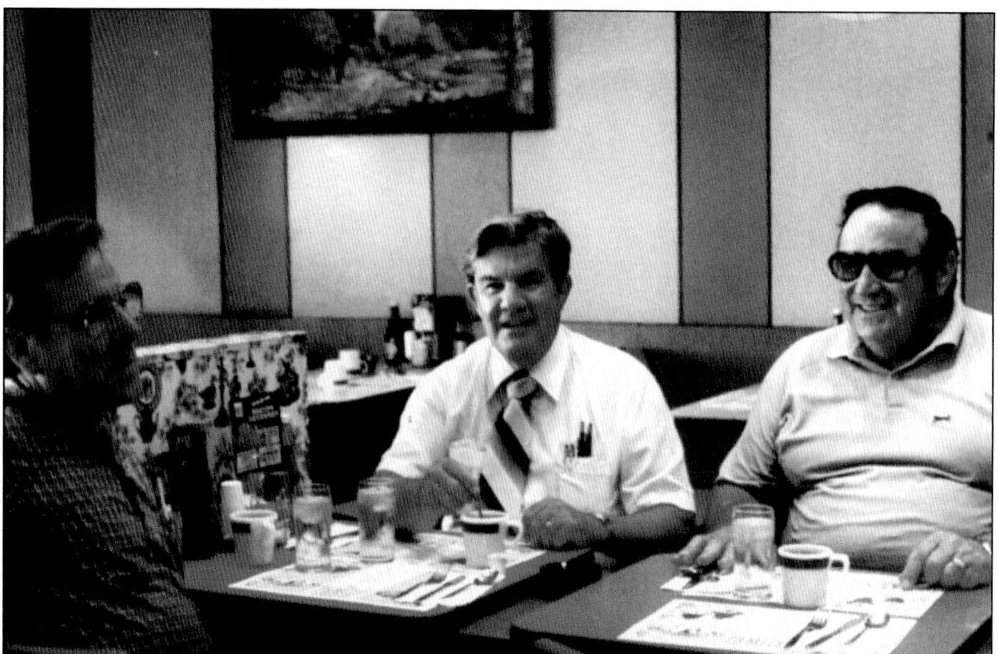

In 1982, Jerry Gould, Larry Duncan, and Paul Terrell enjoyed breakfast in Kmart's restaurant in Stone City Mall on Sixteenth Street in Bedford. The mall is no longer in existence.

Stella Deering taught piano lessons in the 1940s. Her husband, Rudy Deering, taught band and was the music teacher for Bedford High School. For the price of 50¢ per student, she would spend one hour trying to develop and mold the student's talent.

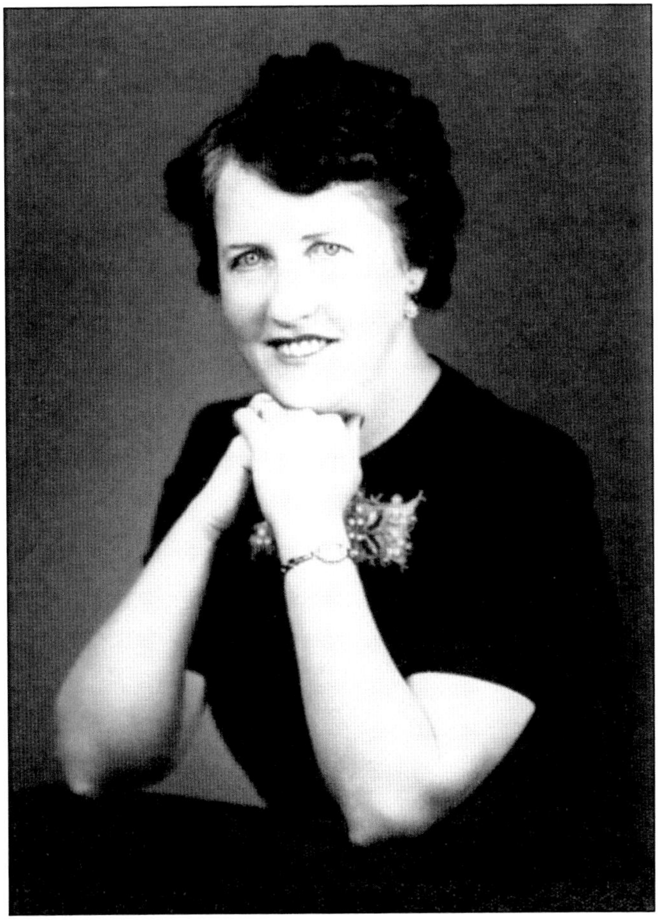

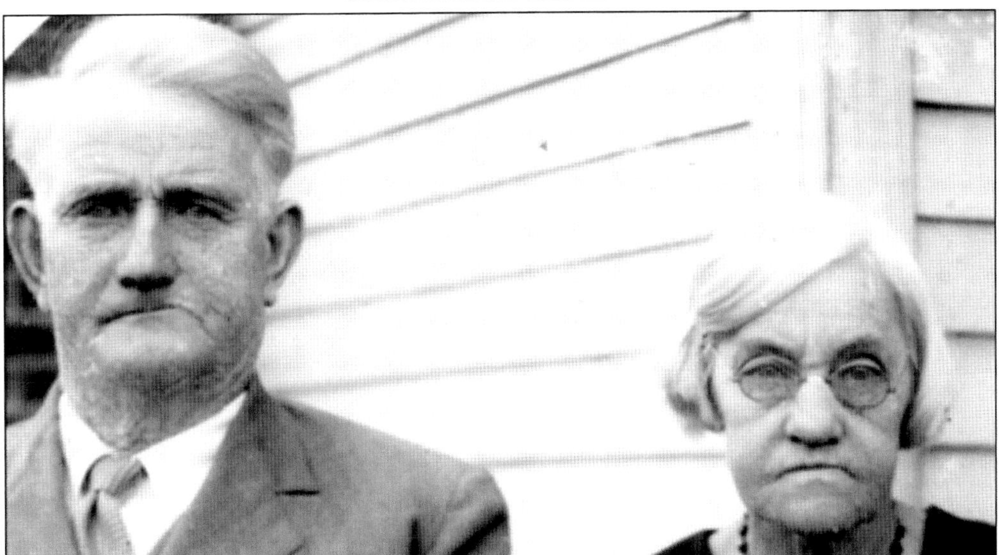

Richard Franklin and Hester Ann Smith Crane were residents of the community of Tunnelton. Richard had the first electric gristmill in the area. They were the parents of six children.

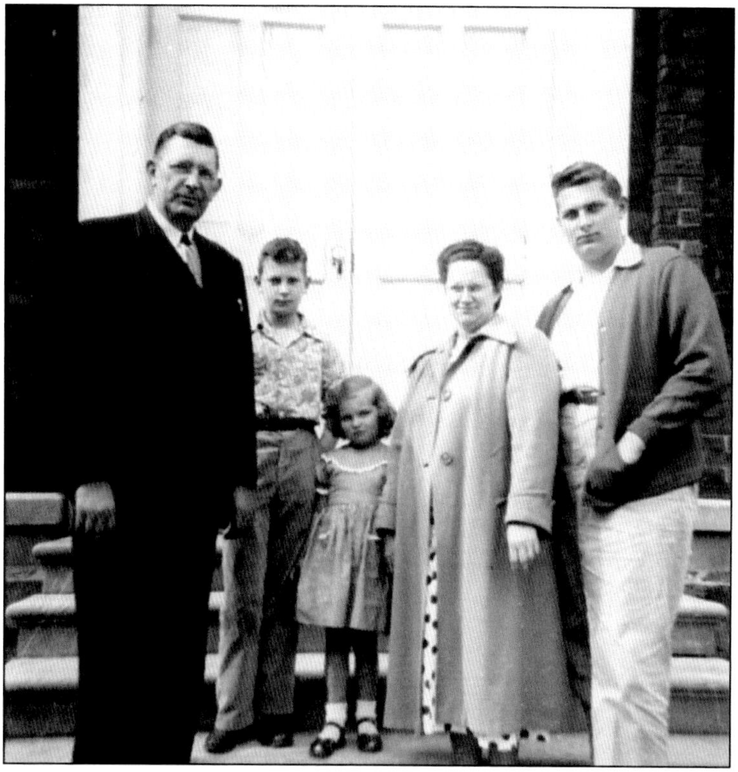

The family of Reverend Stolting stands on the steps of the Grace Methodist Church. Stolting was pastor of the old brick church during the mid-1940s. A new stone church was later constructed on the site.

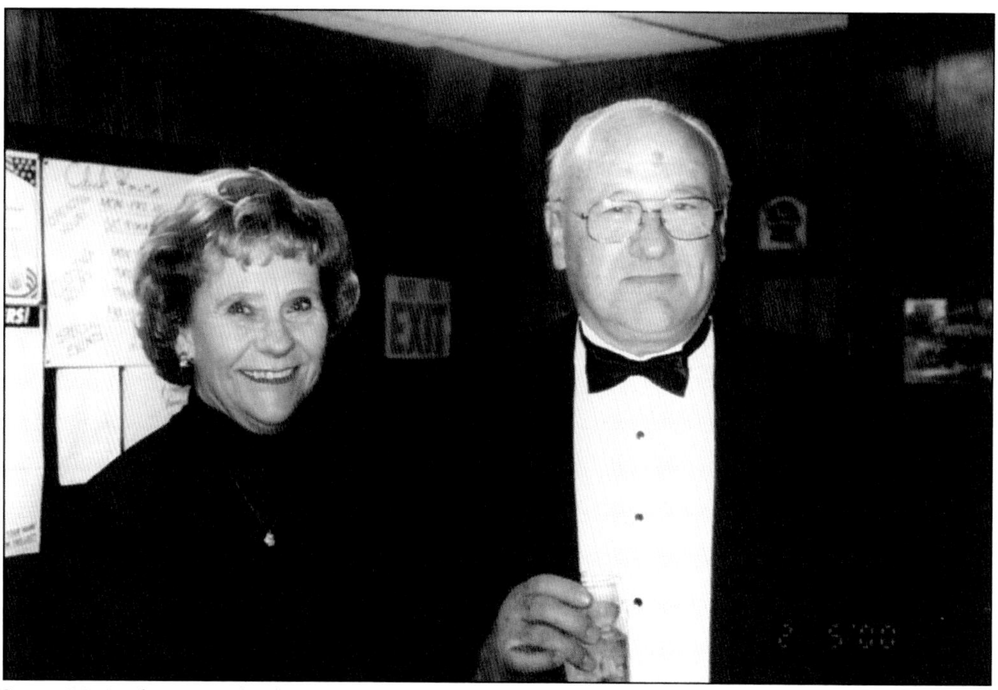

James H. Anderson and Edna Anderson (née Gulbrandsen) once owned the Red Barrel drive-in restaurant on East Sixteenth Street. James later got involved with real estate and land development. (Courtesy of Jim Anderson.)

State police detective Sam Kruse lived in Lawrence County and served the people for 32 years until his death in 2001.

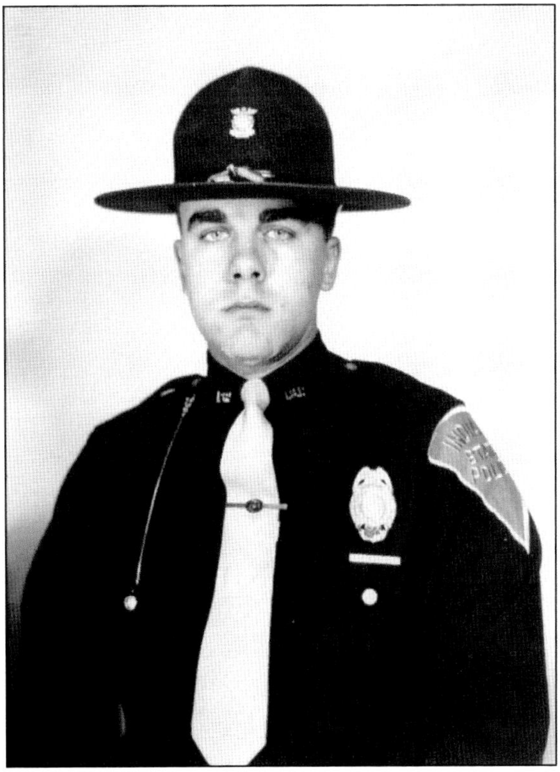

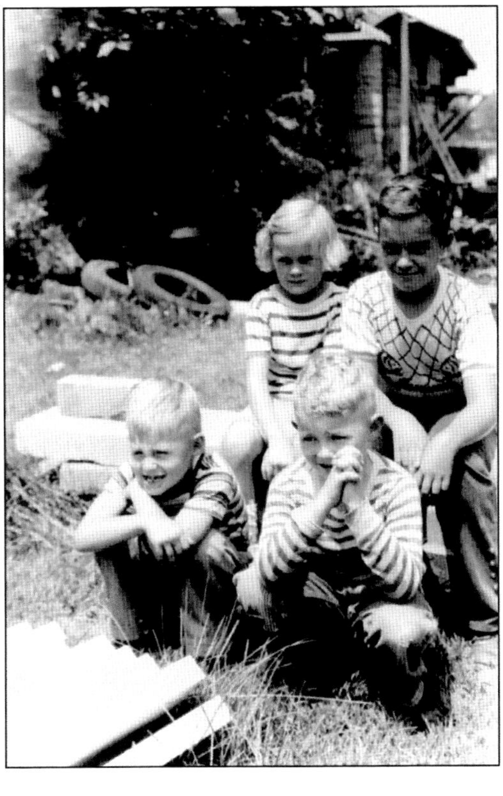

The young Overton brothers are sitting in the first row, and the Manzenberger children are in the back. These children from the north end of town have stopped their play, around 1940, to pose for this picture. They went to Madden School, located on Sixth Street.

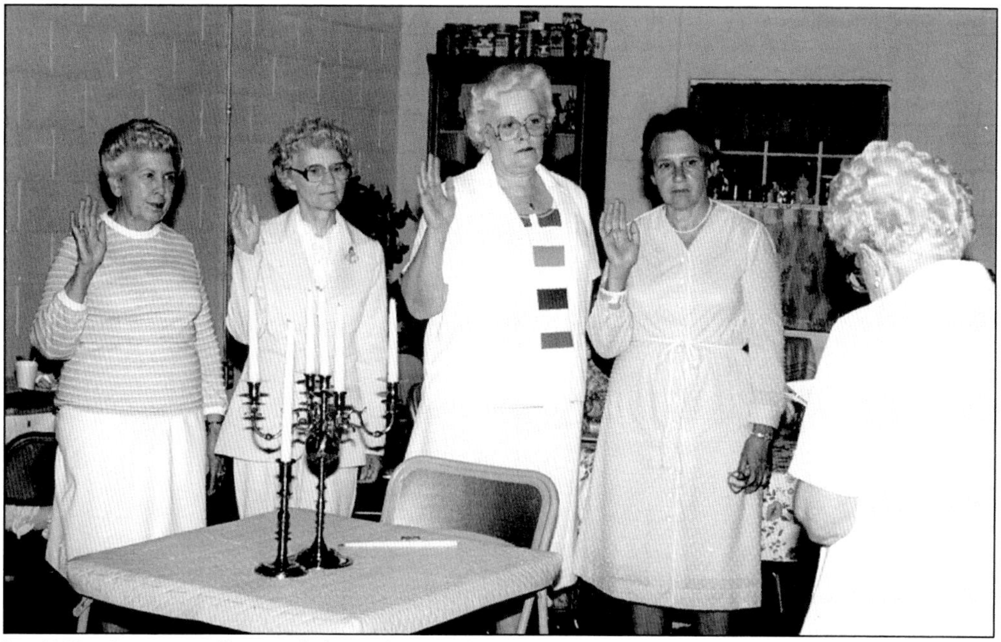

In 1982, the new officers of the John Wallace Chapter National Society Daughters of the American Revolution are being sworn in. The woman in the center dressed in white is the new regent, Norma Brock.

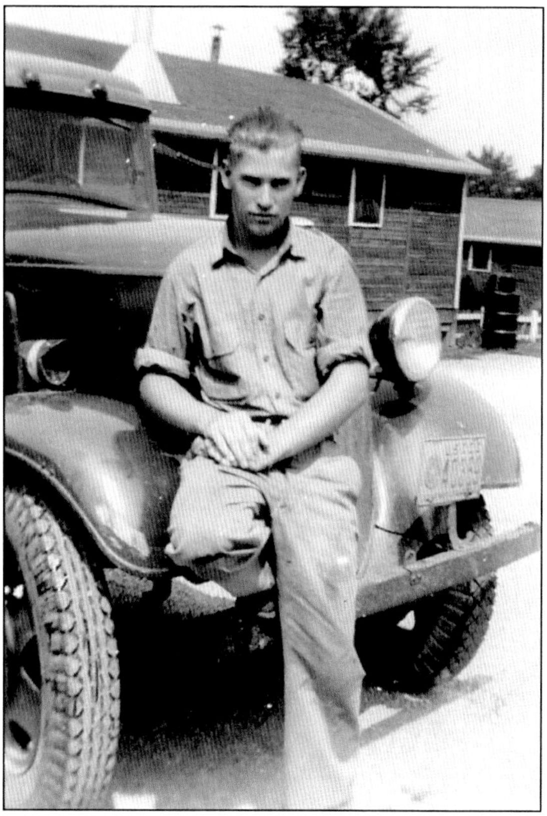

George Hilderbran is shown in front of Civilian Conservation Corps Camp No. 1594 where he served in the years of 1939–1940.

Ben Hitchcock and his wife Audry are shown in front of their home in Bedford. Ben, the son of Jacob Mancel Hitchcock and Charlotte Hitchcock (née Crane), was a businessman and a farmer.

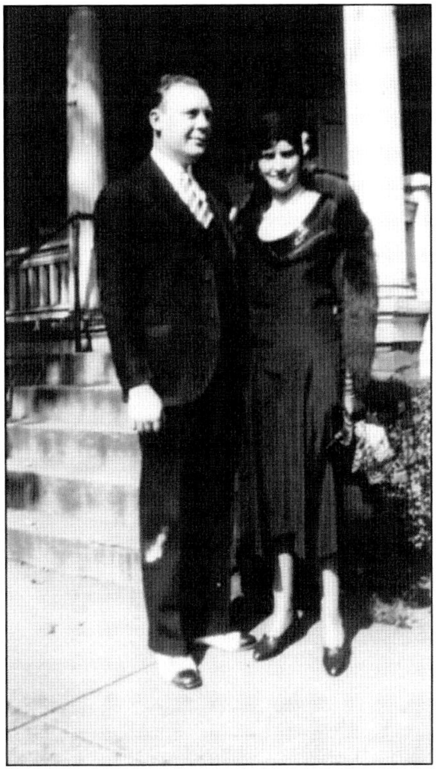

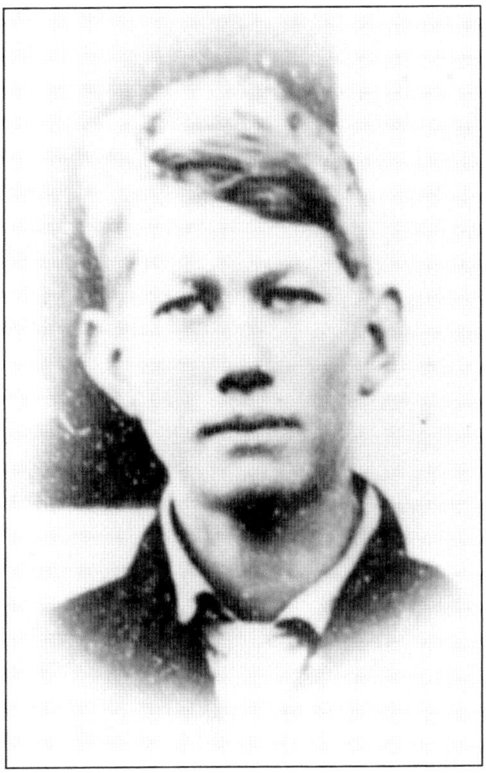

This is a photograph taken in 1919 of Frank Chiles. Postcard photographs were very popular at this time.

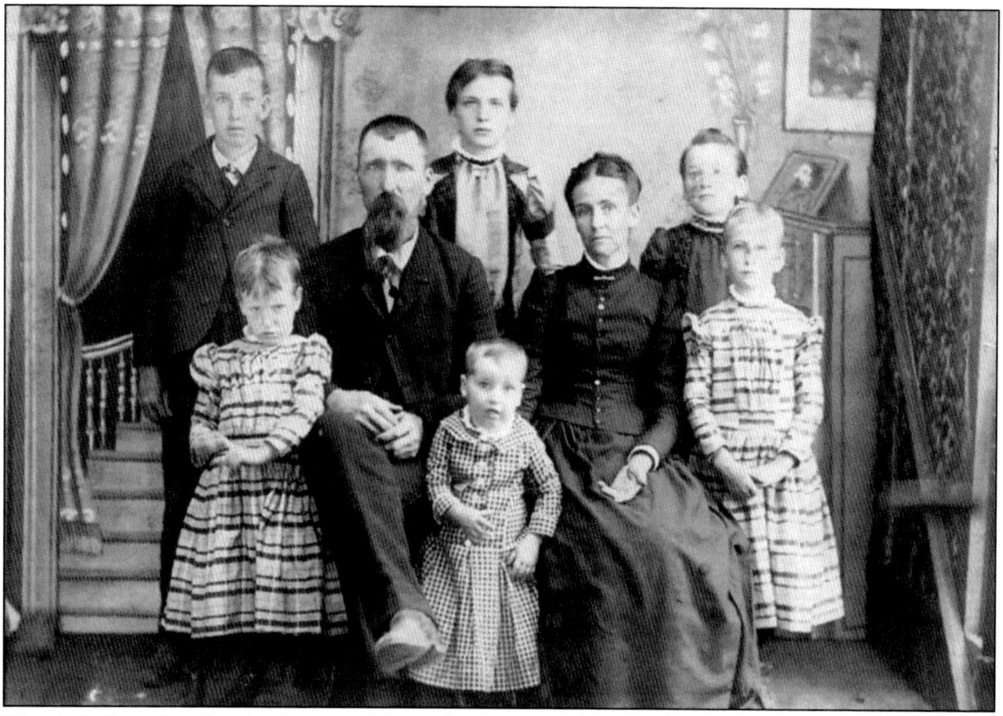

This is believed to be the family of Ben Hotz and Emily Hotz (née Smith). The names of the children are not known. This picture was taken around 1900.

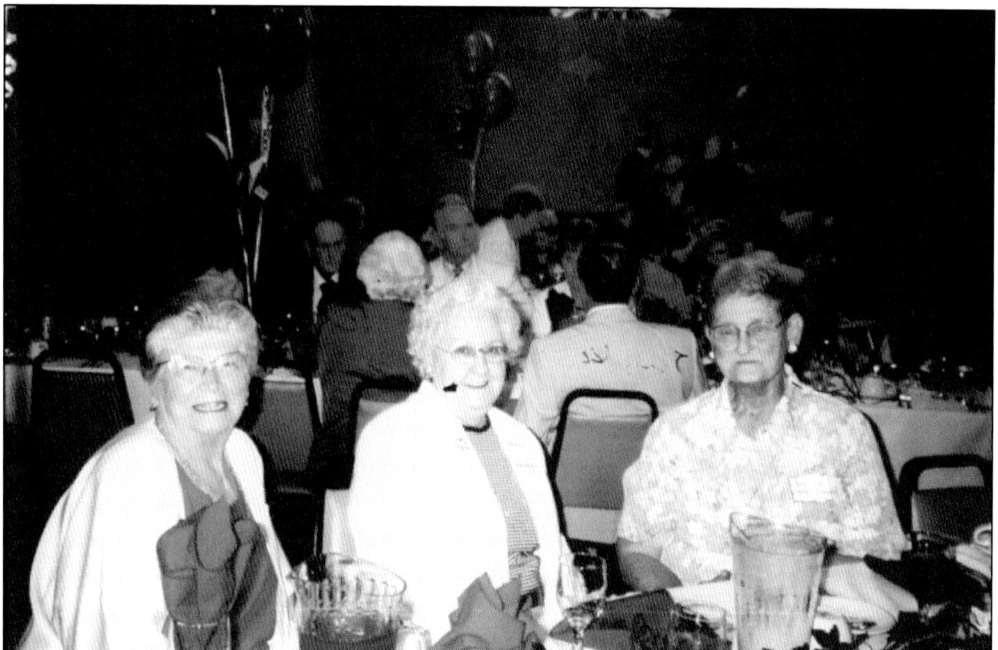

From left to right, Ann Miller (née Winterhalter), Catherine Bowden (née Adamson), and Betty Bodkins (née Ikerd) are enjoying their 50th Bedford High School reunion at the Stonehenge Lodge in Bedford in 1997.

Two

TRANSPORTATION AND TRAVEL

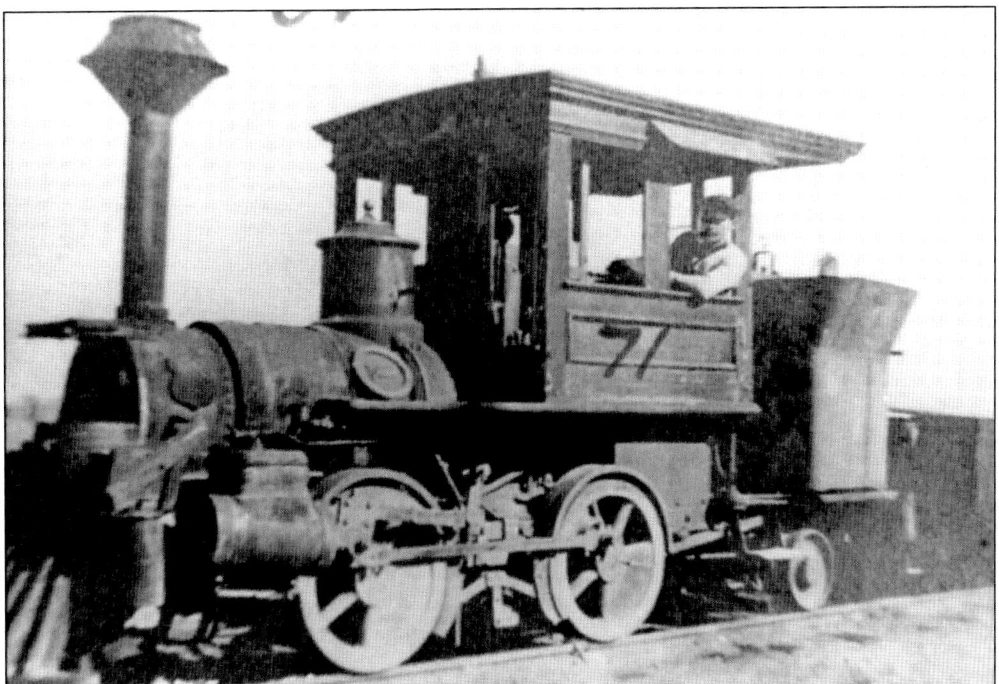

One of the early locomotives stopped for this photograph. The engineer is unidentified. Bedford has a railroad track going through the downtown square.

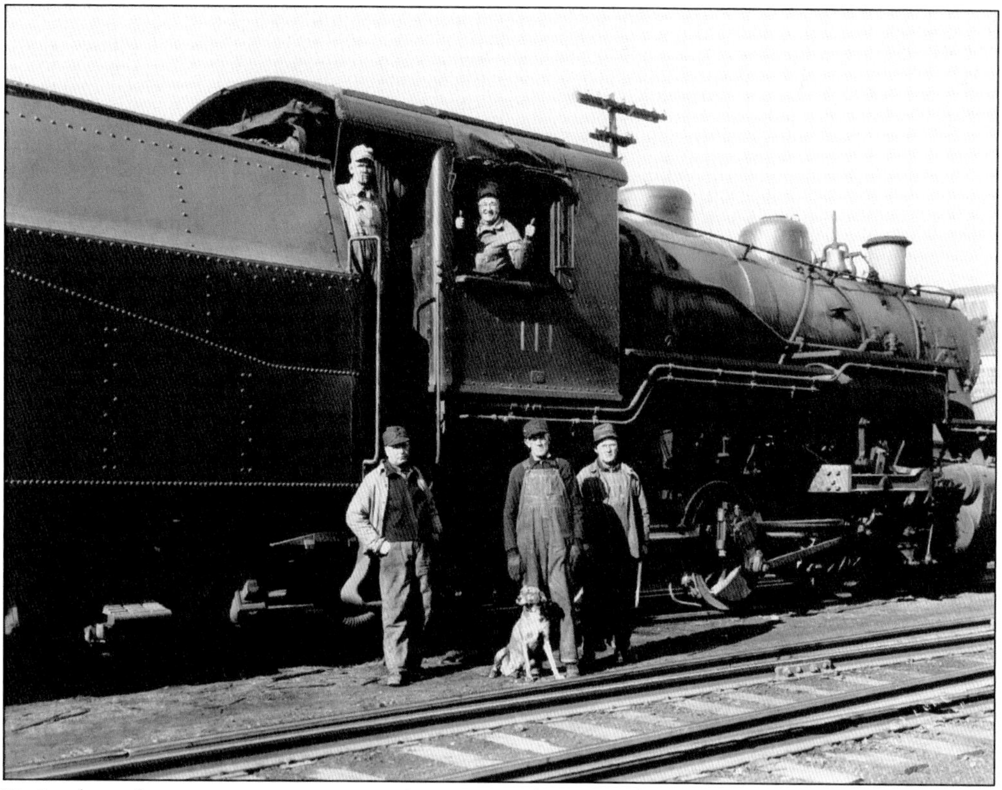

Trains have been very important to this area and were welcome; both as transportation for people and to ship limestone to all parts of the country. During the war years, railroads were used to transport troops. The Monon tracks run along J Street in downtown Bedford.

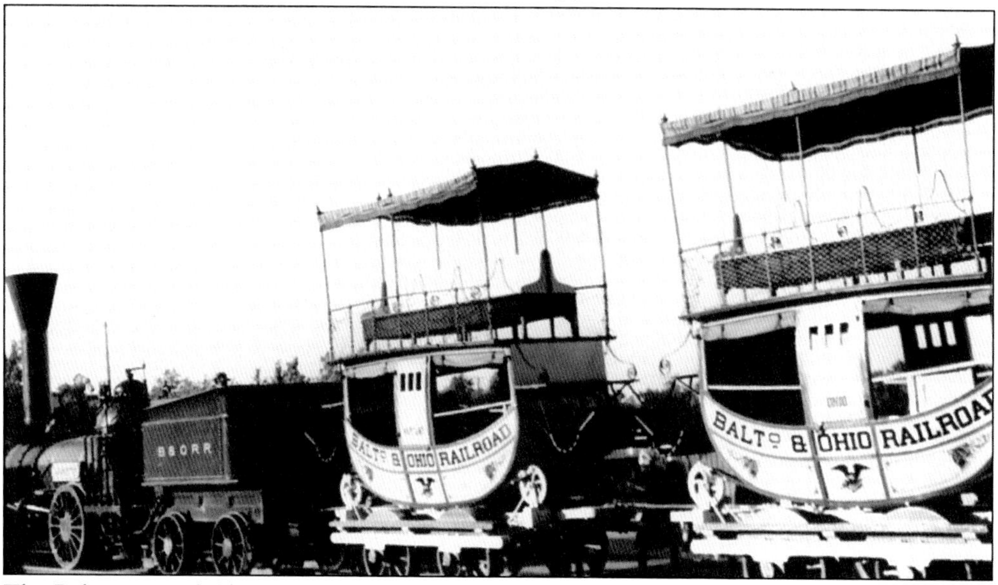

The Baltimore and Ohio train rolled through town in celebration. In the late 1890s and early 1900s, the Baltimore and Ohio Railroad, which goes through Mitchell, was quite important to the growth of the county.

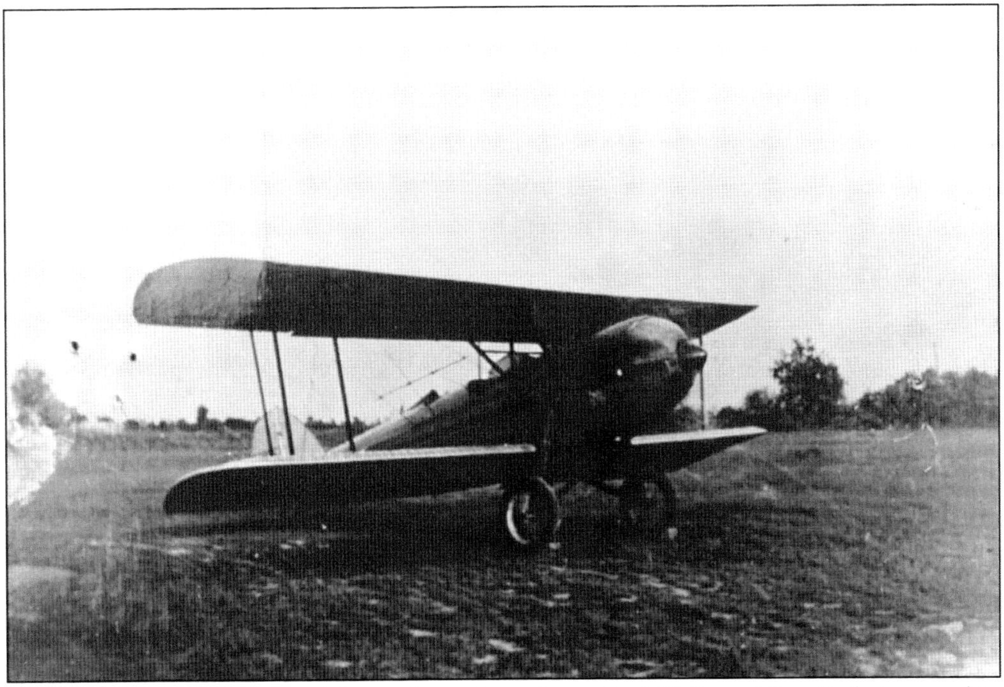

In 1938, Mac McClord owned this early airplane. Later, Bud Walls and Jim Guthrie owned it. Walls was in the insurance business and Guthrie worked at a Bedford bank before retiring and becoming an authority on Lawrence County history.

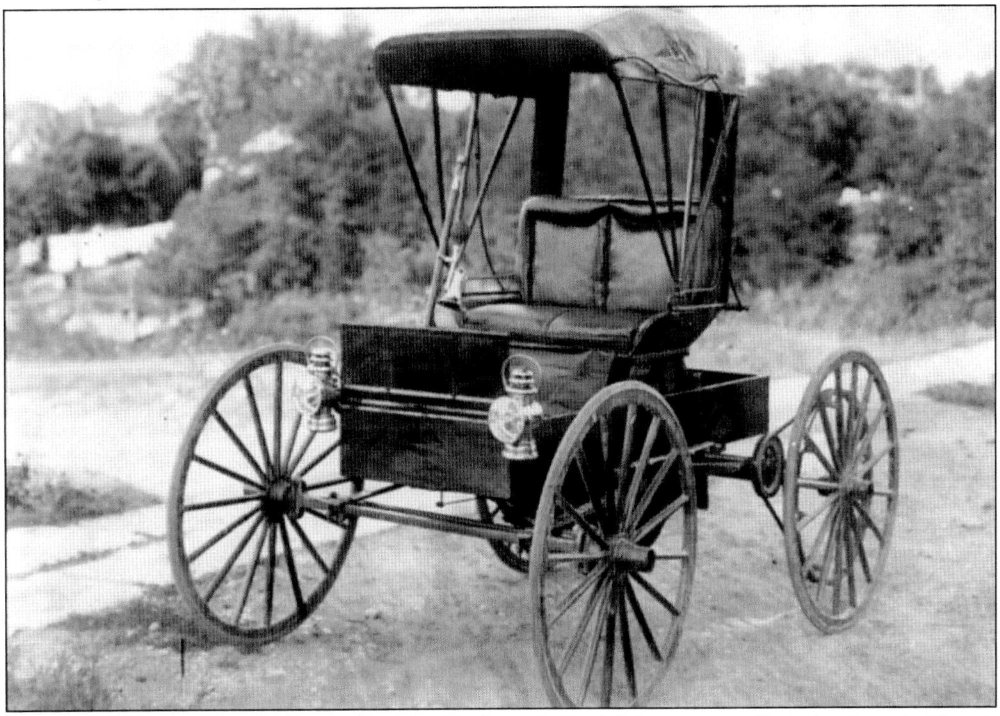

An automobile was manufactured in Bedford in 1908–1909. It was called the Postal. This is believed to be a picture of the early car.

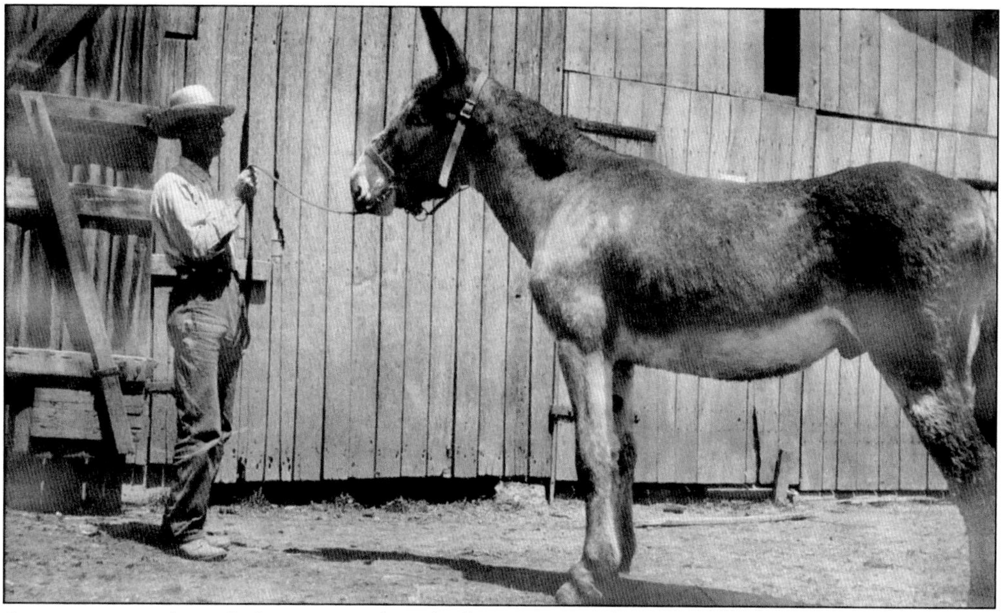

A common southern Indiana animal in the late 1890s and early 1900s was the mule. This jack is nine years old. Miles Standish, who had a farm on South I Street, raised mules for the coal mines and to be used by the U.S. Army in World War I.

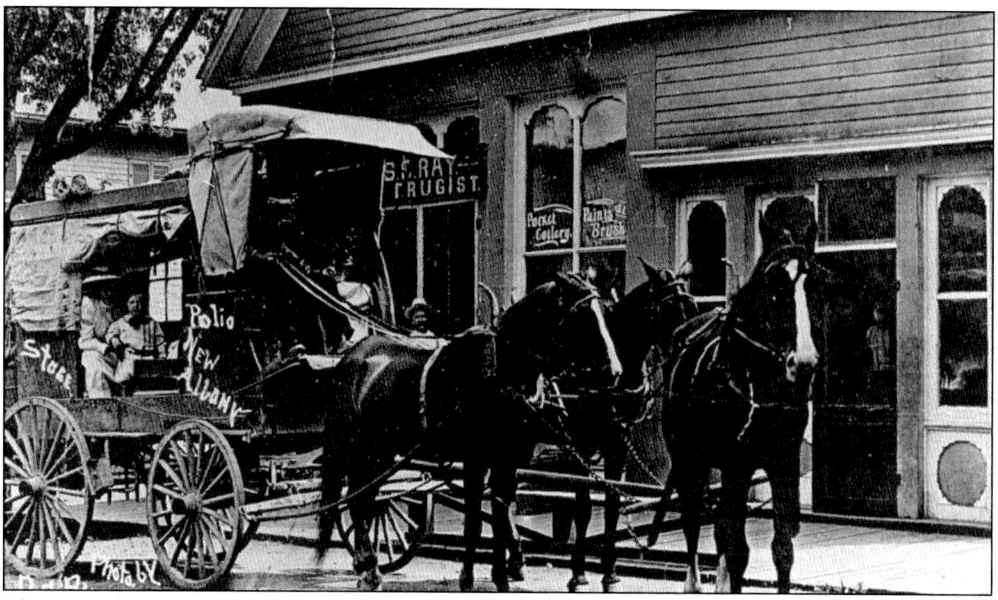

This is a photograph of the New Albany Stagecoach that has stopped for passengers in 1913. There are two passengers shown in the coach checking out the city.

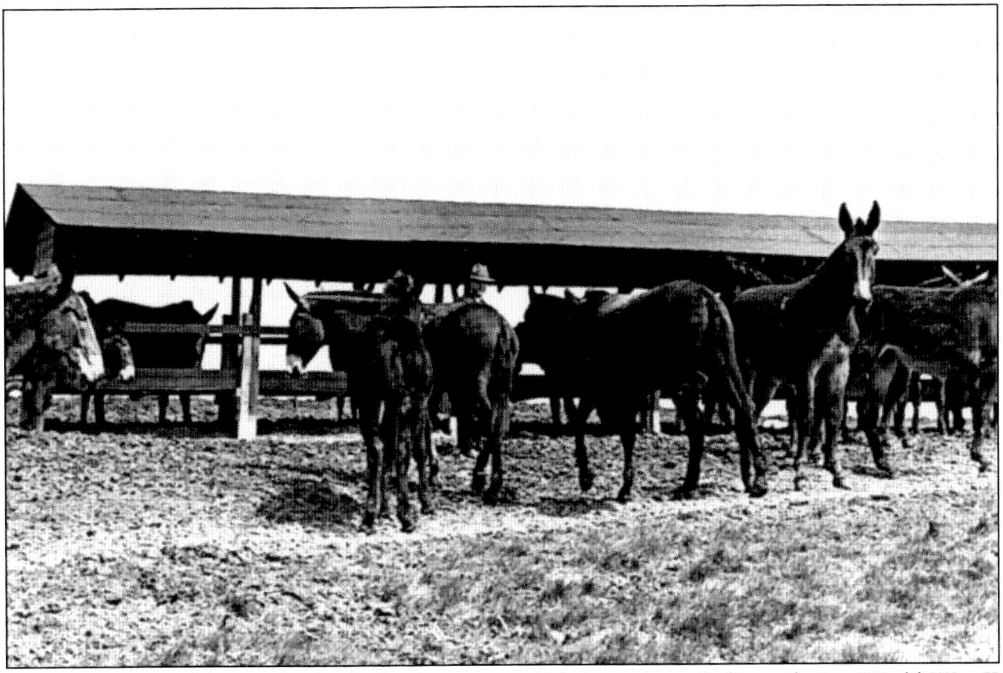

Jim Anderson and his uncle Doyle Anderson traveled throughout Indiana during World War II buying mules that were sold to the U.S. Army. Doyle bought 55 gallon barrels of black strap molasses to mix with grain and feed to the mules. This gave them a glossy coat and fattened them. (Courtesy of Jim Anderson.)

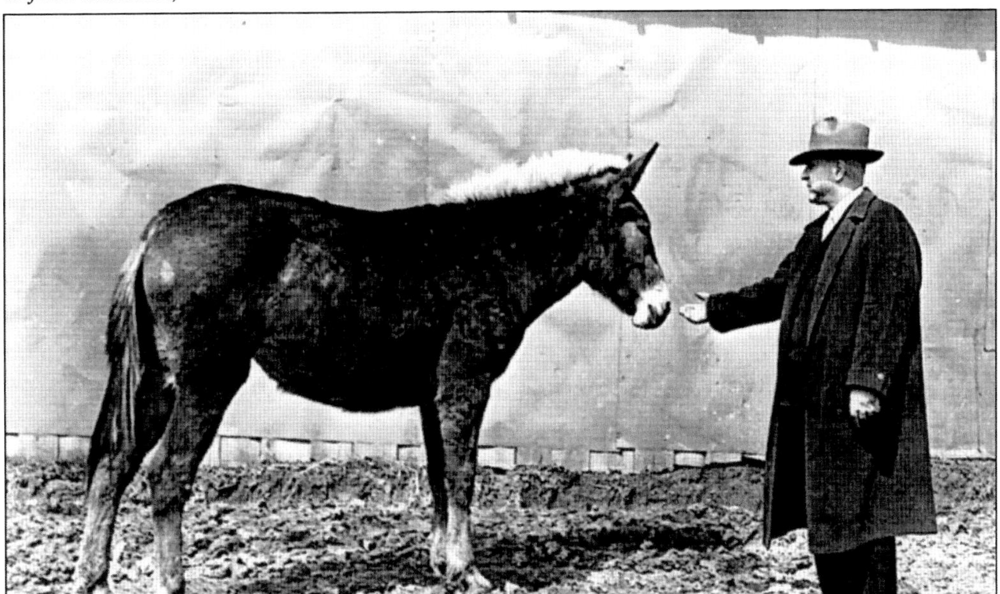

Doyle Anderson, pictured with one of his mules, owned the first Coca-Cola plant in Bedford. It was located on the southwest corner of Fourteenth and I Streets. He sold the plant in 1928 and moved to Fort Wayne, where he built the third largest Coca-Cola plant in the world. (Courtesy of Jim Anderson.)

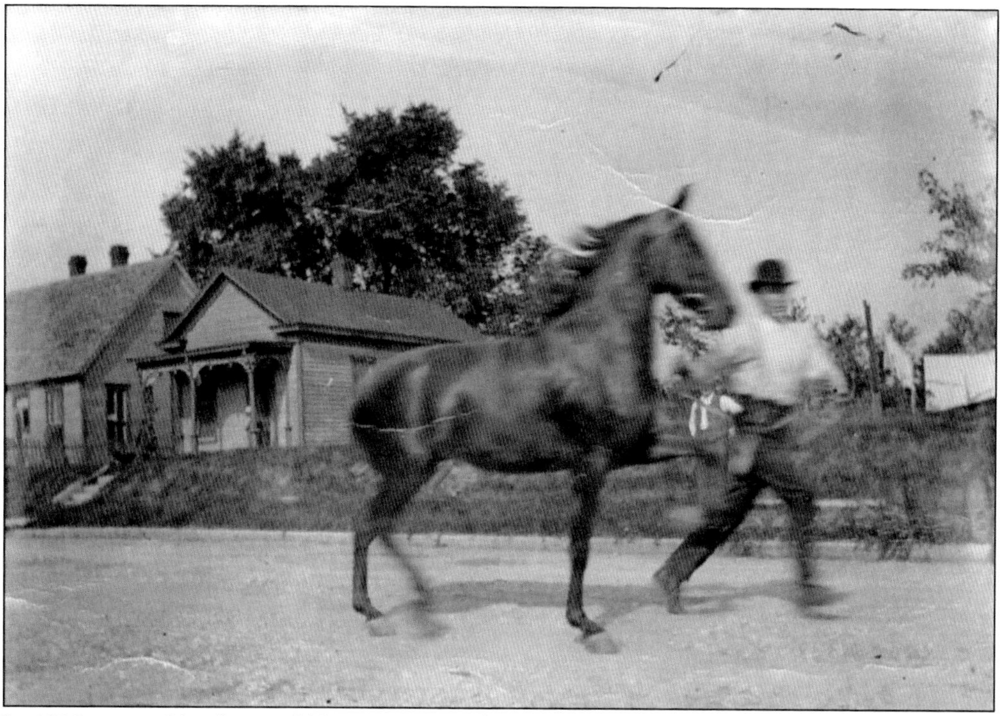

In 1900, scenes like this could be seen quite often in Bedford. It looks as if the horse is about to outdistance the man.

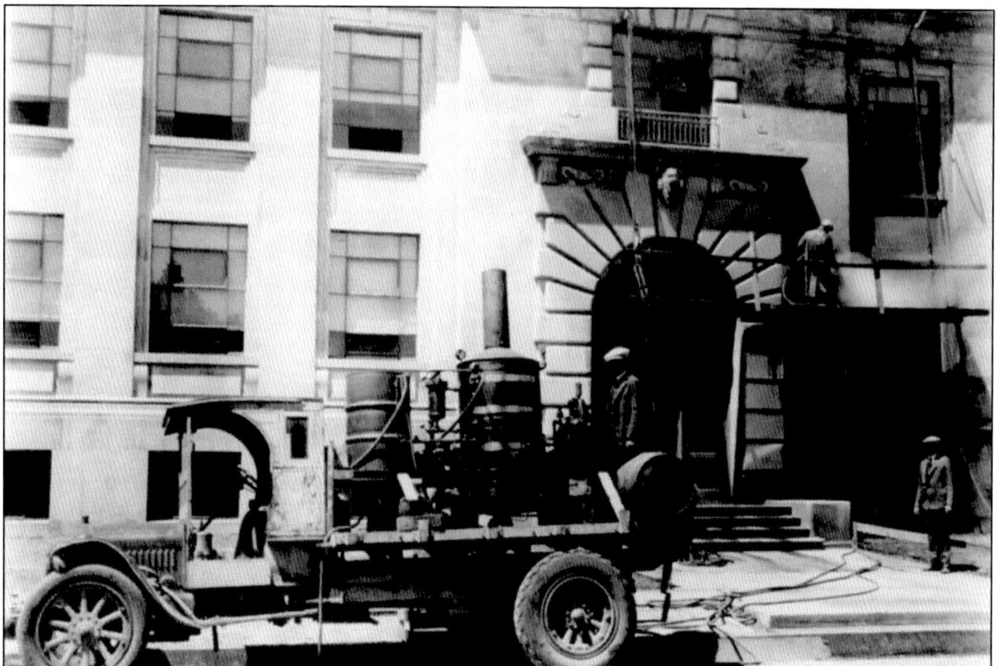

This truck is in front of the Indiana Limestone Company and workers are sandblasting the stone of the exterior of the building. The building is now home to Oakland City College, Bedford, and houses a museum; the Land of Limestone.

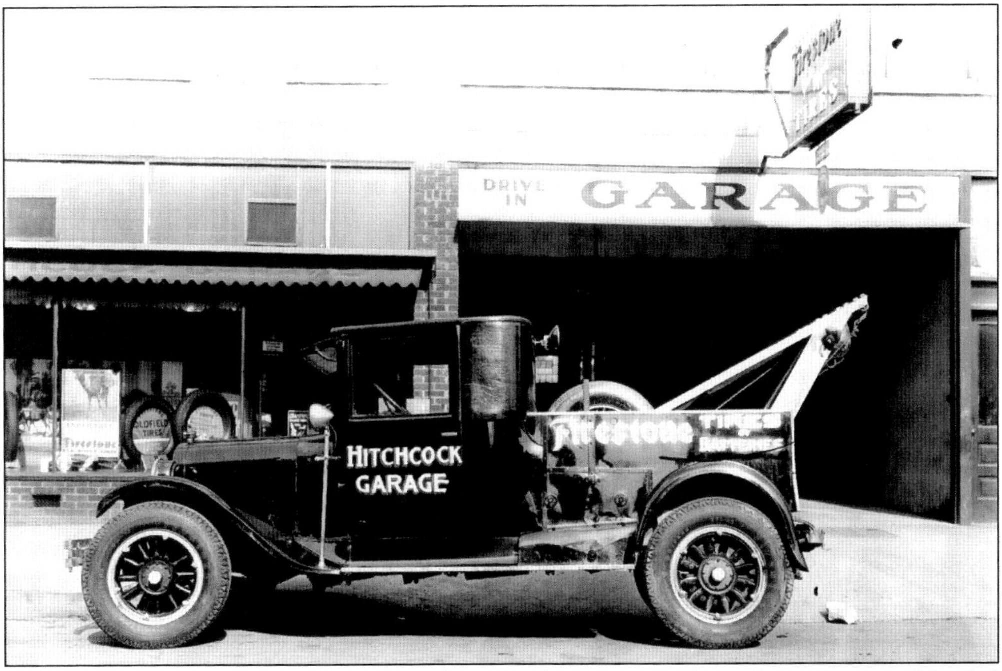

In the 1940s, Ben Hitchcock owned and operated a garage and wrecker service on North I Street in Bedford. He was also a large landowner and had a farm south of town, which stretched approximately 17 miles along White River.

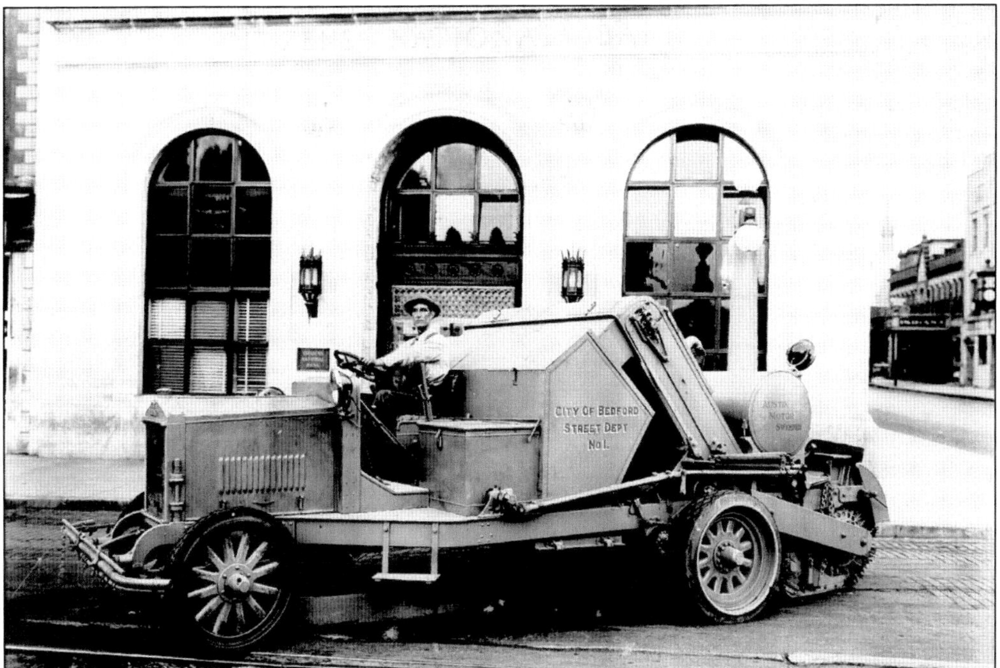

The Bedford Street Department could be seen cleaning the streets each day. This picture was taken at the corner of Fifteenth and J Streets, downtown. Citizens National Bank is in the background.

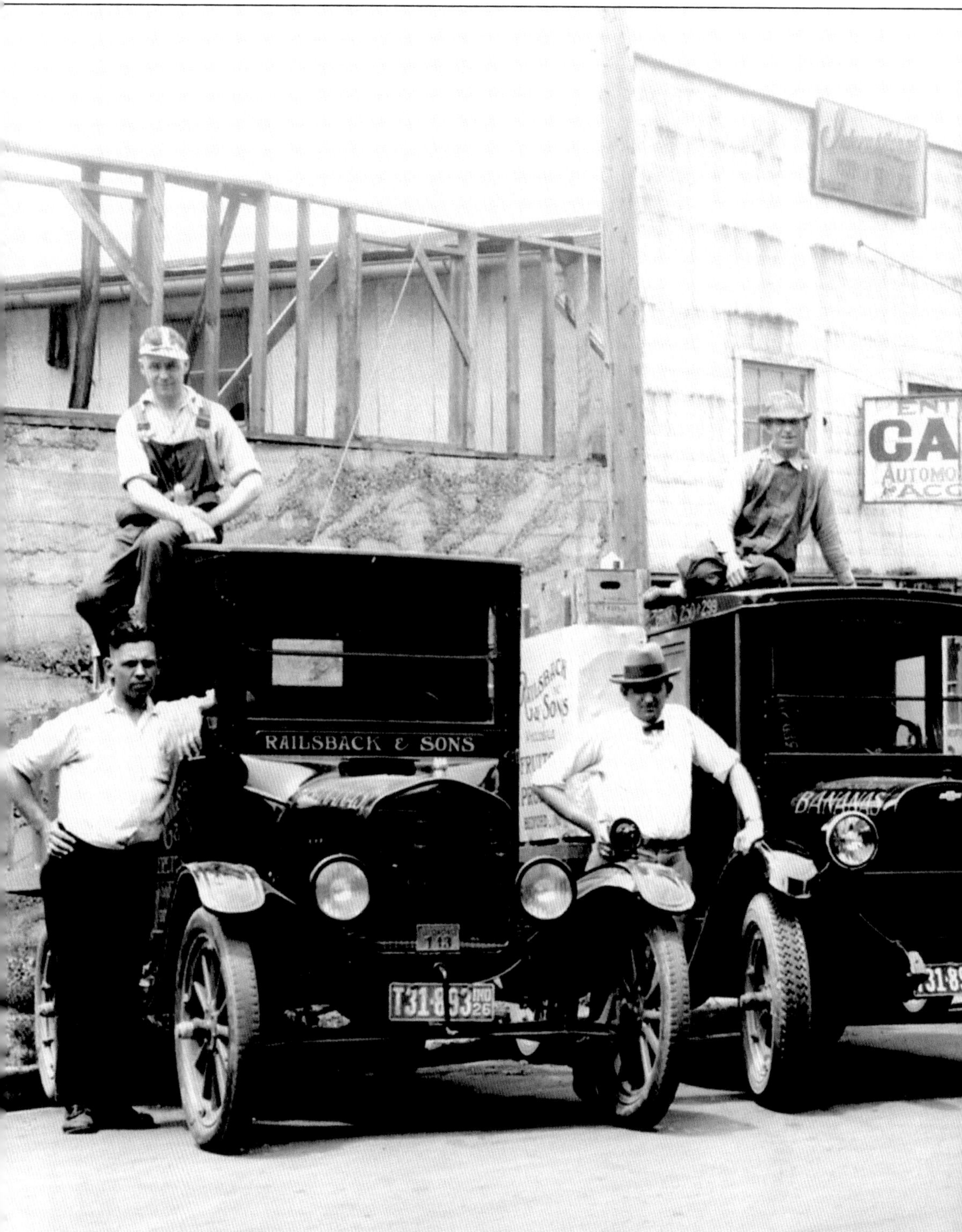

In 1926, Enterprise Garage–Automobile Access Company was located in Bedford. These young men worked at Railsback and Sons who operated a group of produce trucks. They are posing

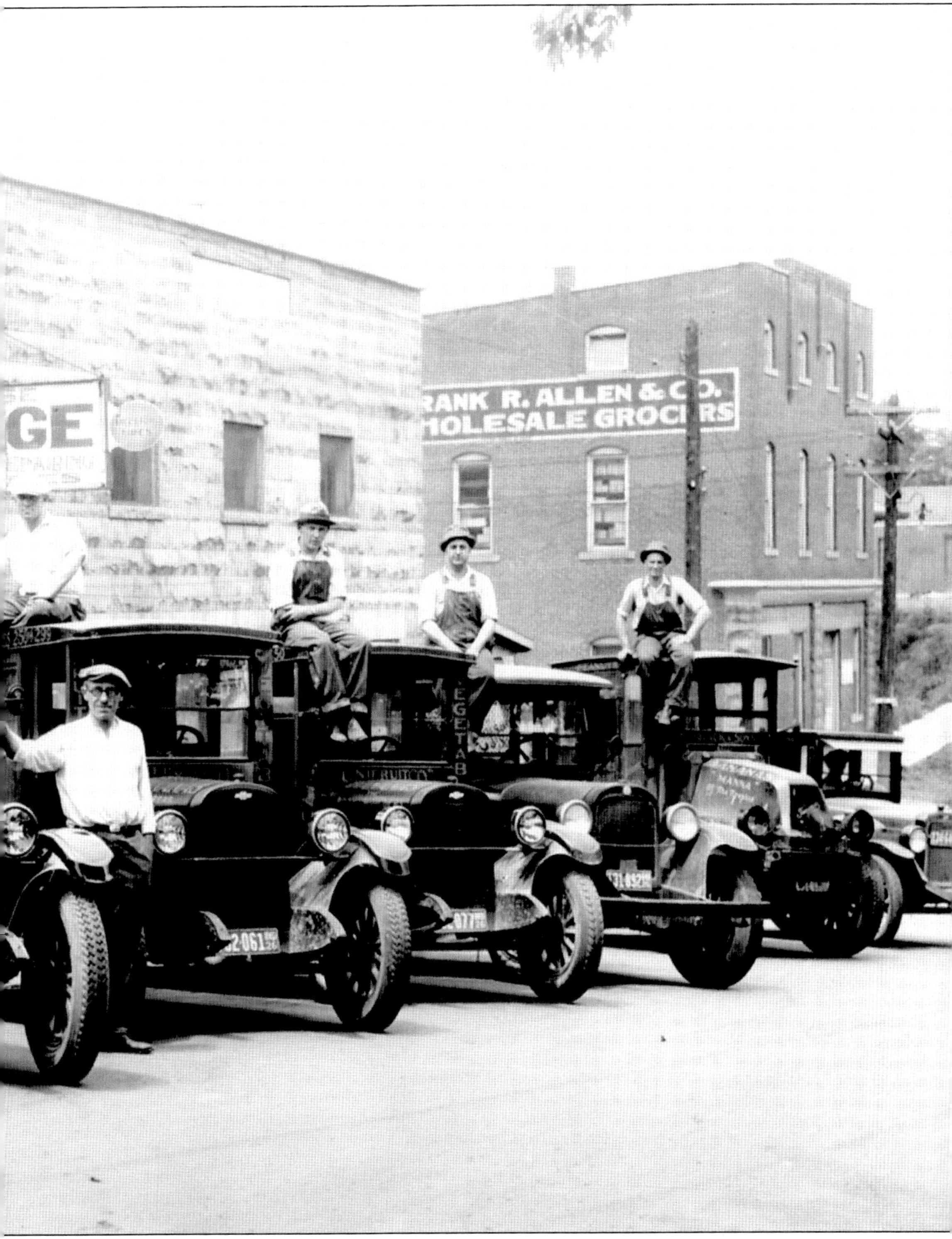

beside their vehicles. In the distance, notice the Frank R. Allen and Company Wholesale Grocers. Neither business exists today.

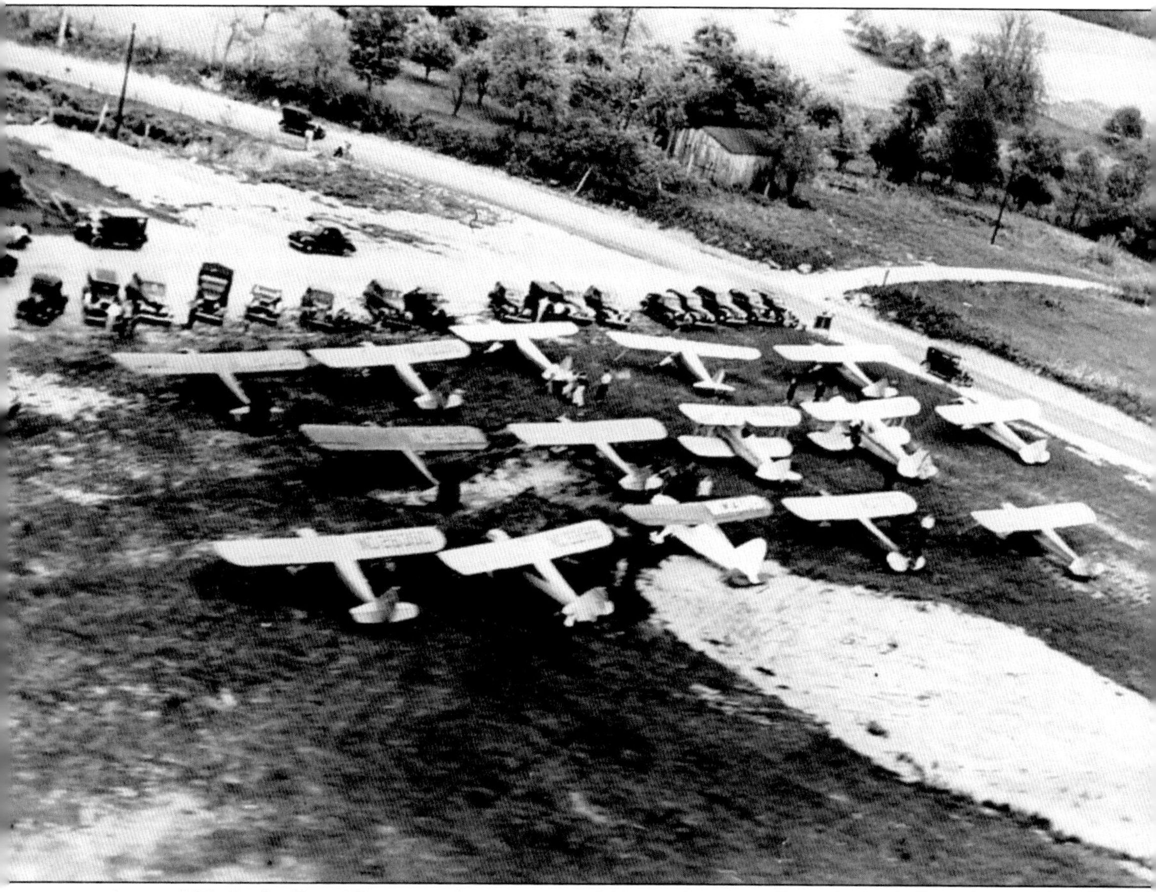

Around 1940, the Fort Wayne, Indiana, Aero Club came to Bedford and was at Harbaugh Field, the county's airport. At one time, there were two small airports in the county; the other was located in the Englewood neighborhood. The latter no longer exists. Just after the astronaut Virgil "Gus" Grissom was killed in the Apollo fire, the name of Harbaugh was changed to the Grissom Airport. It is located just outside of Bedford on Tunnelton Road. Several years ago, this airport was hit by a tornado.

Three

DOWNTOWN SQUARE, BUSINESSES, AND STREETS

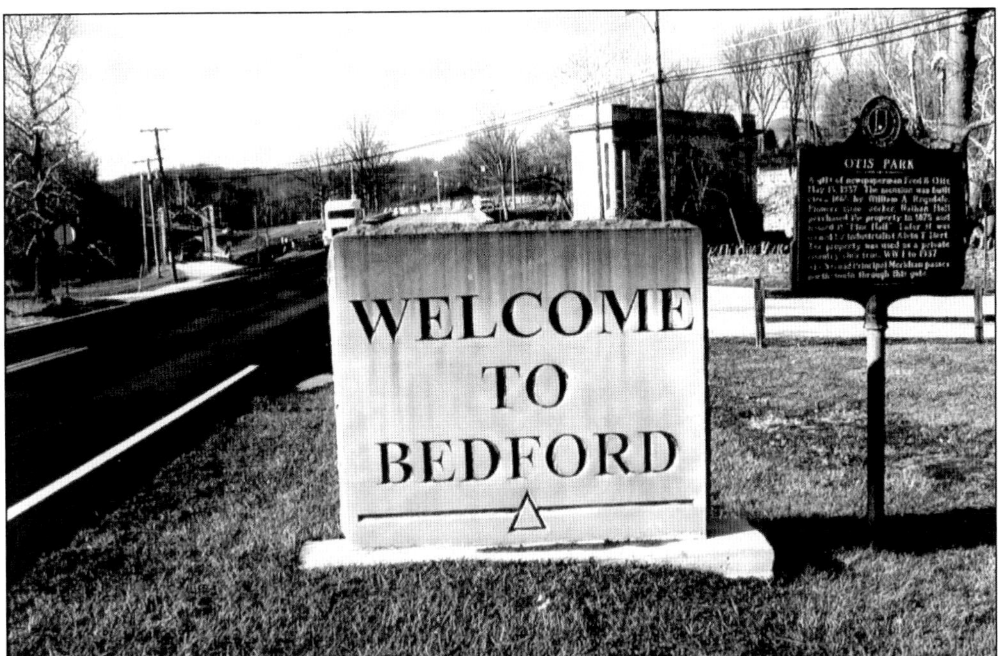

Bedford is located in south central Indiana. The city can be reached by traveling Indiana Highway 37 or U.S. Route 50. A limestone panel, such as that above, welcomes people to the city.

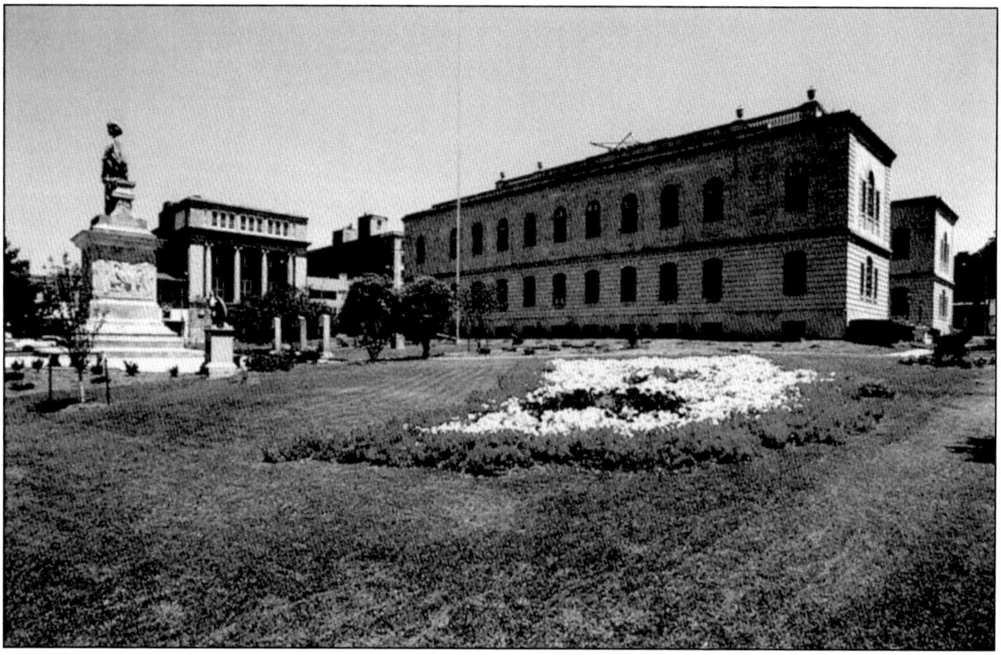

The Lawrence County Courthouse is located in the center of the Bedford public square. The county seat was located in Bedford in 1825. Portions of the present building were built in the late 1870s, and major remodeling was done in the 1930s.

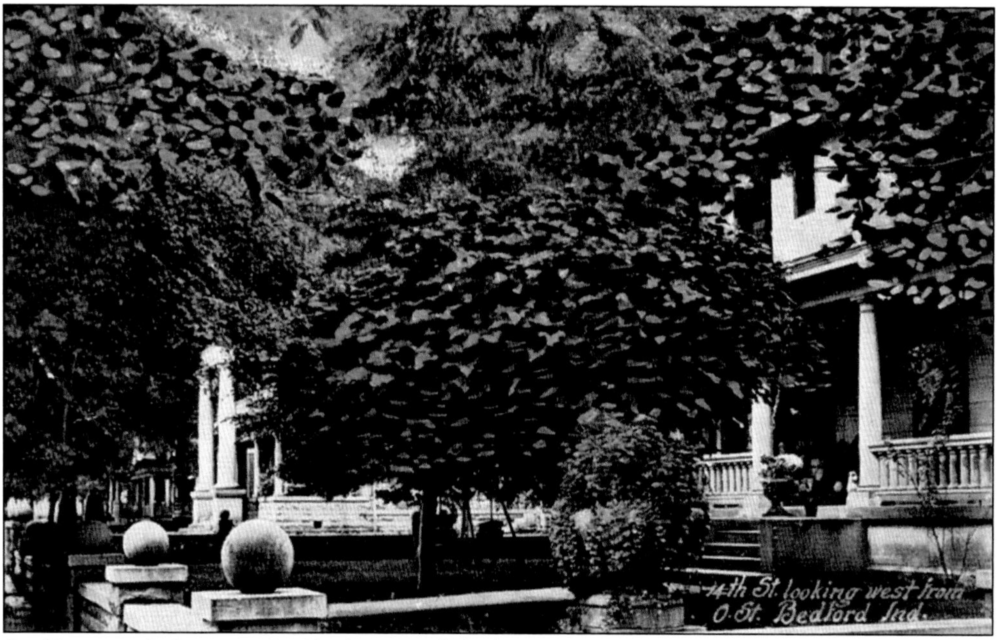

On Fourteenth Street in Bedford, one will find several solid stone houses that were owned by limestone company executives and owners at one time. These homes now have new owners.

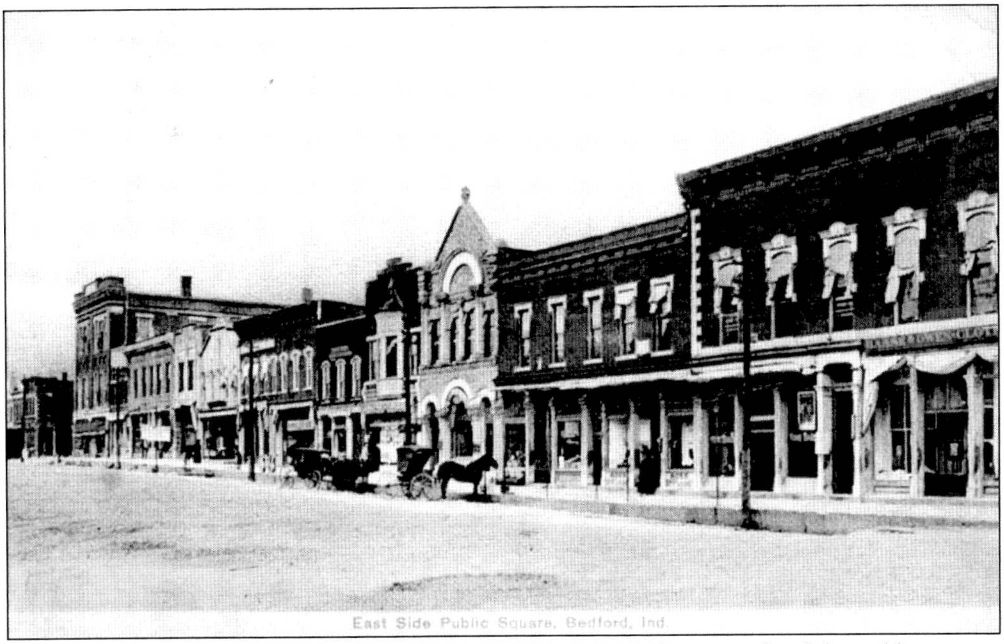

In 1909, this postcard shows the stores that were located on the east side of the public square. Notice the two horses with buggies parked in the picture.

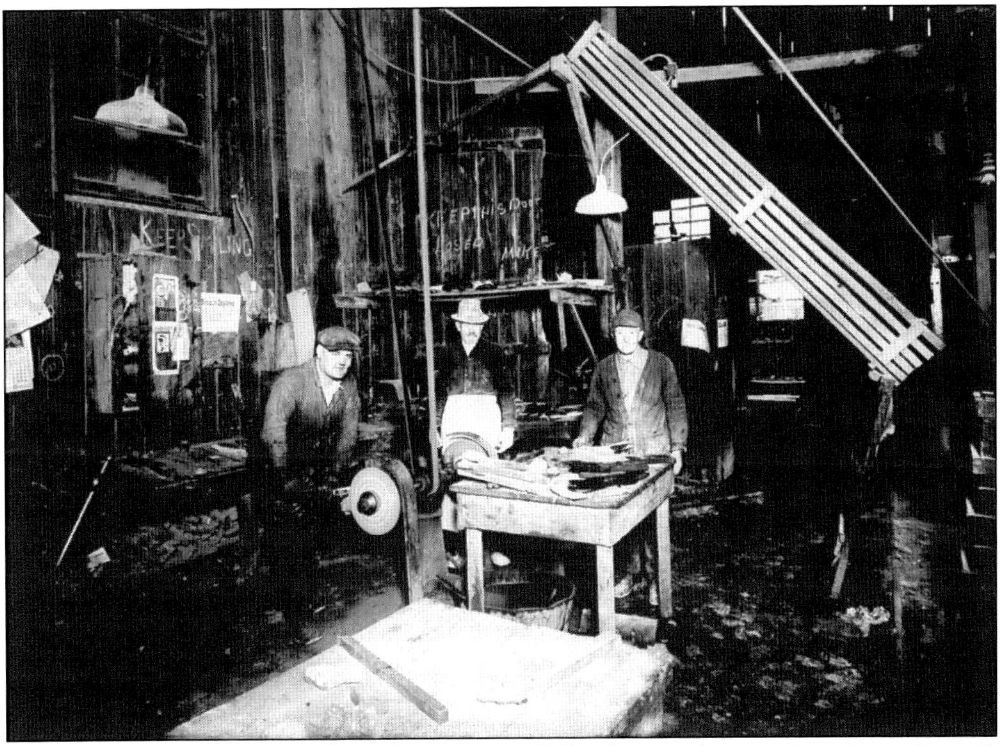

This is a photograph of an early workshop in the 1900s. It is not known where it was located. The photograph came from the Erwin-Johnson estate.

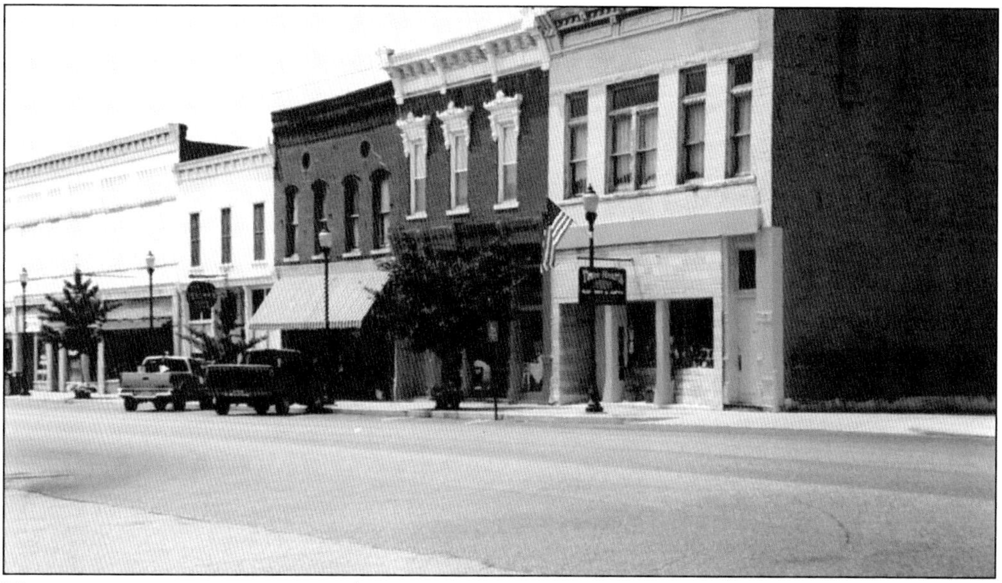

There are many antique stores in the area. Main Street of Mitchell, just south of Bedford, is filled with antique shops. This is the hometown of Virgil "Gus" Grissom.

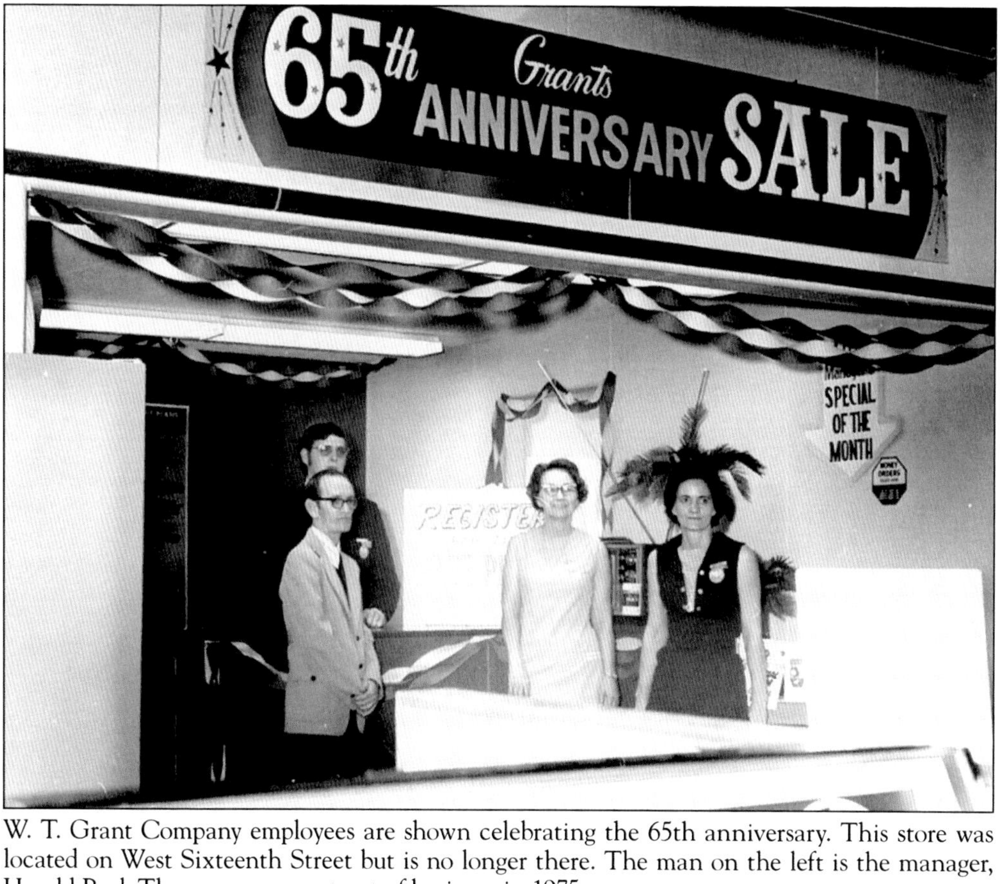

W. T. Grant Company employees are shown celebrating the 65th anniversary. This store was located on West Sixteenth Street but is no longer there. The man on the left is the manager, Harold Paul. The company went out of business in 1975.

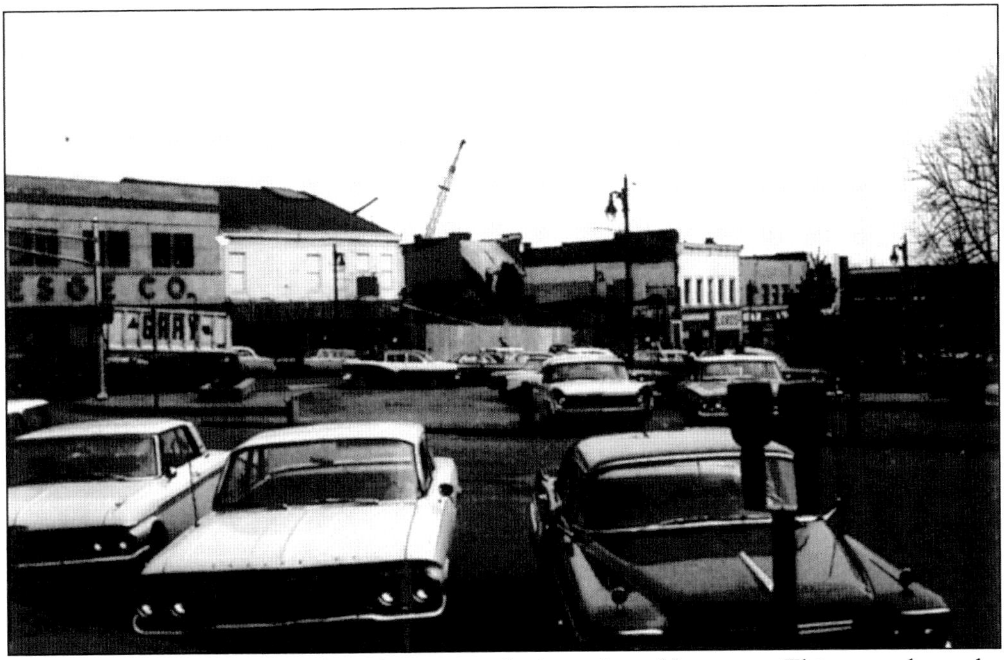

In the 1960s, a new W. F. Woolworth Store was built on the public square. This scene shows the demolition of other stores to make room for the new store. The stores torn down were; the old Woolworth, Montgomery Ward, Singer Sewing Company, and Franklin's Drug Store. (Courtesy of Jim Anderson.)

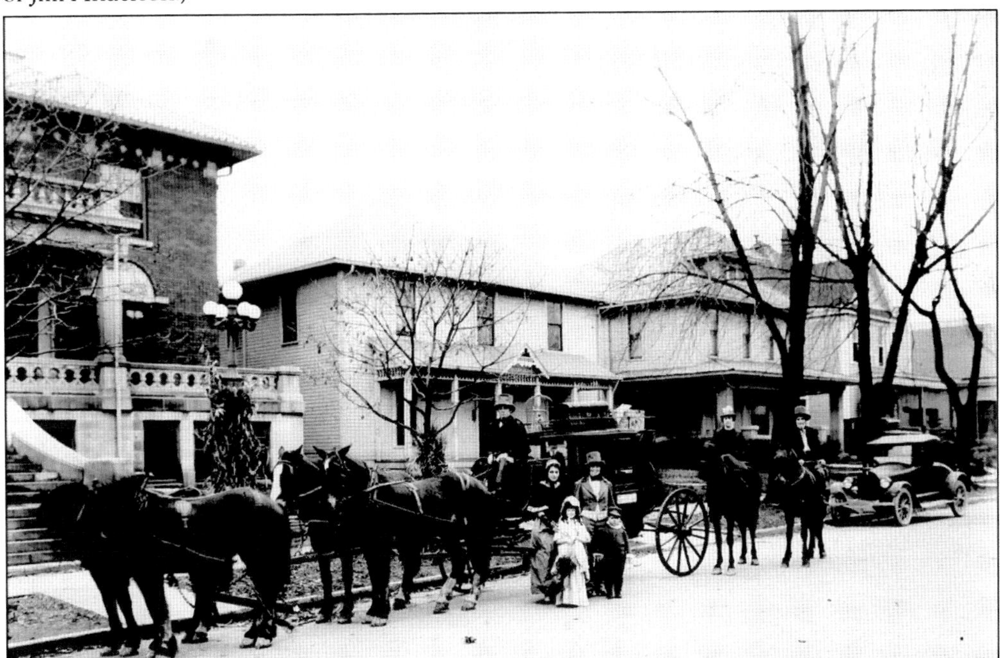

This photograph was taken during the centennial celebration in Bedford in 1925. The Tri Kappa entry is shown in front of the brick and stone Elks Club building, which is located on Fifteenth Street. The people in the picture are unidentified.

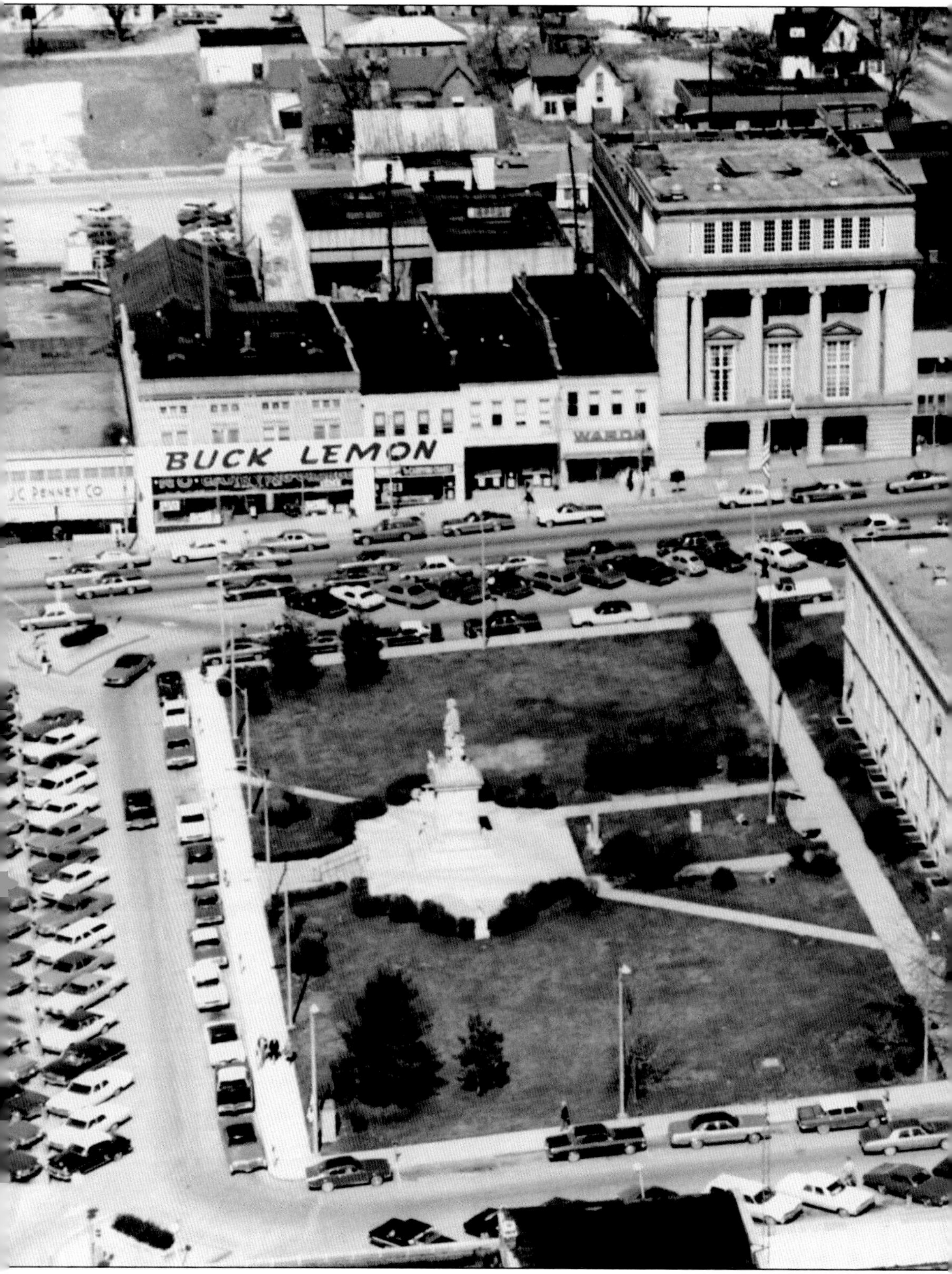
BUCK LEMON
J.C. PENNEY CO

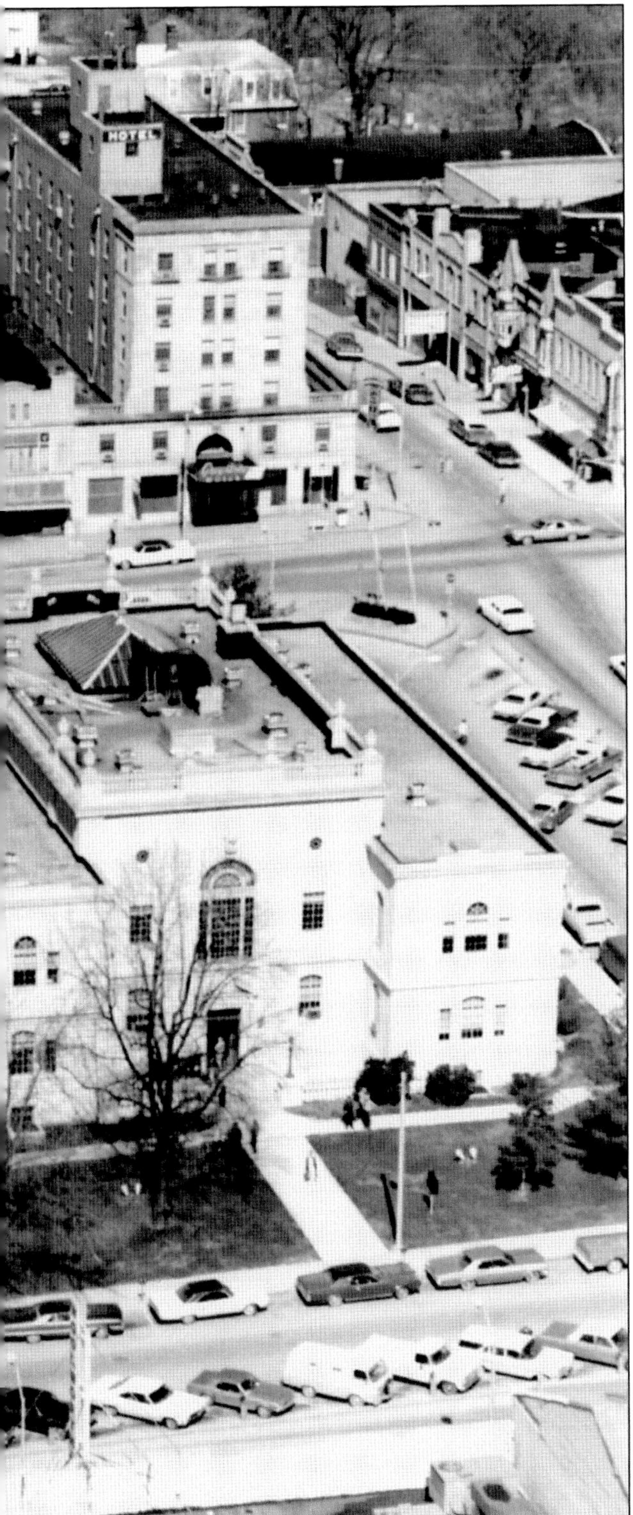

This is an aerial survey picture of the downtown public square of Bedford. Lawrence County Courthouse is shown in the center. The tall building on the left is the Masonic lodge and the tall one on the right is the Greystone Hotel. The Buck Lemon building is now home to a museum and research library. The Greystone Hotel caught fire twice, was torn down, and a new building went up in its place. Most of the old stores are no longer around and have been replaced with offices. Many downtowns have given way to malls and strip centers; Bedford is no exception.

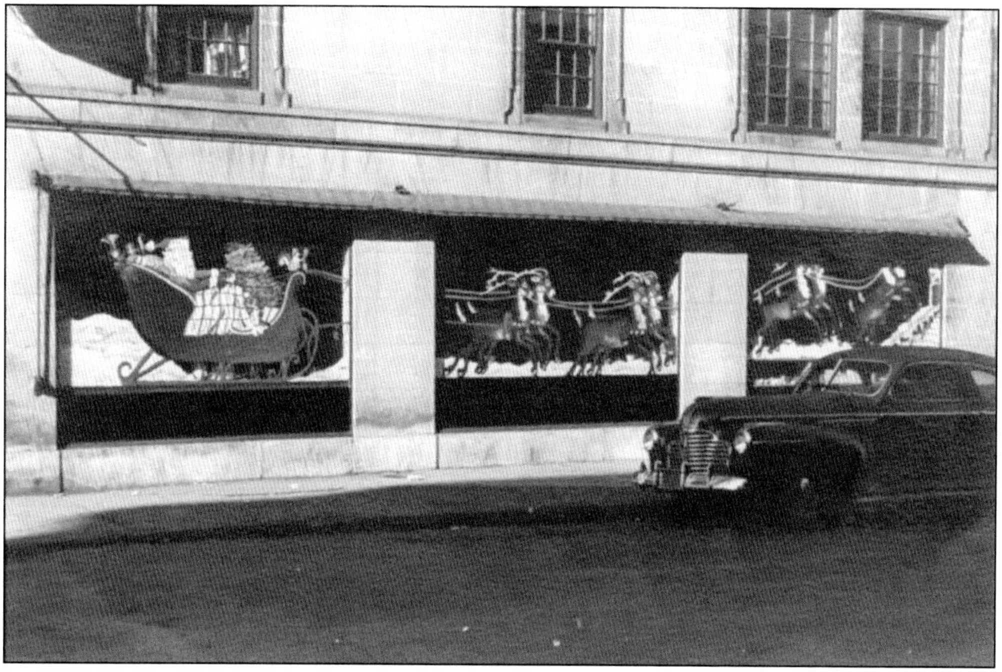

In 1947, Bedford High School senior Maxine Crane painted this Christmas scene on the windows of the Greystone Gift Shoppe, which was part of the Greystone Hotel. The hotel was built around 1929 and was advertised as the finest in southern Indiana.

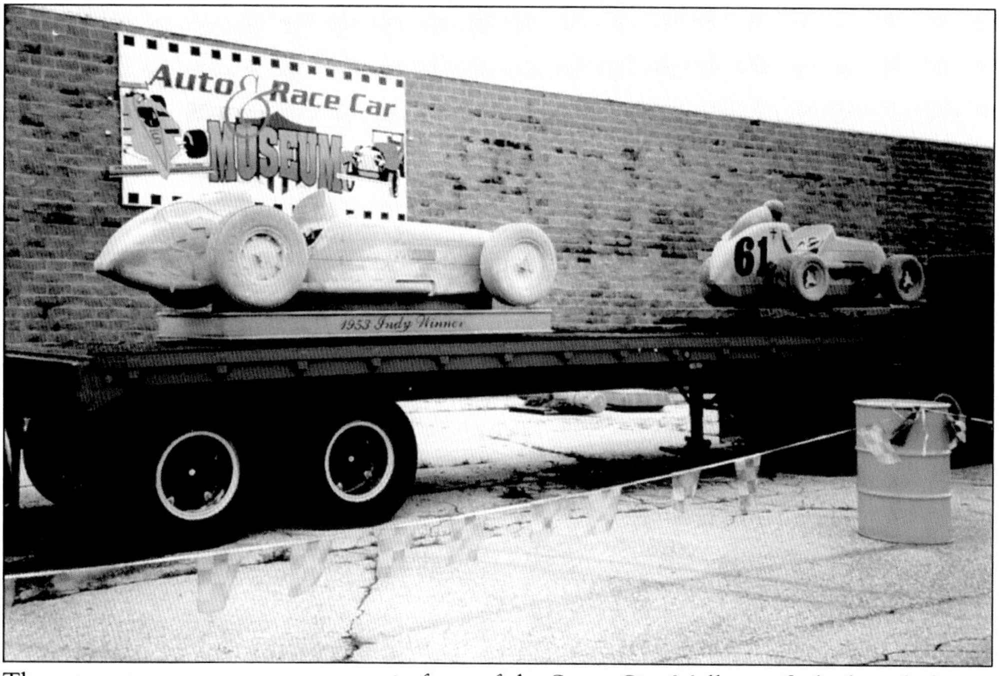

These two stone race cars were once in front of the Stone City Mall on a flatbed truck during the 1990s. Owner Eddie Evans had the Antique and Race Car Museum until the mall was sold in the late 1990s. Evans was the owner of Architectural Stone Company. His son John Evans carved the Indianapolis 500 race car models.

Four

Limestone Mills and Quarries

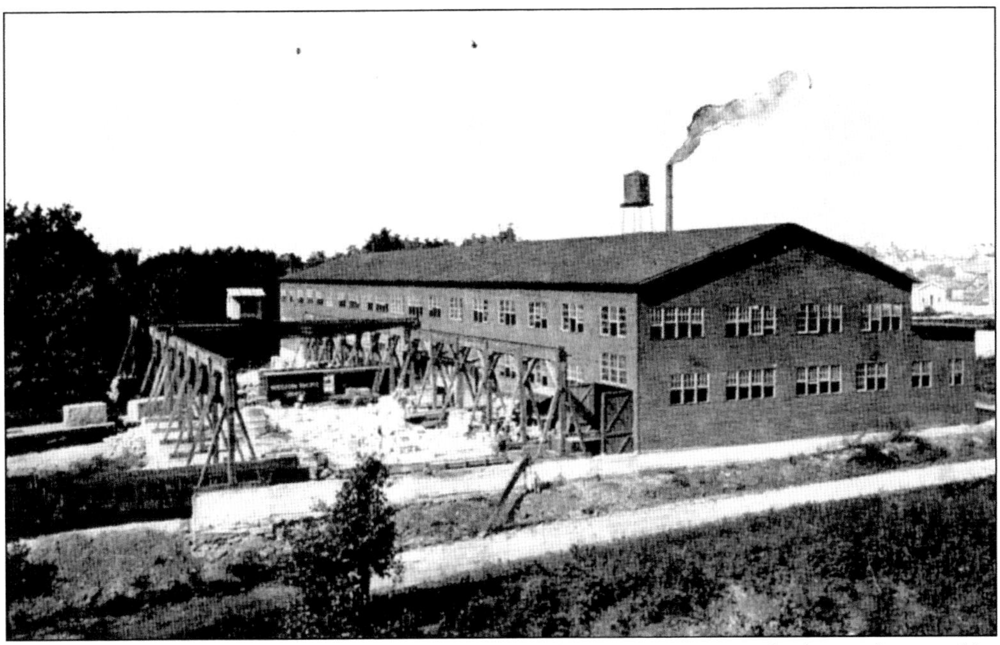

This is believed to be the Ingalls Stone Mill, located on Garvey Lane, which was destroyed by fire on November 10, 1918. The loss was $250,000, more than twice the insurance value. It was the largest and best mill in the district. The mill, filled with stone for shipping, was destroyed. Arson was believed to have been involved. C. C. Ingalls, the operator, was distraught.

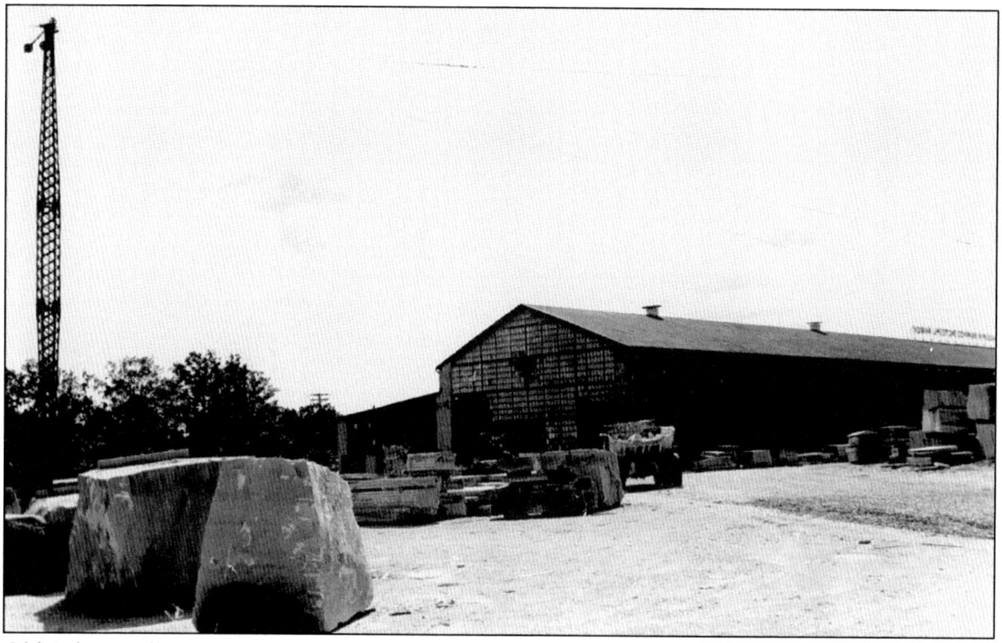

Old Salem Mill was one of the local limestone mills in the 1920s and 1930s. This photograph is believed to be of that mill. There were approximately 23 mills in the area at one time.

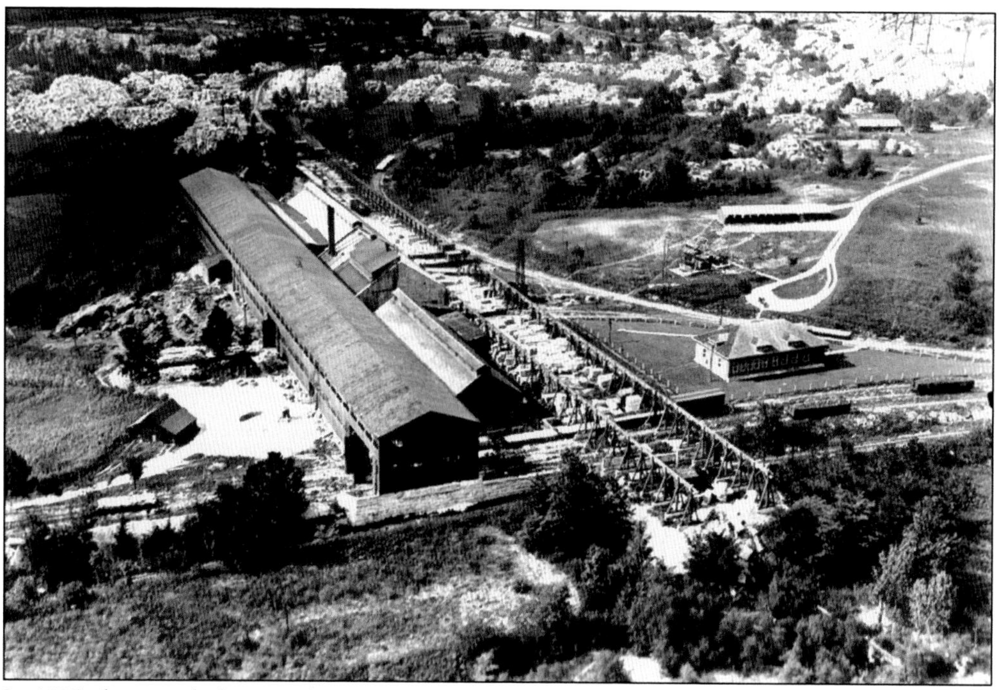

In 1935, this aerial photograph was taken of Indiana Limestone Company Office and Hoosier Mill. This stone company was the largest in the Bedford area.

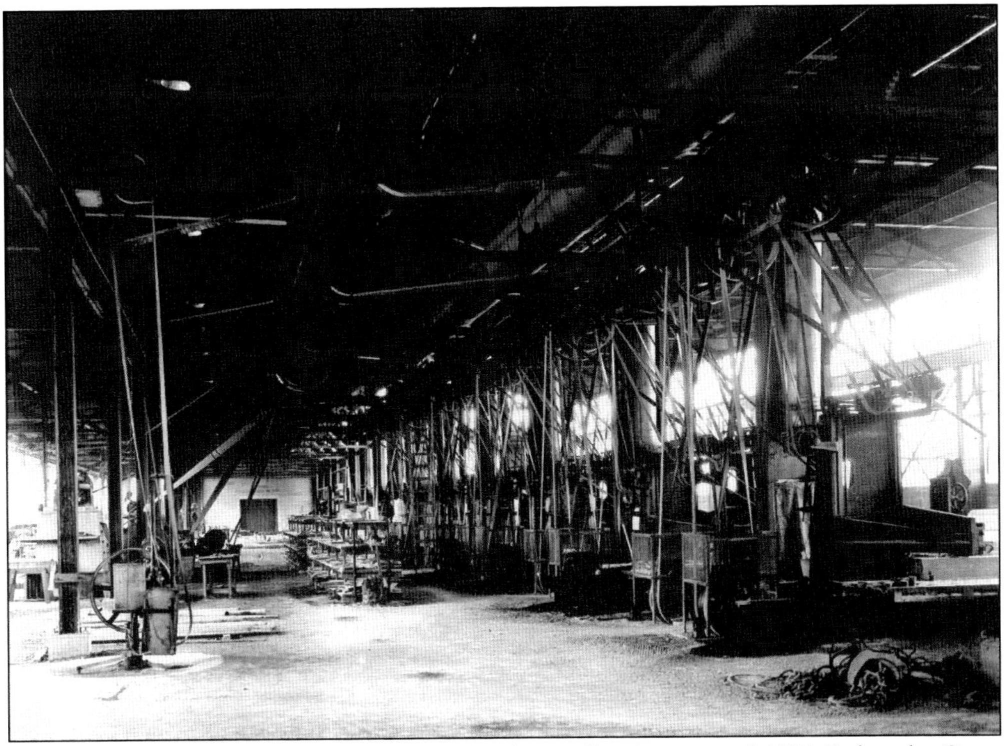

This photograph is of the interior of the old Salem Mill, taken around 1930. Before the Great Depression, the limestone business was booming. The main market at that time was in the East and it remains there today.

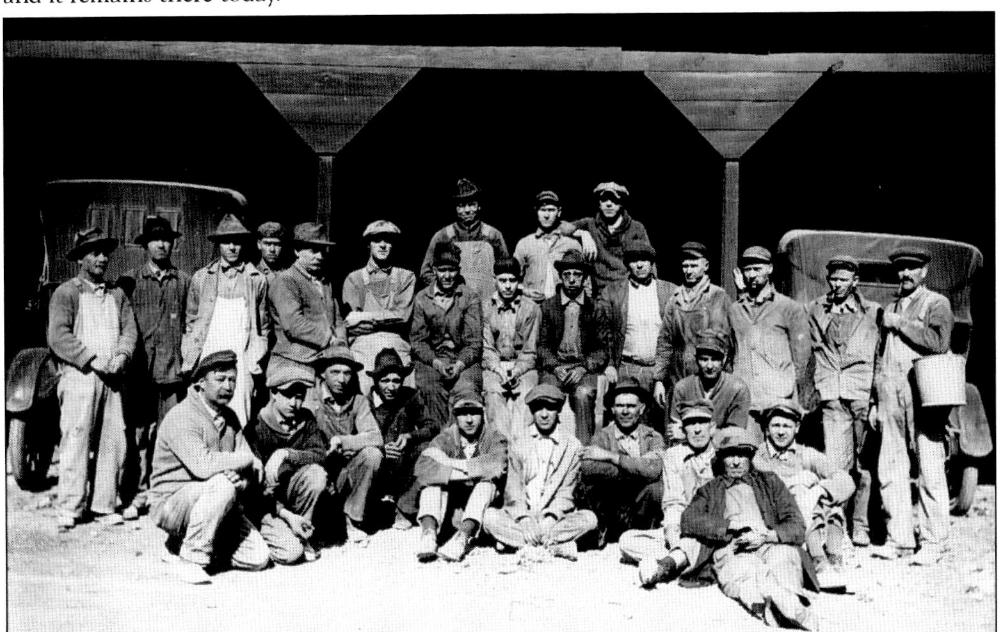

It is believed that this is a group of local stone workers in the early 1900s. Notice the stone dust on their hats and shoes. Stone dust is not as harmful as the coal dust in the mines.

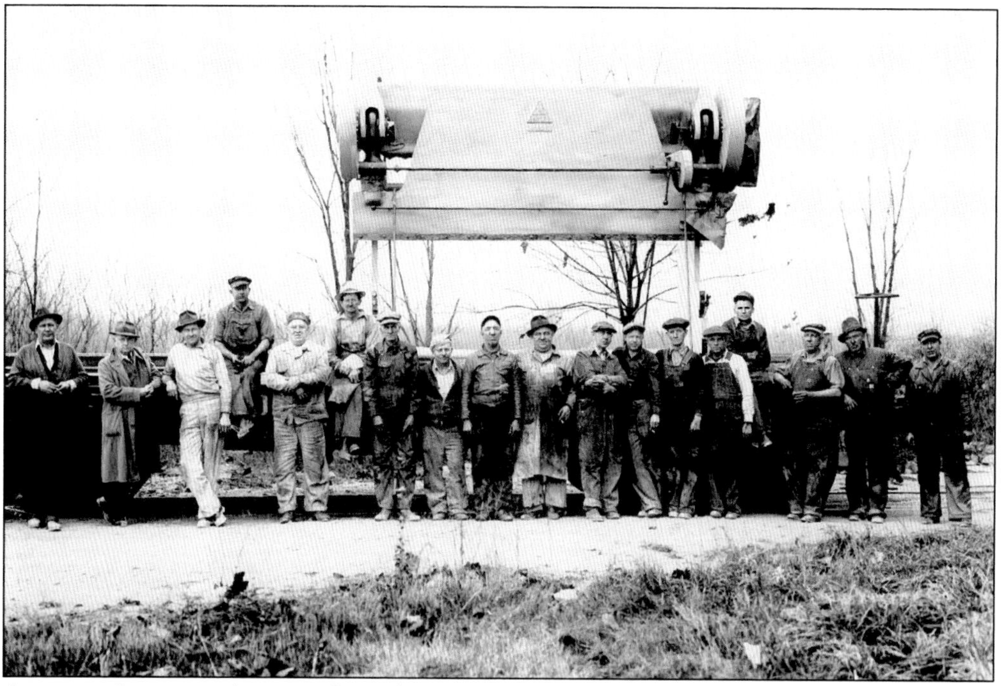

A group of stone workers stands in front of a railroad car. The man fourth from the left is Howard "Snowball" Anderson. The piece of machinery in the back is believed to be a breaker, a tool used in the stone industry. (Courtesy of Jim Anderson.)

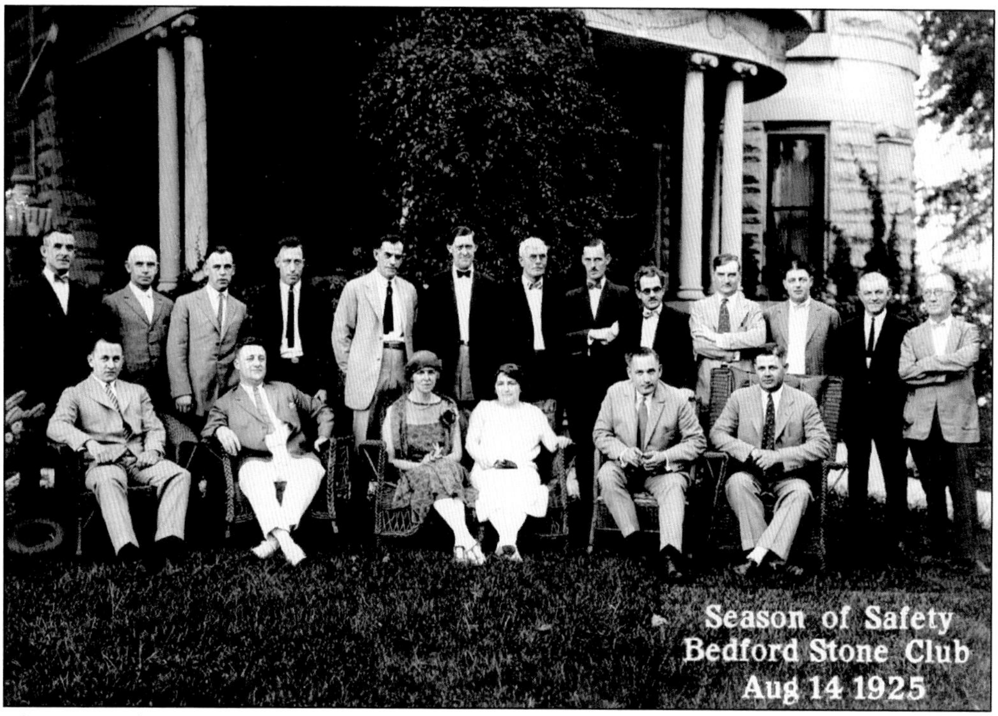

This is a gathering of stone men and women, posing for this picture in 1925 in front of the Norton Mansion, a solid stone house for offices used by the Bedford Stone Club.

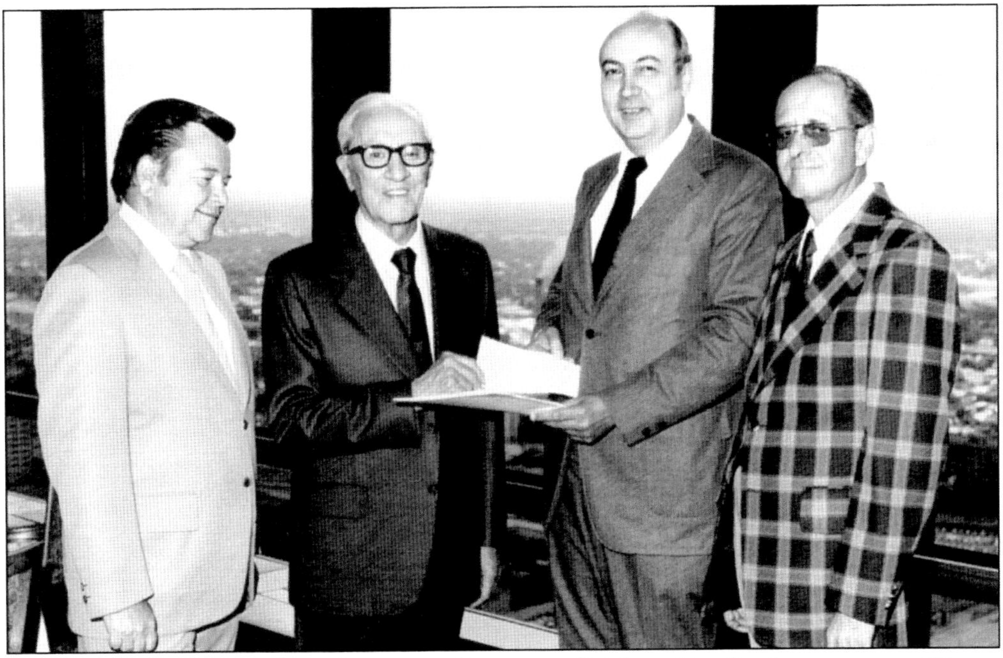

This is a photograph of Indiana Limestone Company officials making final payment on a 30-year mortgage of $2.5 million to the trustee of the Indiana National Bank in Indianapolis. Pictured are John Tucker, president of Indiana Limestone; H. H. Sackell, president of Indiana National Bank; and K. W. Johnson, secretary and treasurer of Indiana Limestone.

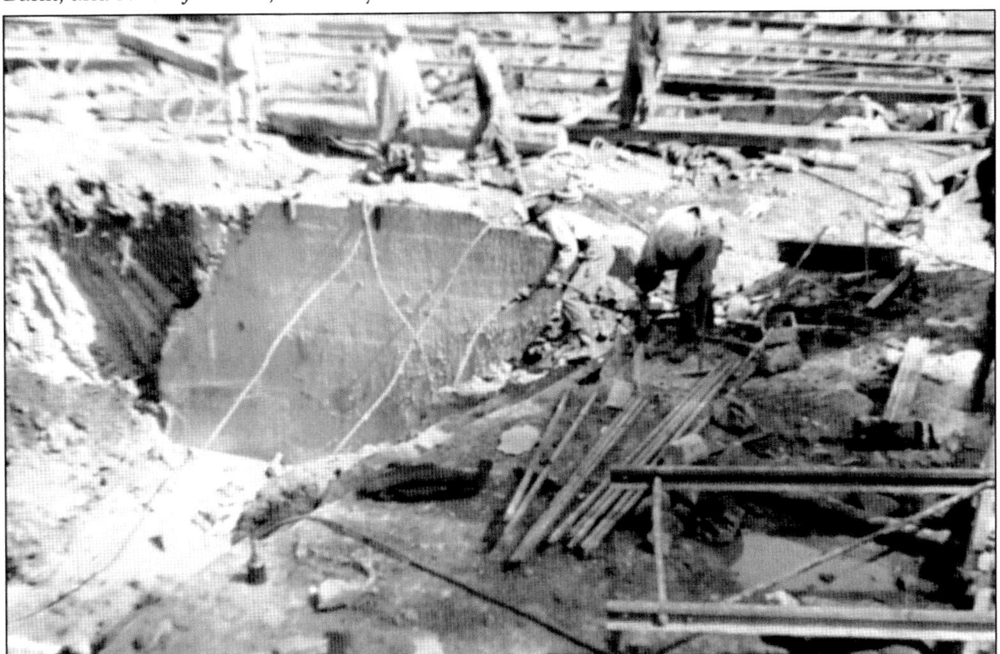

Quarry workers are busy preparing to cut the stone from this early limestone quarry. There are many quarries in the county, filled with clear blue-green water, that are no longer in use. They are a temptation for swimmers.

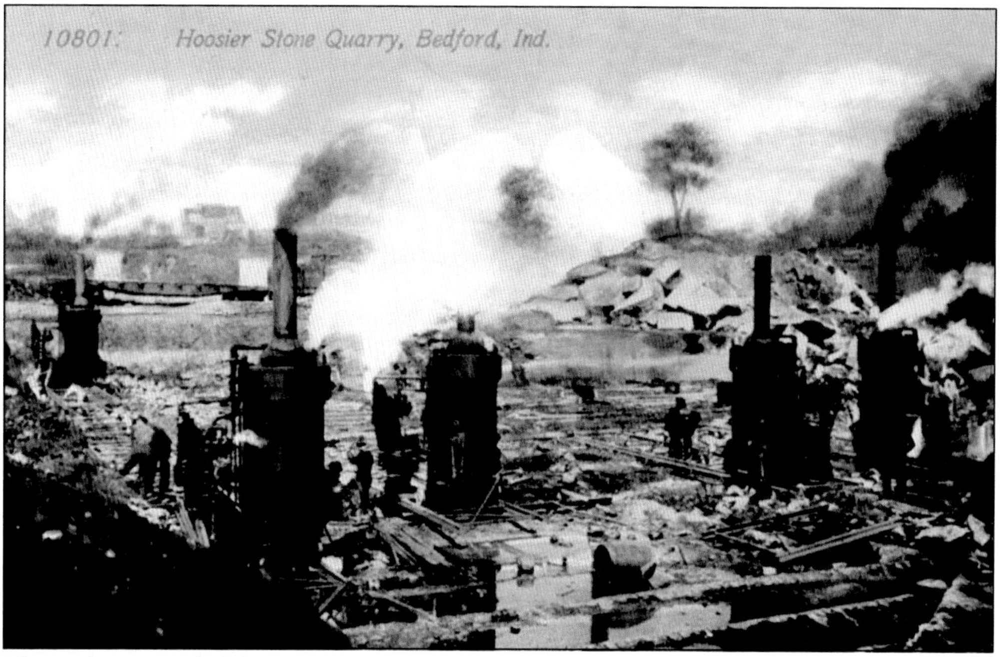

This early postcard of the Hoosier Stone Quarry shows steam channelers used to cut the stone. Modern machinery is much faster. Hoosier Stone Company was one of approximately 23 limestone companies in Bedford in the 1920s and 1930s.

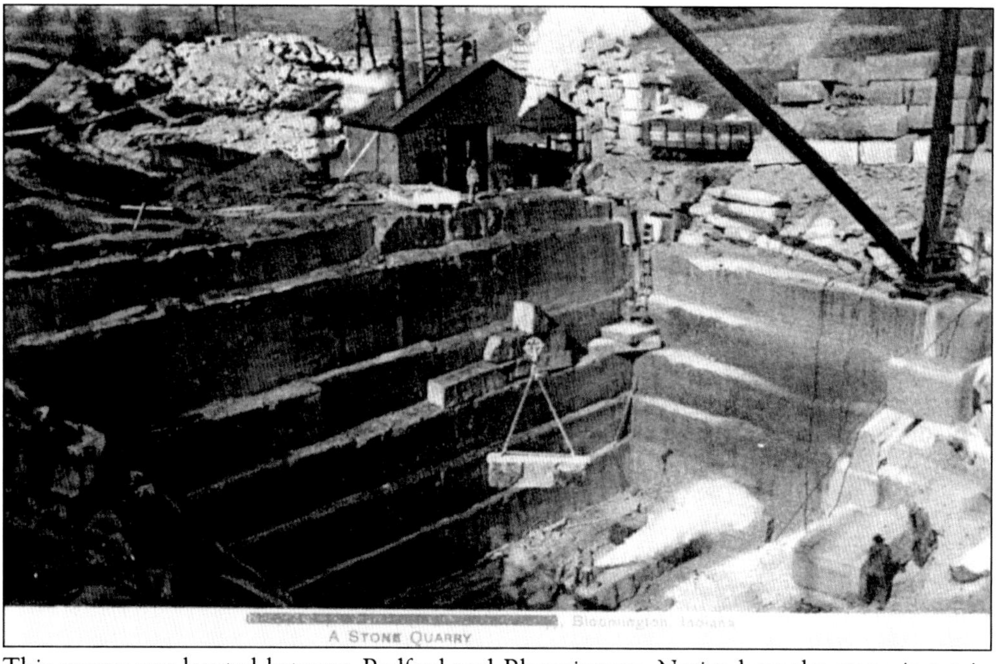

This quarry was located between Bedford and Bloomington. Notice how the stone is cut in layers and the mill blocks are removed by derricks.

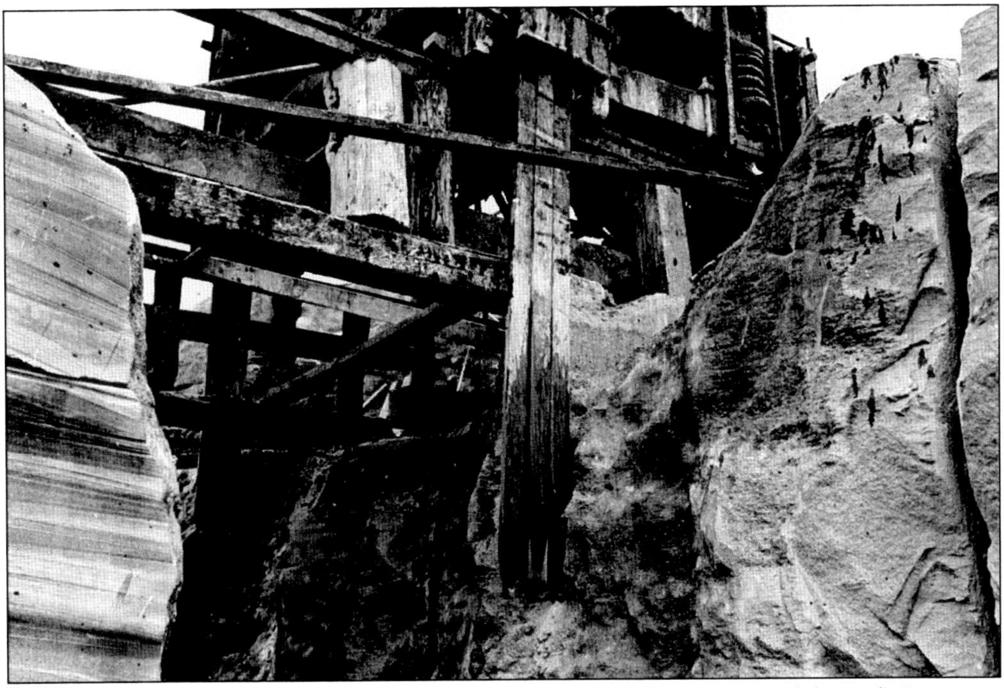

This wooden framing device houses a steam-channeling machine in one of the early Lawrence County quarries.

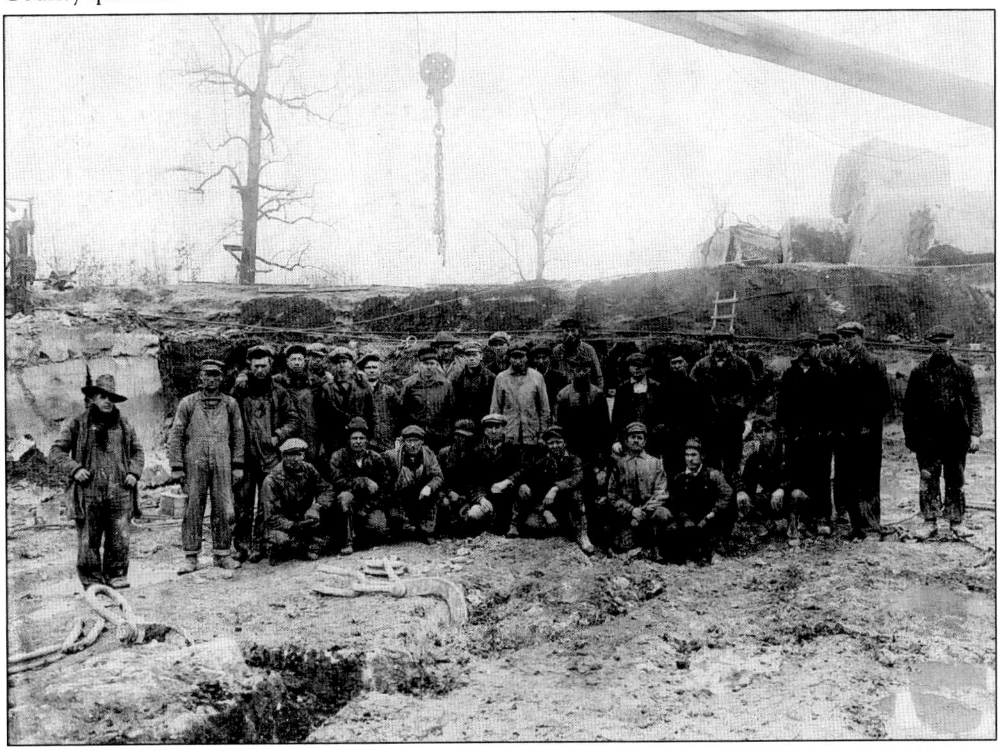

In 1915, this group of unidentified stone workers poses for this picture at one of the Ingall Stone Company quarries. The quarries did not operate during the winter months due to ice and snow.

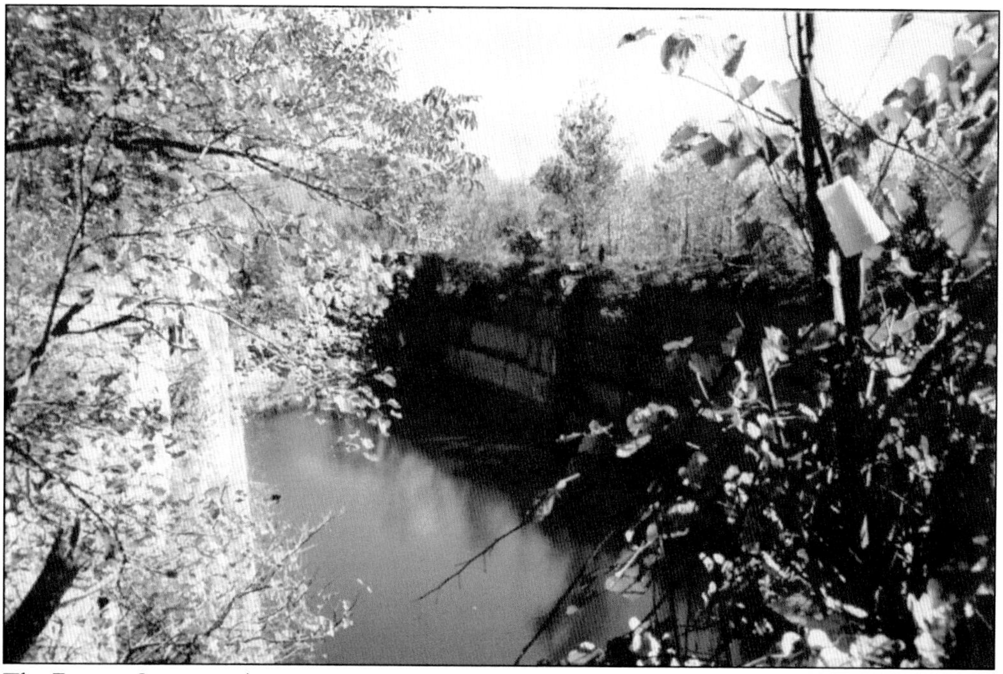

The Empire Quarry is the most famous of all the quarry holes in the county. From it, stone was quarried for the Empire State Building in New York City. In the past, it served as a swimming hole for the young people.

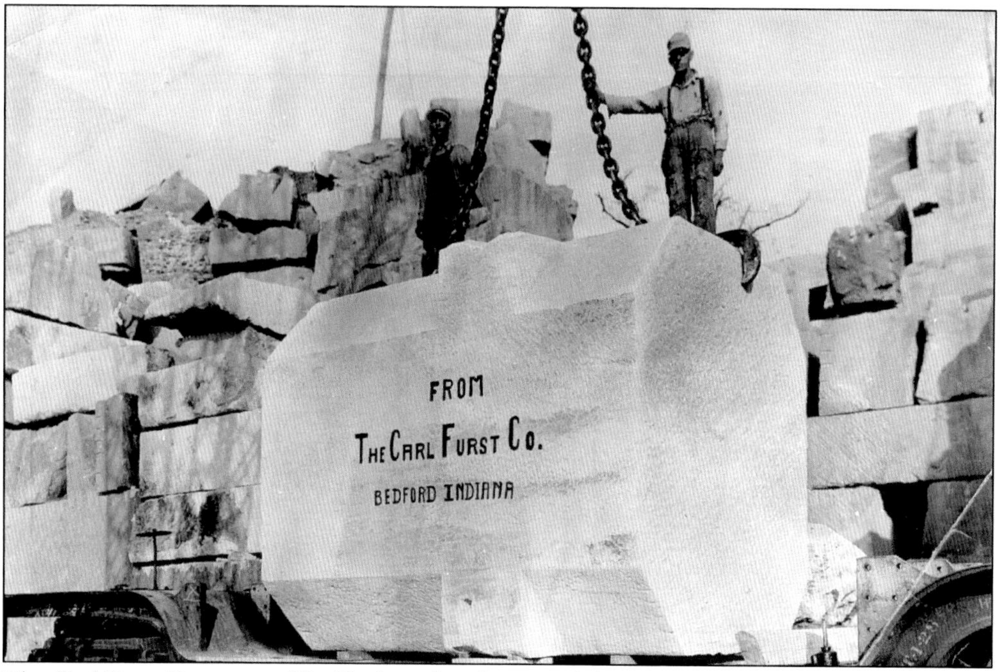

The Carl Furst Company of Bedford produced some of the stone that was shipped to the East between 1860 and 1920. The stone industry was at its greatest with more than 23 mills in the area. Stone men and builders recognized the superior quality, appearance, and endurance of Indiana limestone to many of its competitors.

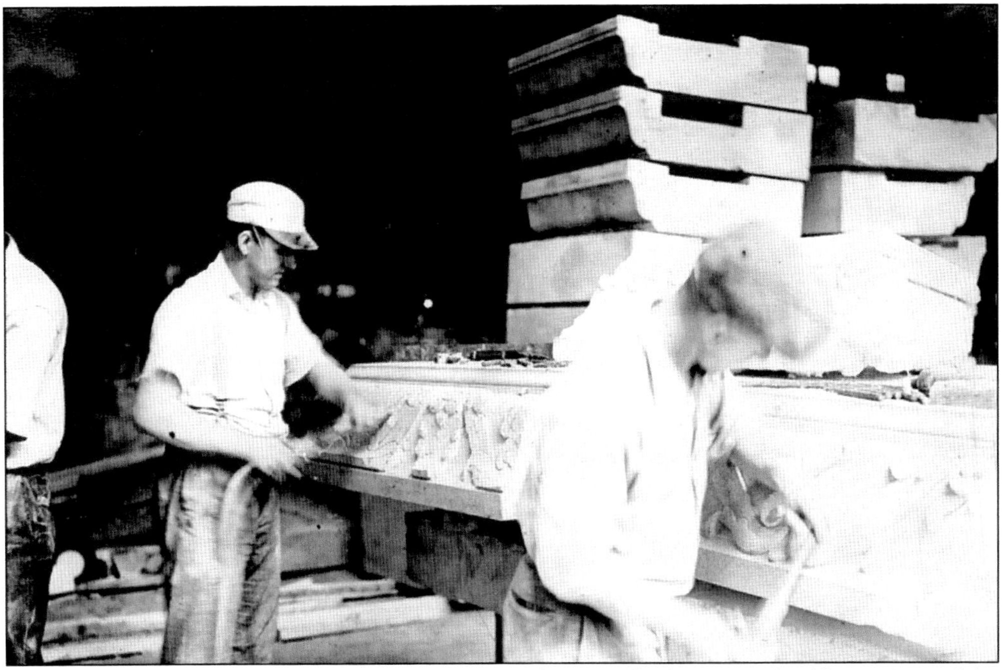

Two stone carvers are working on an intricate panel that will adorn some building. Many of the buildings in the nation's capitol are structured with Indiana limestone. Much of the carving on these structures is the work of master carvers from this area.

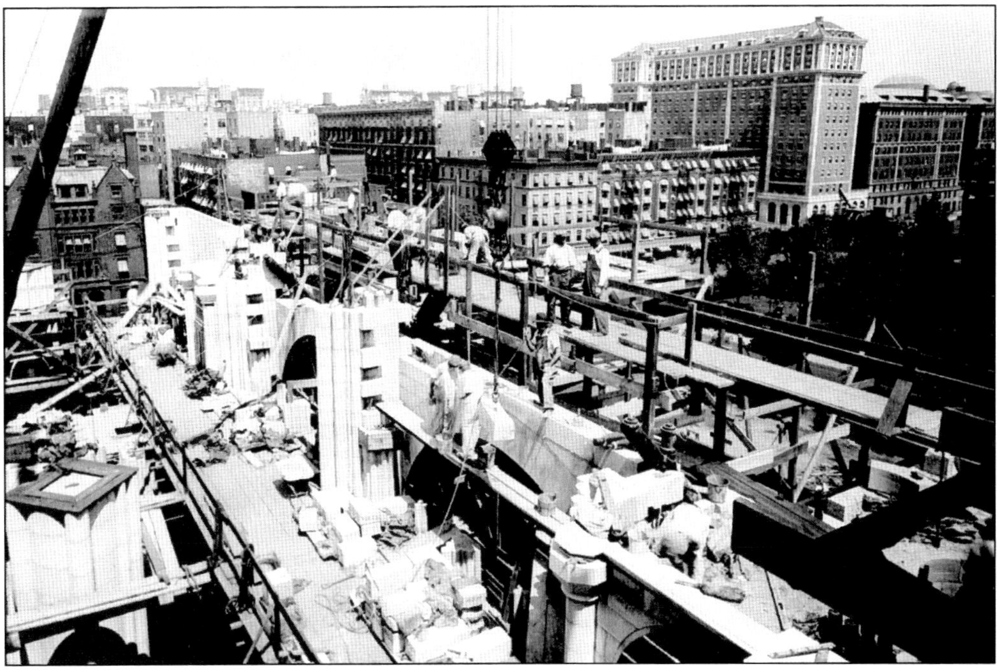

High above the city, contractors are erecting an Indiana limestone building, which will be fire resistant. Codes demand materials that are predictable and dependable. John A. Rowe, who became familiar with Indiana limestone after visiting Bedford, later went to Chicago to promote the stone to architects and builders.

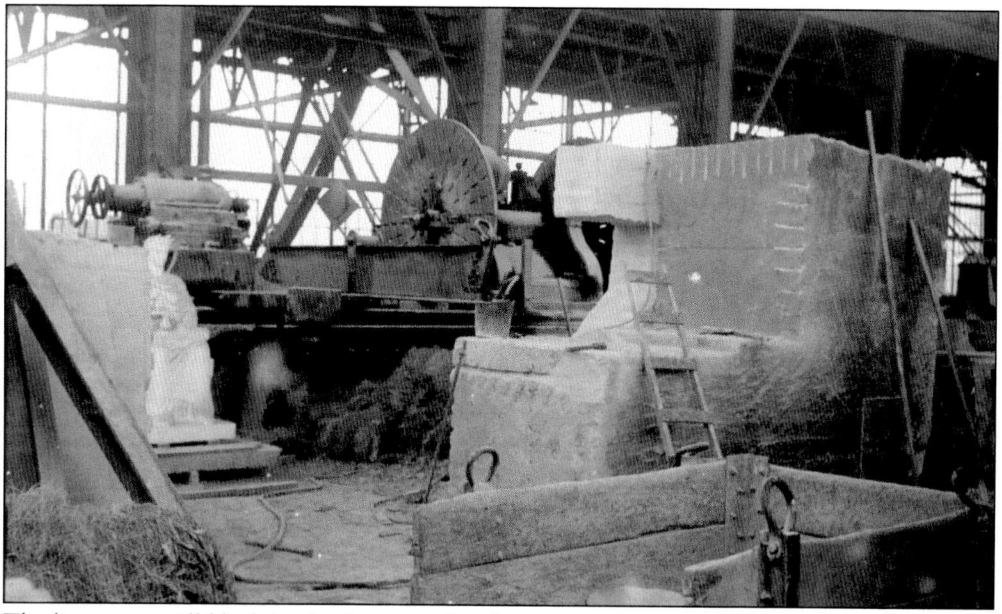

The limestone mill block in the foreground is destined to be cut and designed to specifications before shipping to its destination. Each block, weighing tons, has a job number of the project and where it is located.

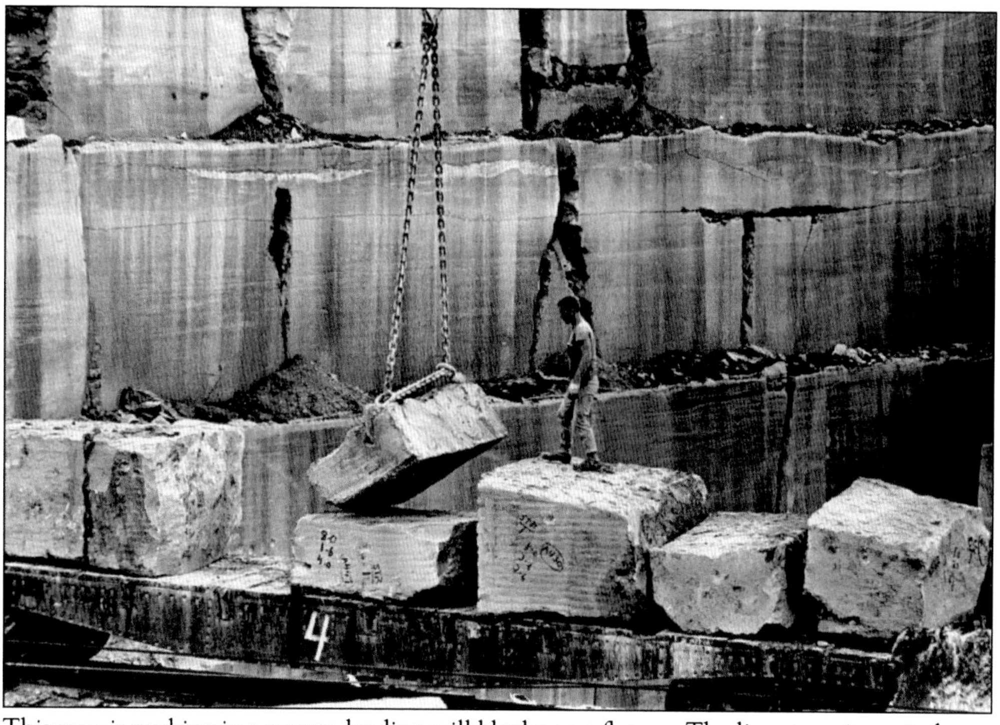

This man is working in a quarry, loading mill blocks on a flat car. The limestone is cut in layers and a mill block can be of any size depending on the job. Quarries usually do not work during the winter months because frost and snow make the stone slick and hazardous.

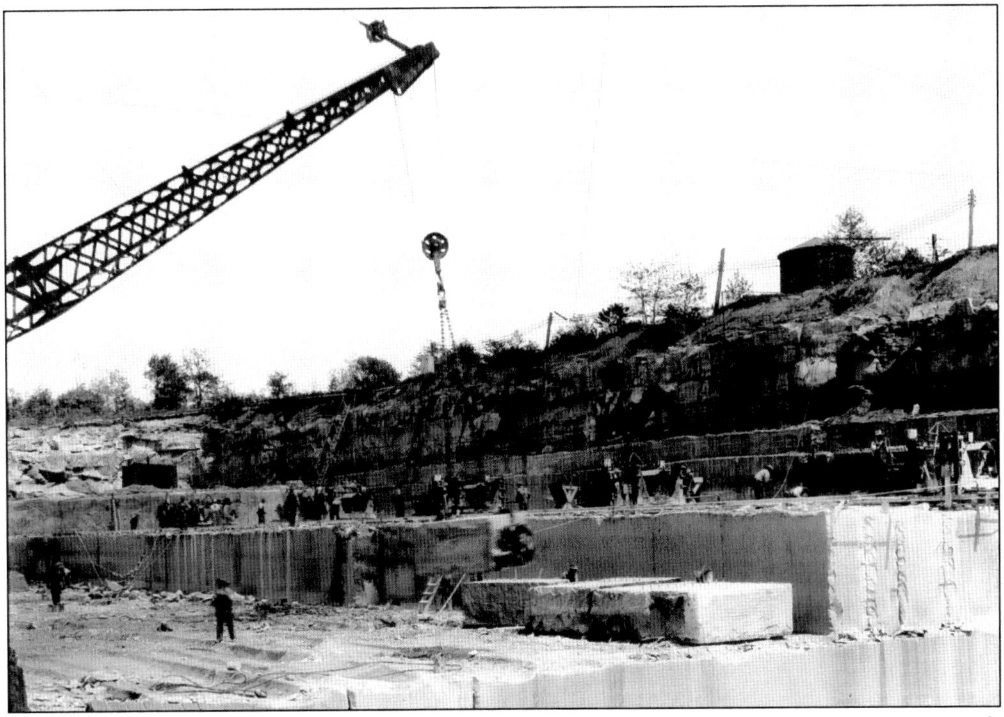

Dark Hollow Quarry produced gray stone. The stone for the Vanderbilt mansion in North Carolina came from this quarry. Mill blocks are cut in layers and lifted by derricks.

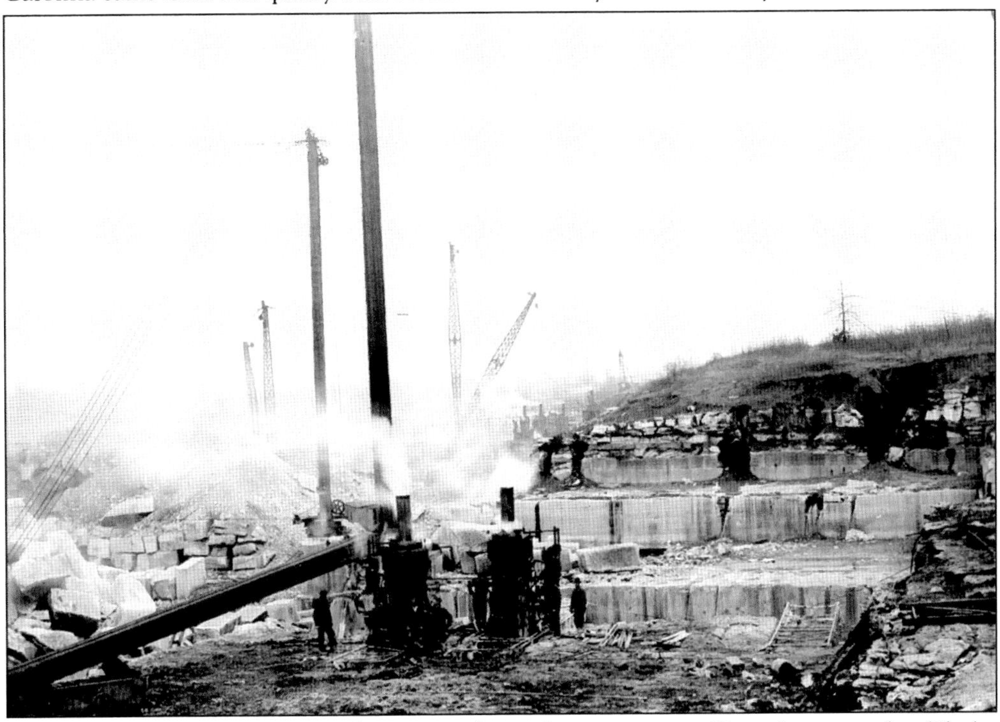

Steam channeling machines can be seen in this early quarry scene. Derricks are used to lift the heavy stone blocks.

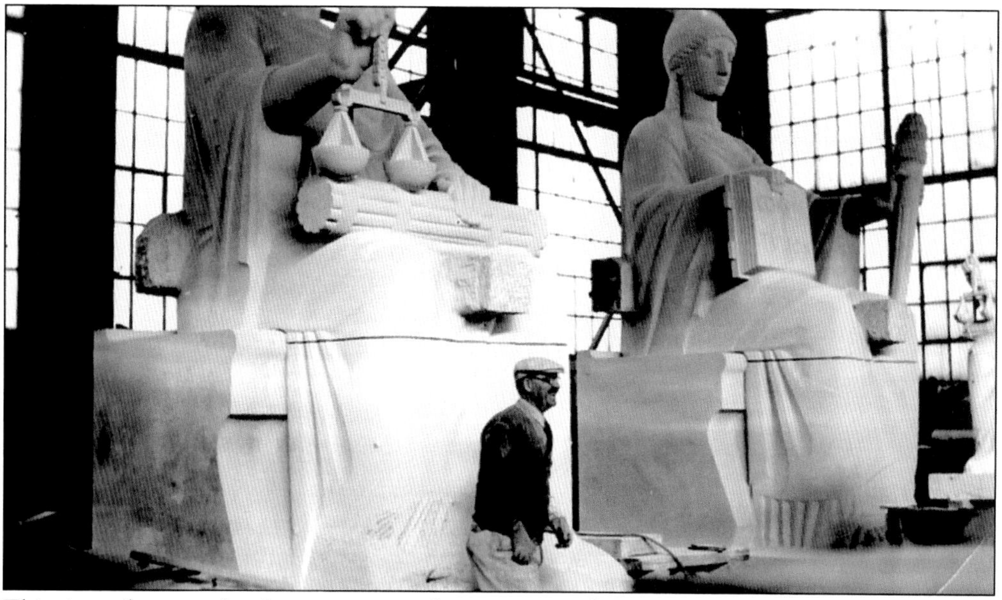

This is a photograph of two carvings being prepared for a U.S. customs building and a courthouse. The justice artwork at the left is nearly finished. The liberty carving at the right has been completed. The two pieces are enclosed inside the Walters Mill owned by the Indiana Limestone Company.

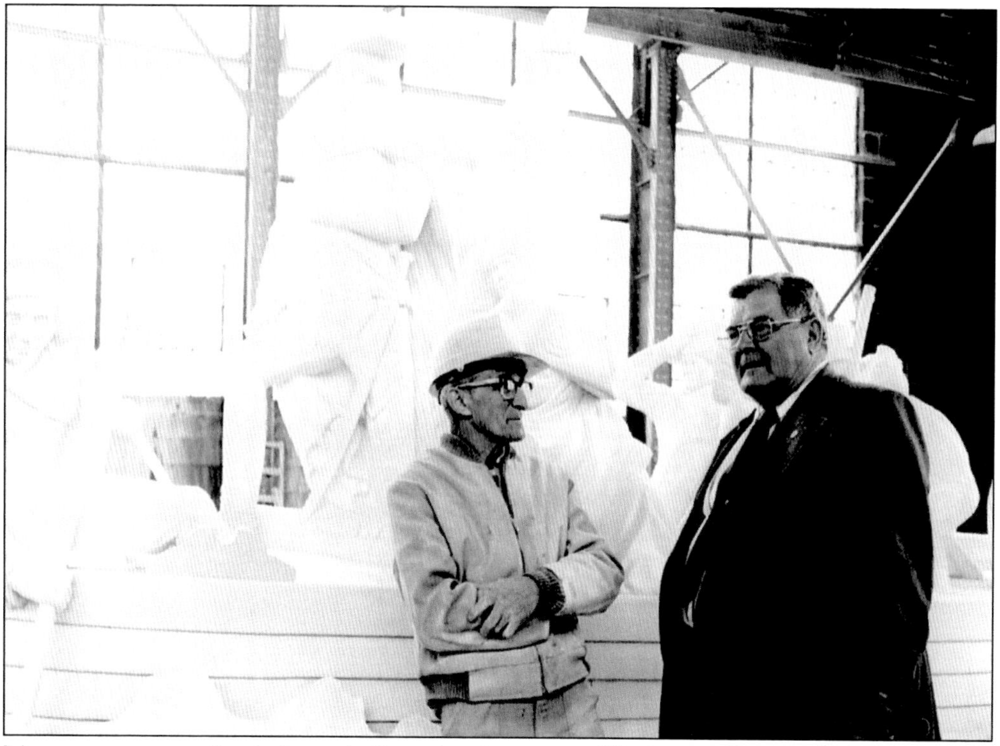

Master stone carver Frank Arena is discussing the carving *Washington Crossing the Delaware* with the executive director of the Bedford Area Chamber of Commerce Merle Edington. In 1976, this statue was given to the nation. It now stands at Washington Crossing, Pennsylvania.

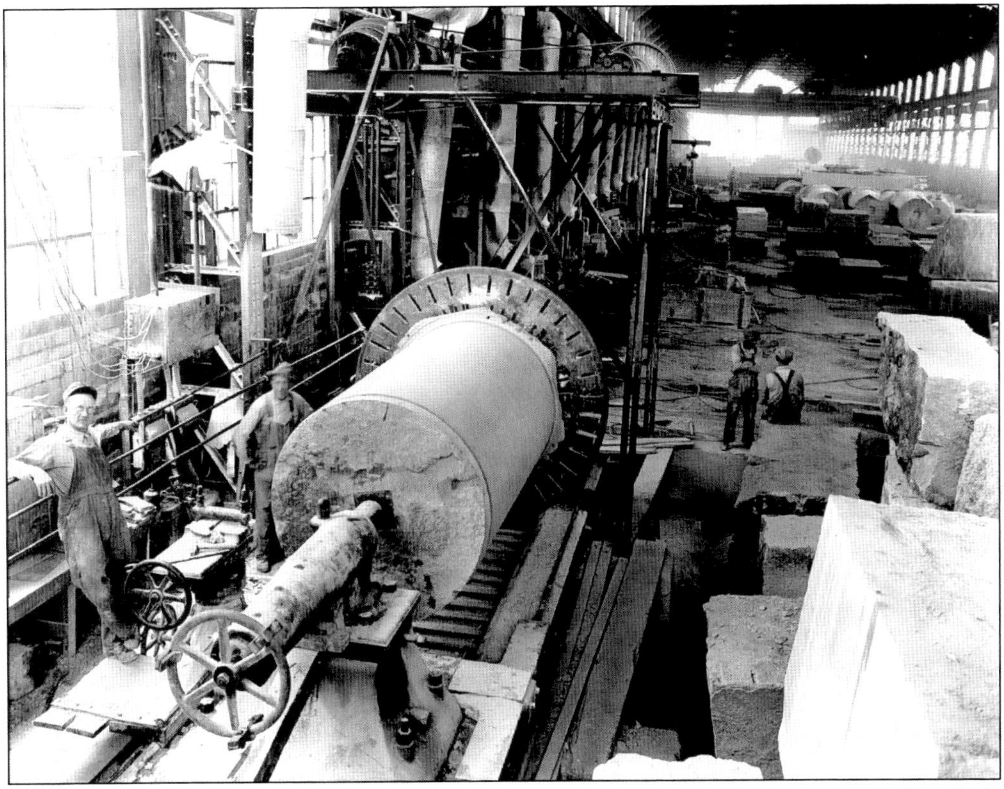

This picture was taken inside the Dickinson Mill in Bedford. The stone workers are unidentified.

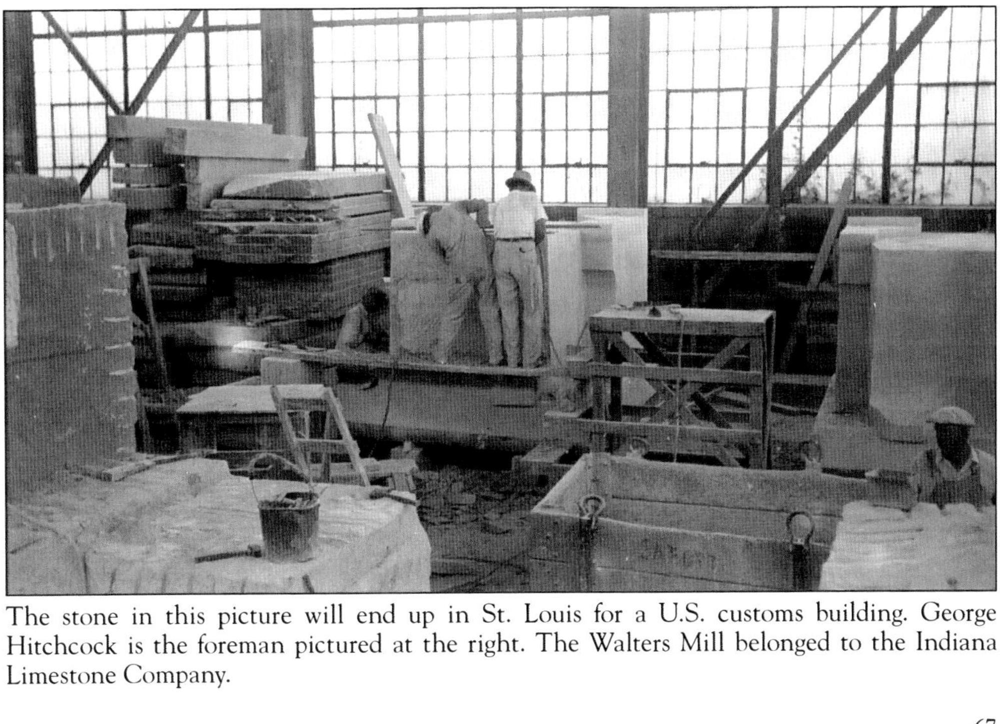

The stone in this picture will end up in St. Louis for a U.S. customs building. George Hitchcock is the foreman pictured at the right. The Walters Mill belonged to the Indiana Limestone Company.

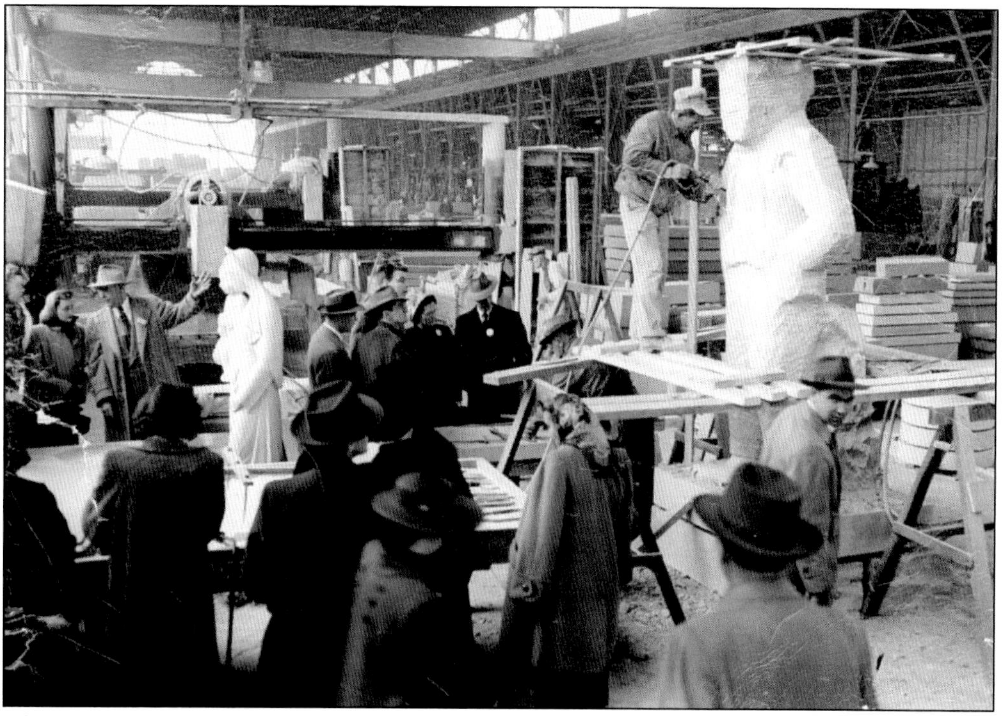

Glen Quackenbush and architects and their wives are observing the carving of cartoon character Steve Canyon, an aviation hero created by Milton Caniff.

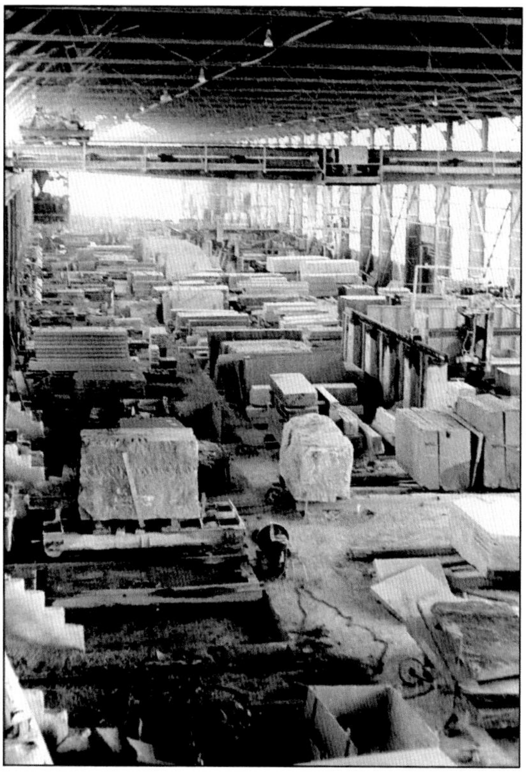

The interior of this mill is filled with mill blocks that will be fabricated for a special job. Stone comes in three colors: buff, the most popular and the color used for carvings; gray, the Biltmore mansion in North Carolina is made of this color; and variegated.

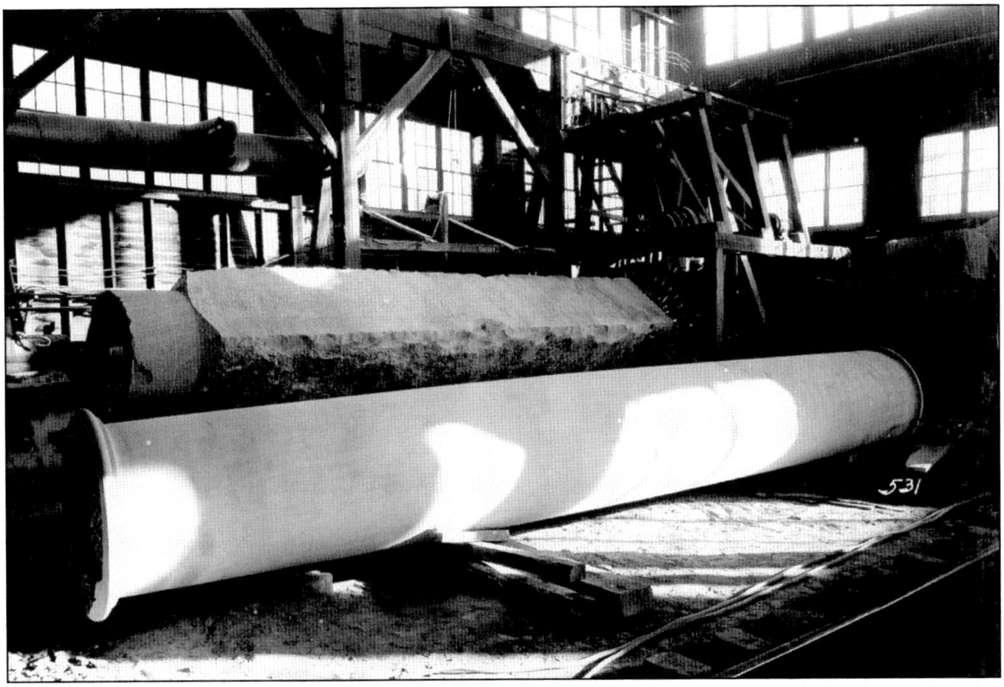

It is unknown where these huge two columns will be going. They will probably be shipped to the eastern market and possibly for a government building. Most of the early government buildings were made of Indiana limestone.

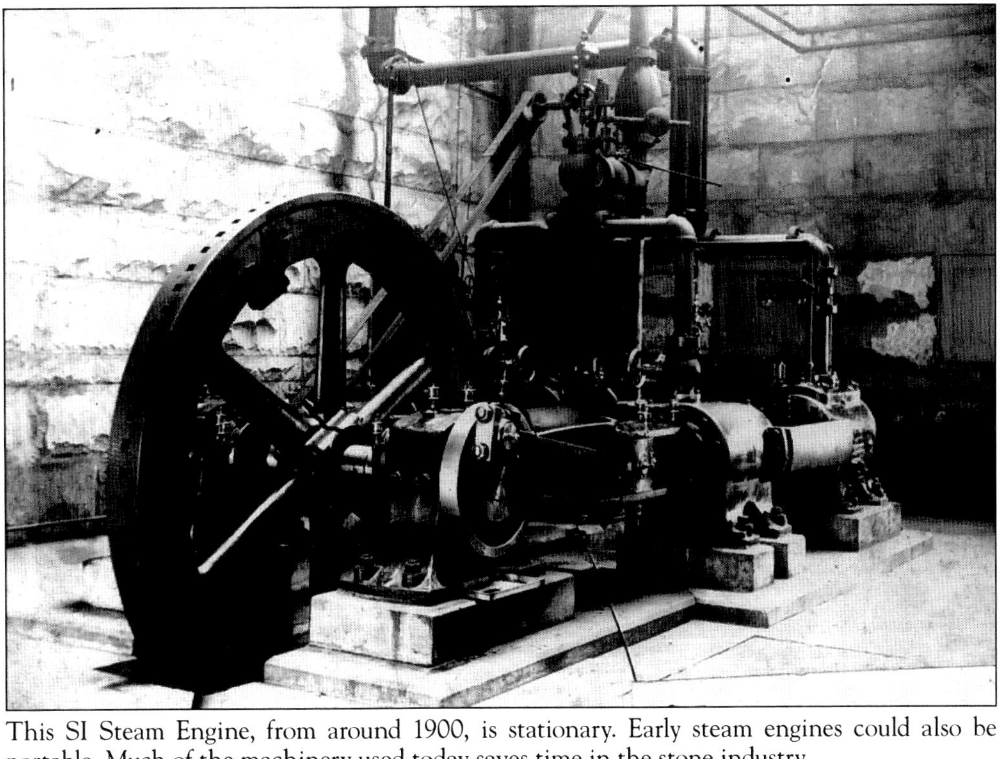

This SI Steam Engine, from around 1900, is stationary. Early steam engines could also be portable. Much of the machinery used today saves time in the stone industry.

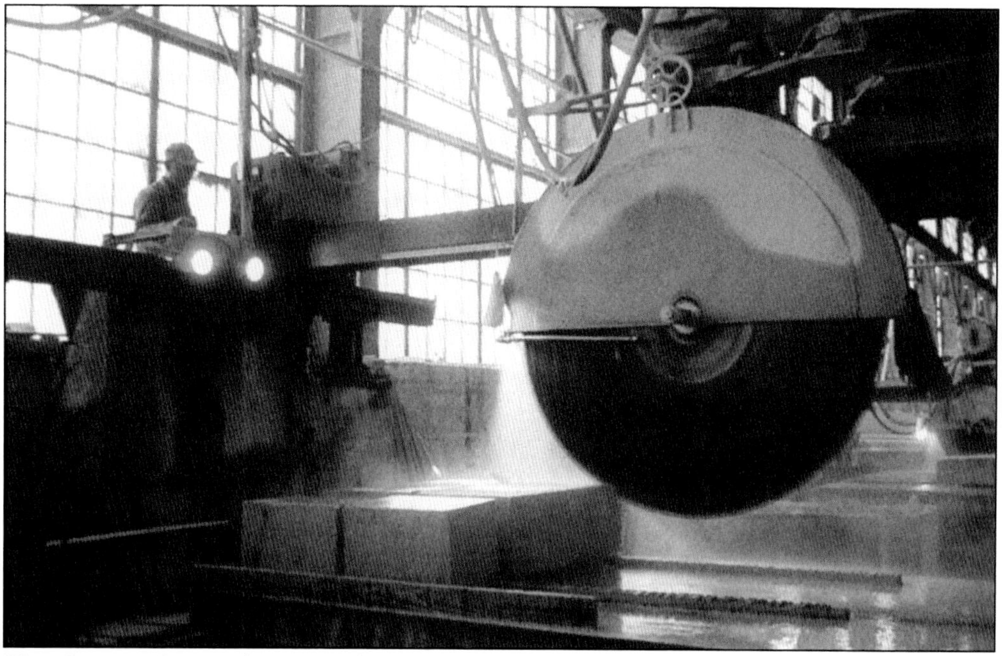

This photograph was taken around 1985 in one of the many limestone mills in the area. A radial saw smoothly cuts limestone in the fabrication of building stone.

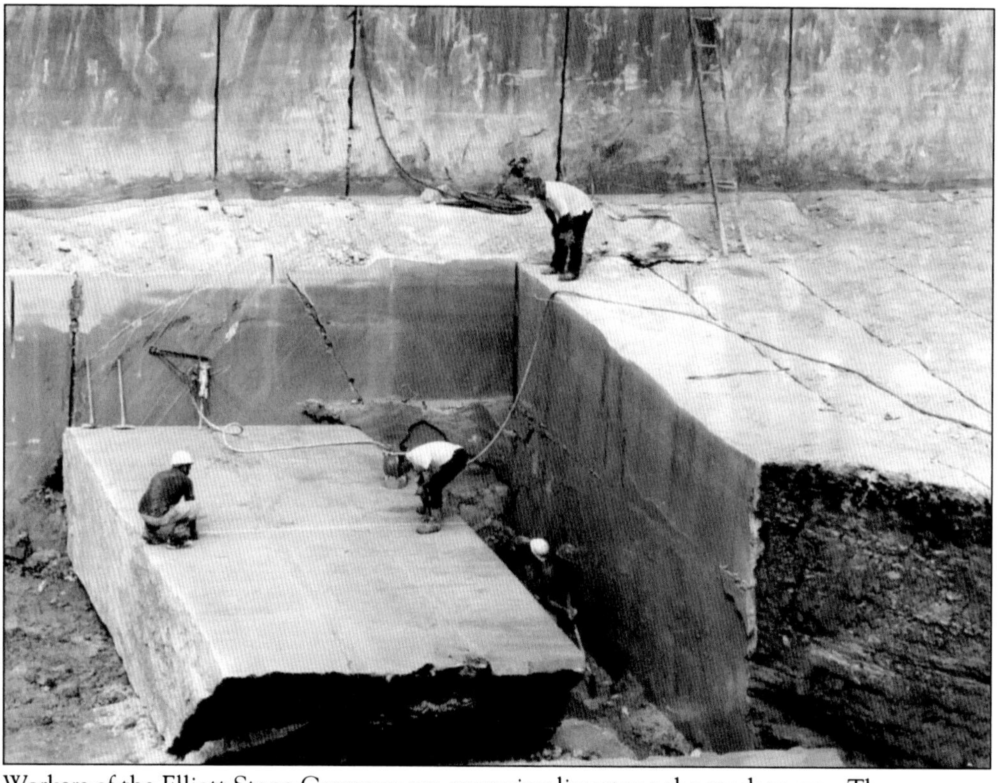

Workers of the Elliott Stone Company are quarrying limestone the modern way. The company also owns an underground quarry. It is the only one of its kind in the county.

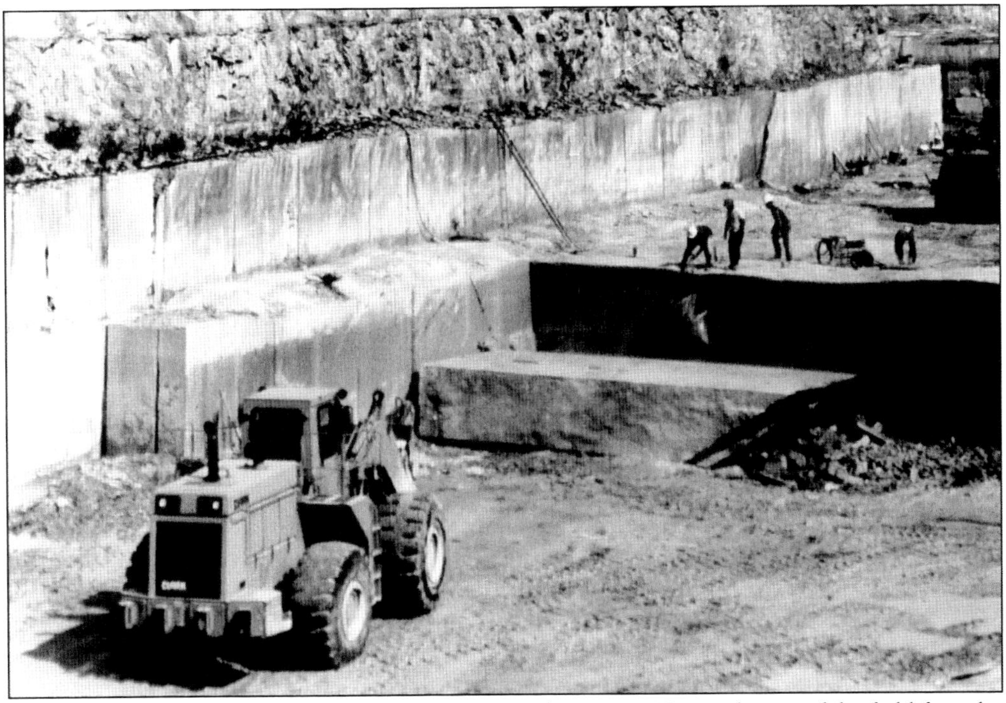

This photograph shows the modern way of quarrying limestone. Notice the use of the forklift in the foreground. It is used to move the stone blocks. This is one of the Elliott Stone Company quarries.

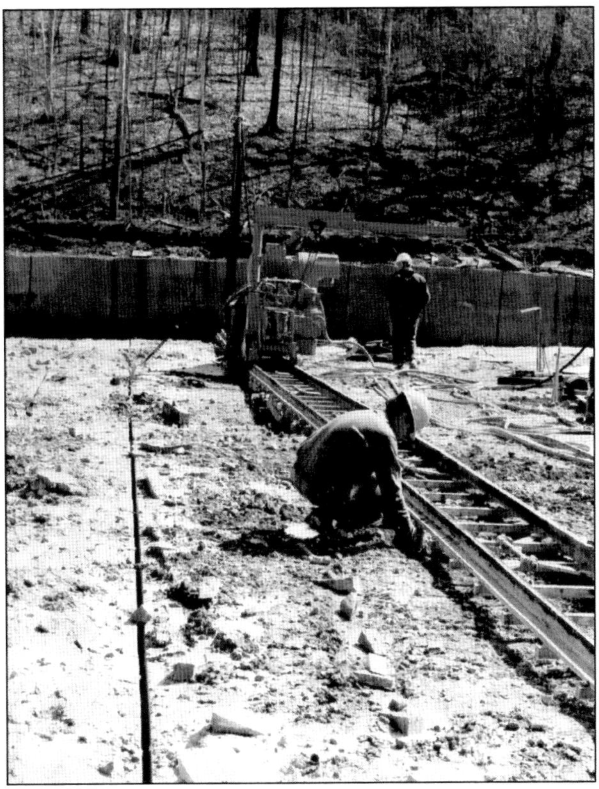

Men at the Elliott Stone Company are using the modern channeling machine to cut stone out of the quarry. In the early days, workers would drill holes and fill them with dynamite to blast the stone away.

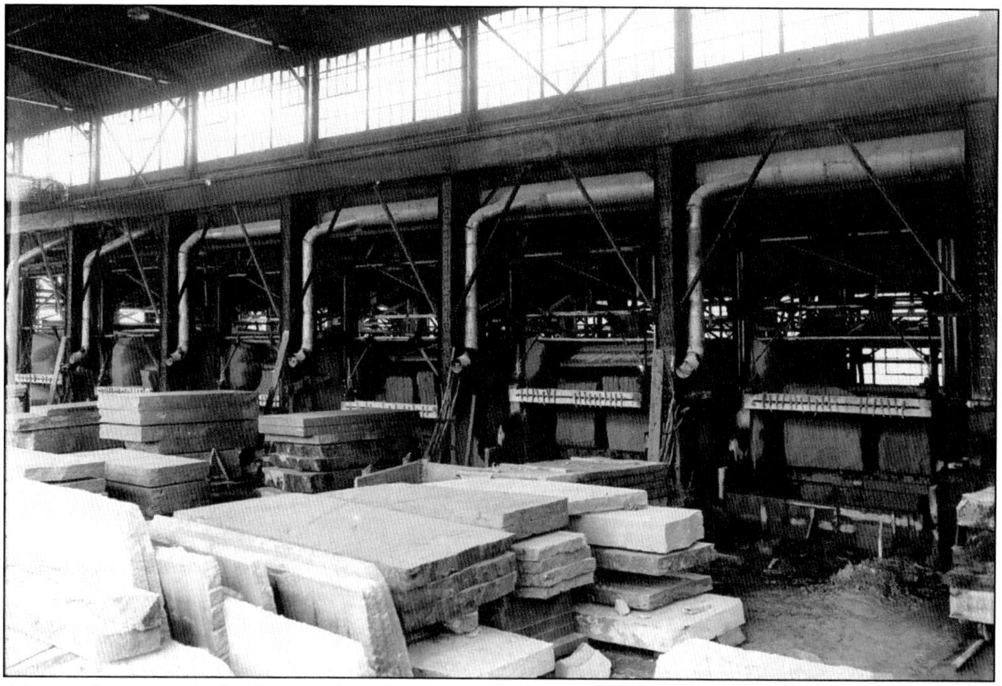

The machines in the background in this photograph are called gang saws, used to cut mill blocks into slabs. In the early days of the limestone industry, it took eight hours to cut a block of stone. Today, with the modern diamond saws, it takes only a few minutes.

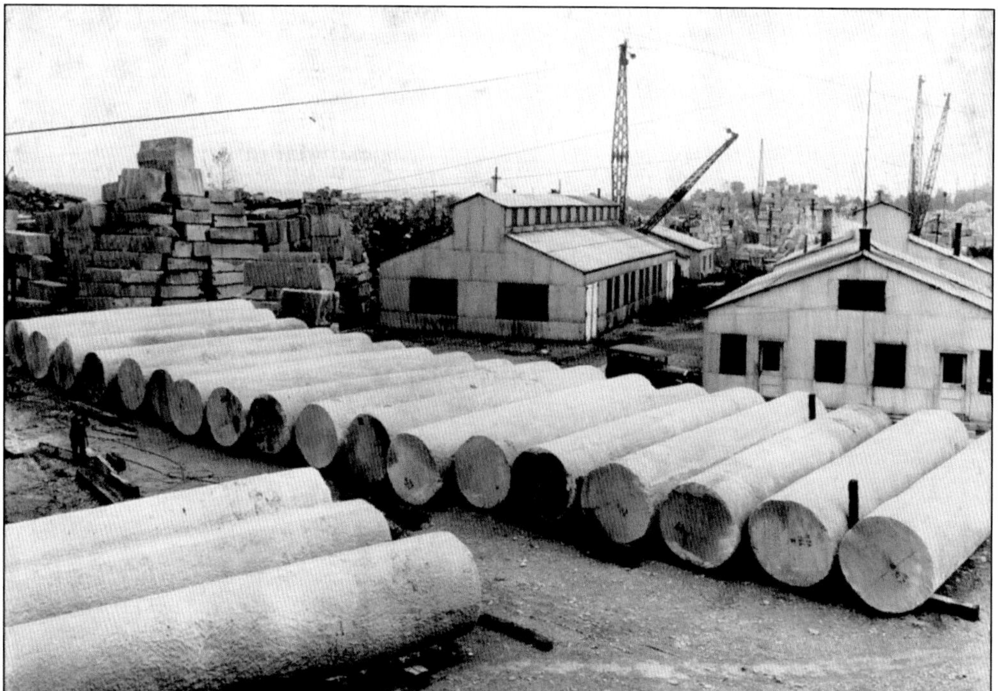

Stone columns lay in the mill yard. These huge circular limestone columns are ready to be shipped to a job in Washington, D.C.

Five

MASTER CARVERS, CUTTERS, AND THEIR WORK

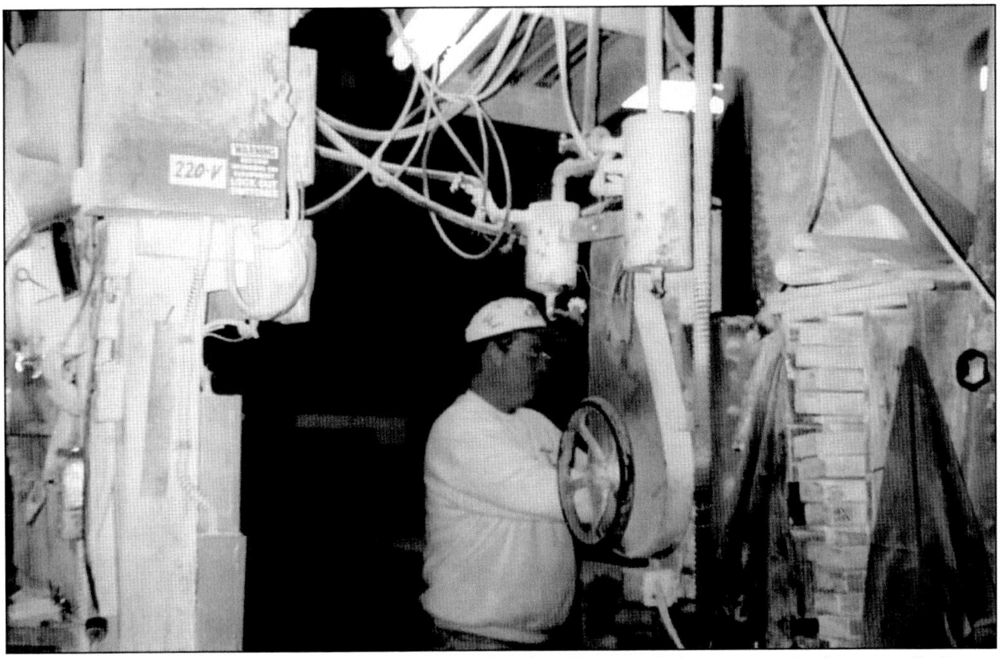

One of the Evans brothers is working at the family-owned business, Architectural Stone Company. This family has been in the stone business for several years. This photograph was taken while a group of tourists visited Bedford in 1990.

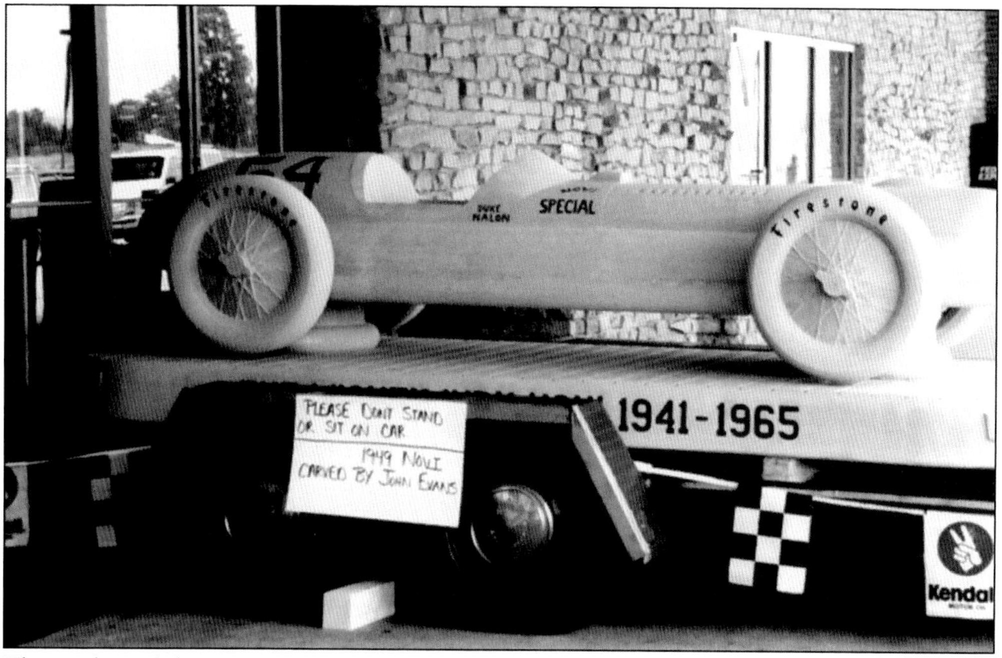

This replica of the 1949 Novi race car, driven by Duke Naylon in the Indianapolis 500, was and still is owned by John Evans of Architectural Stone Company. The Evans family had the Race Car and Antique Auto Museum in Bedford at one time, and Eddie Evans still owns a fine collection of vintage cars.

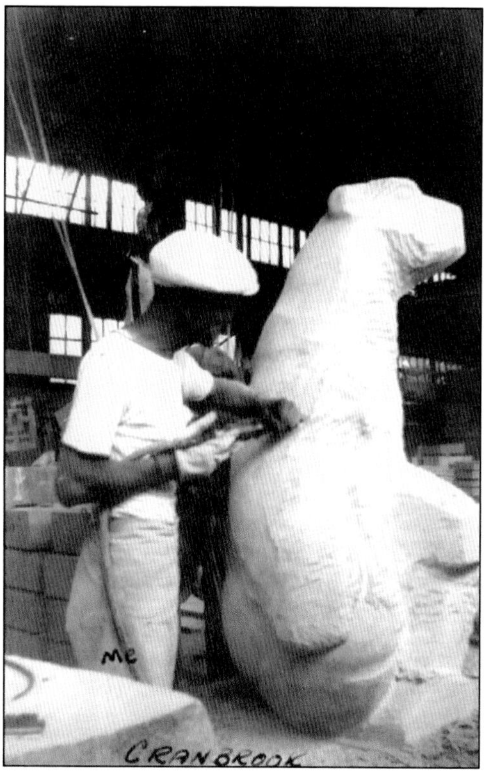

Glen "Curly" O'Brien is roughing out a carving of a bear. It is not known where this piece of art will be going when completed. The date of this work was 1949.

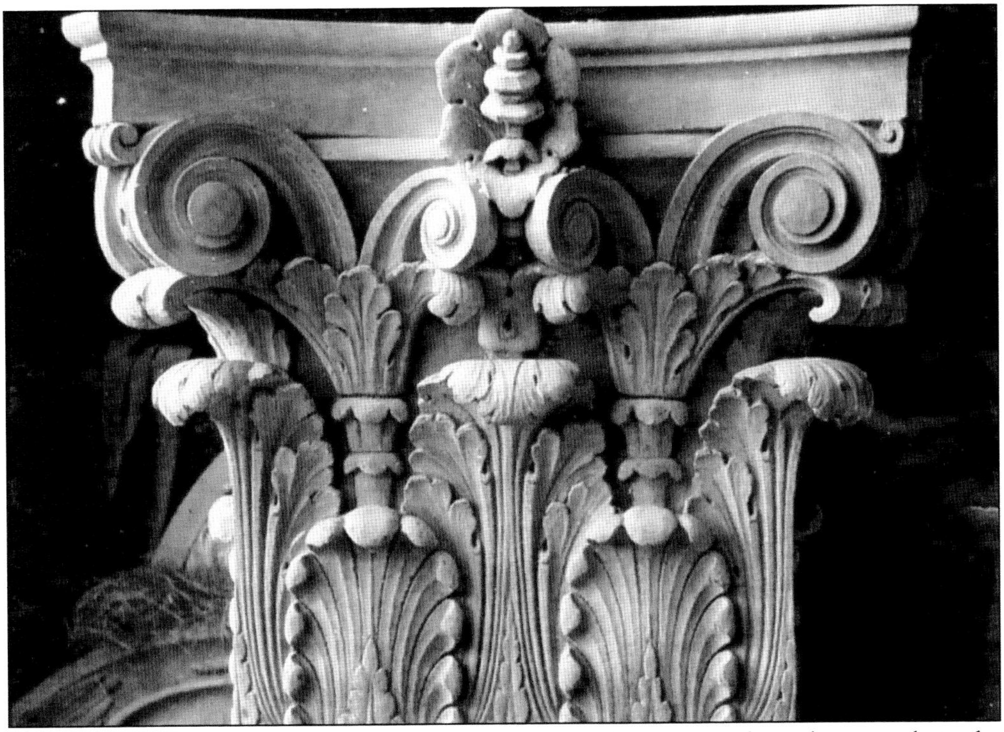

Master carver Virgil Corbin carved this ornate capital. There were at least three people in the Corbin family who were carvers.

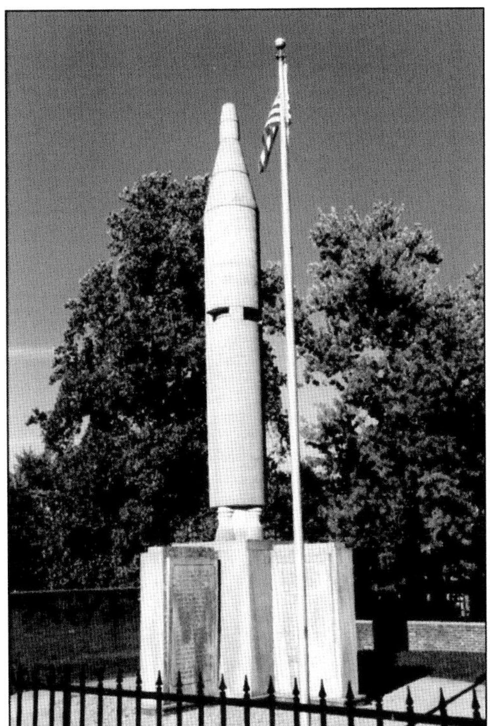

This space capsule copy was designed and carved by Jack Bunch and stands in the town of Mitchell, the home of Virgil "Gus" Grissom. It is a memorial to the famous astronaut.

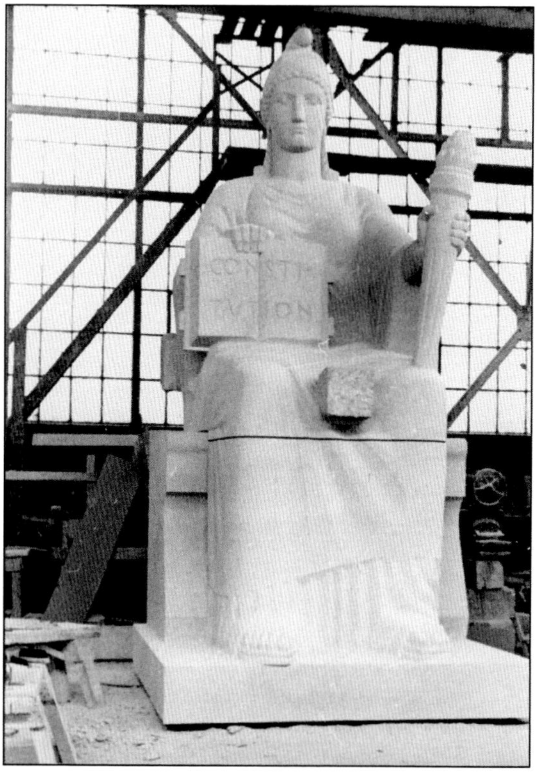

Miss Liberty was completed in 1938 at the Walters Mill, Indiana Limestone Company in Bedford. The statue now stands at the U.S. customs and courthouse in St. Louis. Many of the early customs buildings and courthouses in the United States are made of Indiana limestone.

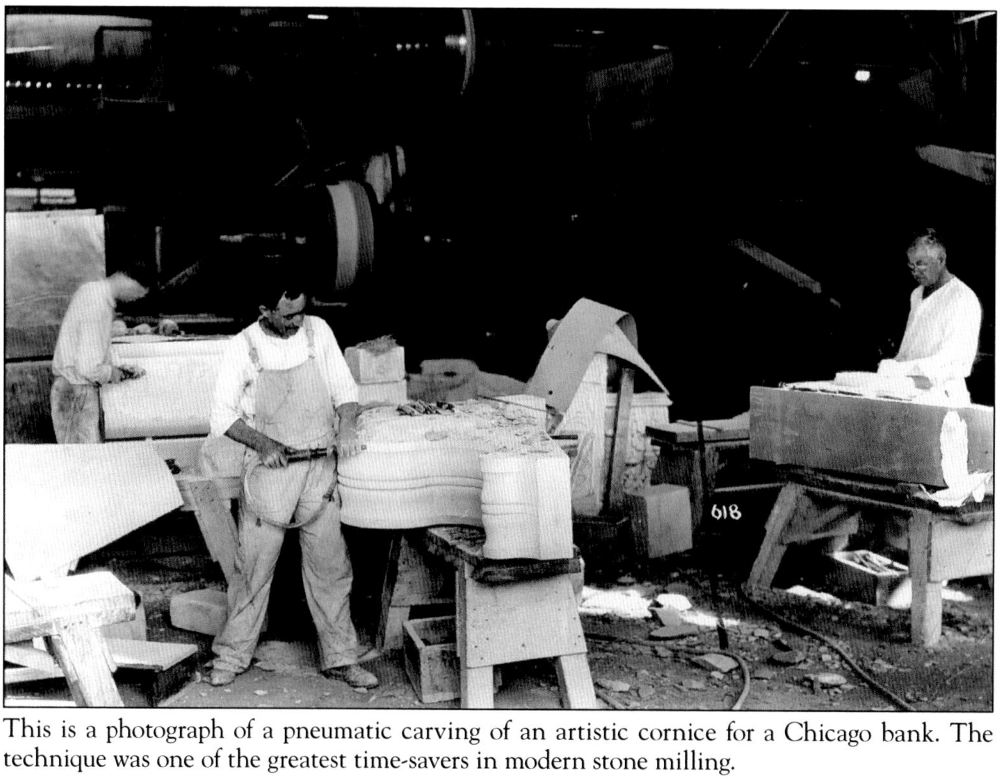

This is a photograph of a pneumatic carving of an artistic cornice for a Chicago bank. The technique was one of the greatest time-savers in modern stone milling.

These stone workers are laying this carved piece high above New York City. It is to be a part of a hotel.

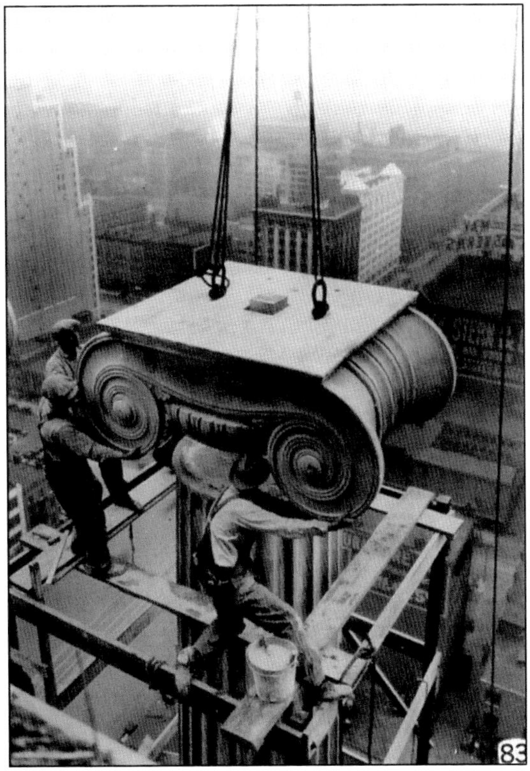

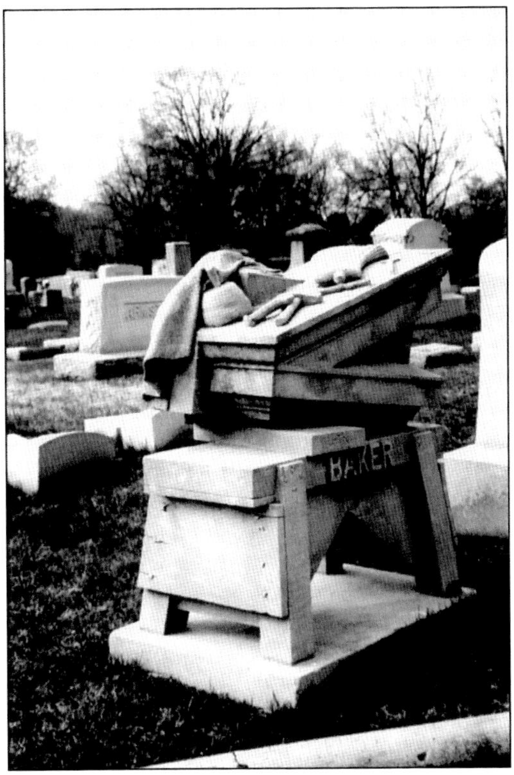

Louis Baker was a stone carver who died of a heart attack while at work in the mill. Fellow carvers carved his bench just as he left it. The tombstone in Green Hill Cemetery in Bedford is famous throughout the country. It was featured on the *Today* show at one time.

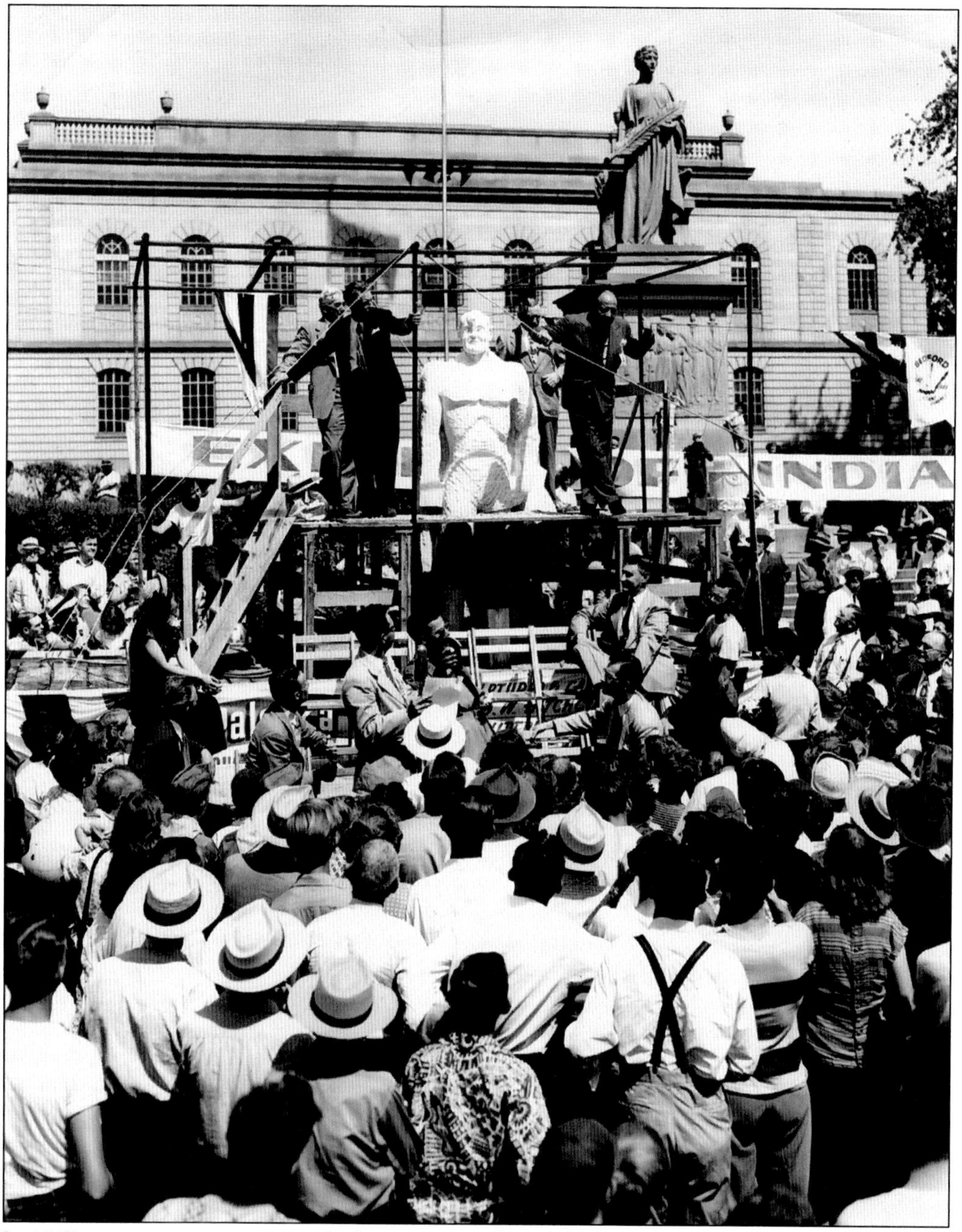

In 1947, master stone carvers worked on a statue of Joe Palooka, a comic strip character who was brought to life by his creator, Ham Fisher of Pennsylvania. The carving took place on a platform on the public square. Fisher was in Bedford for the event. *Joe Palooka* was a very popular comic strip during this period. He was a boxer and an all-American.

This is a face model of Joe Palooka that was used in the carving of the statue by George Hitchcock and Ed Saladee.

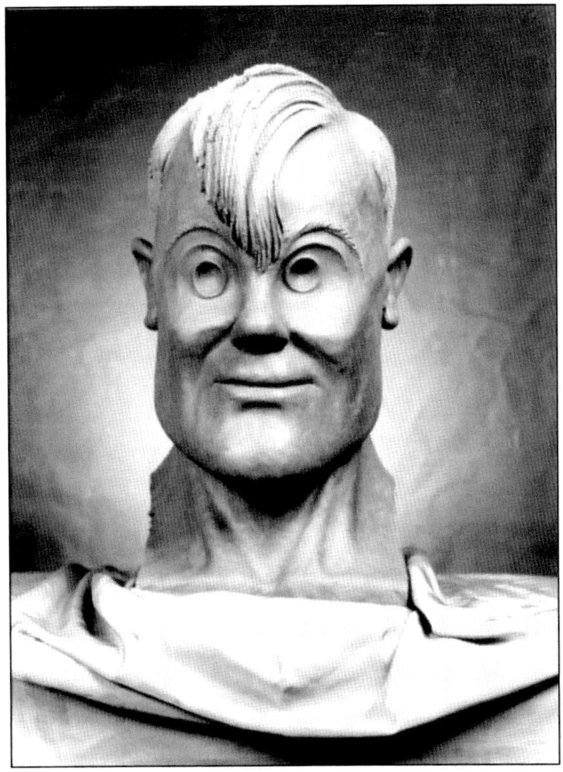

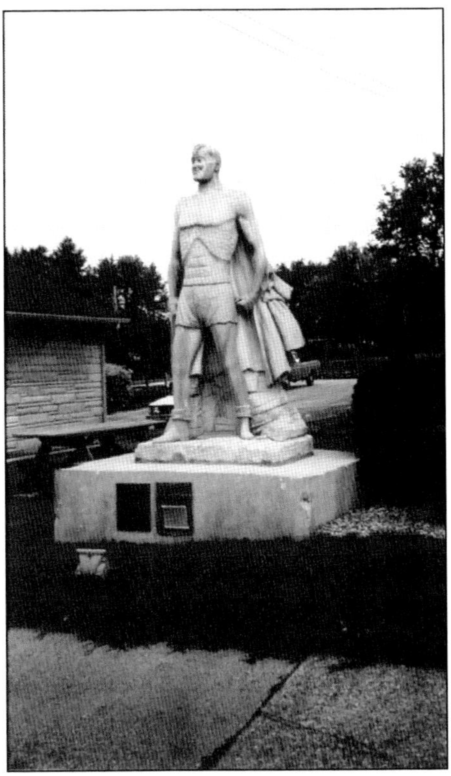

The statue of the comic strip character, Joe Palooka, once stood proudly at the FOP (Fraternal Order of Police) Park in Bedford. Ham Fisher was the creator of the comic strip. When the FOP Park was sold, the statue was moved to a permanent spot in front of the town hall in Oolitic.

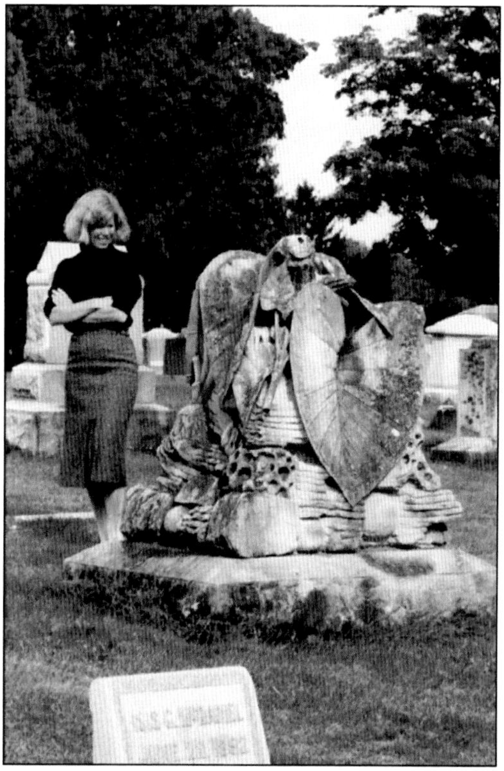

Around 1981, the Smithsonian sent a representative to Bedford to check out some of the stone carvings in Green Hill Cemetery. This unusual carving is called *The Elephant Ear.* At the time, the Smithsonian was making a documentary, *The Stone Carvers.*

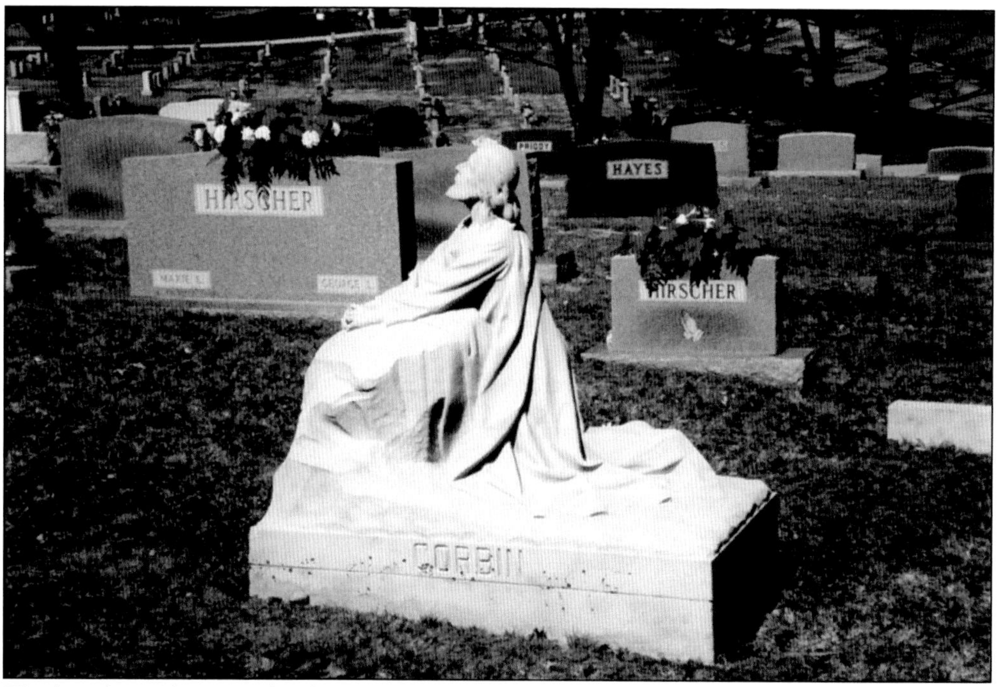

The kneeling Christ marks the graves of the Corbin family. Three of the Corbin men were master stone carvers and carved this stone for the family's resting place. This stone can be found in Green Hill Cemetery.

Michael F. Wallner, wounded by shell fire on July 20, 1918, was a doughboy in World War I. He was wounded shortly after arriving at the front and spent most of his remaining life in a hospital until he died on June 3, 1940. This is one of 35 doughboy carvings in the country.

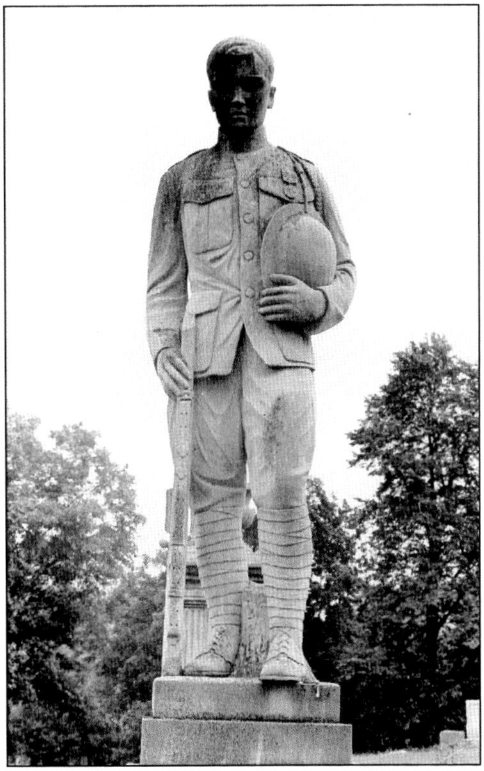

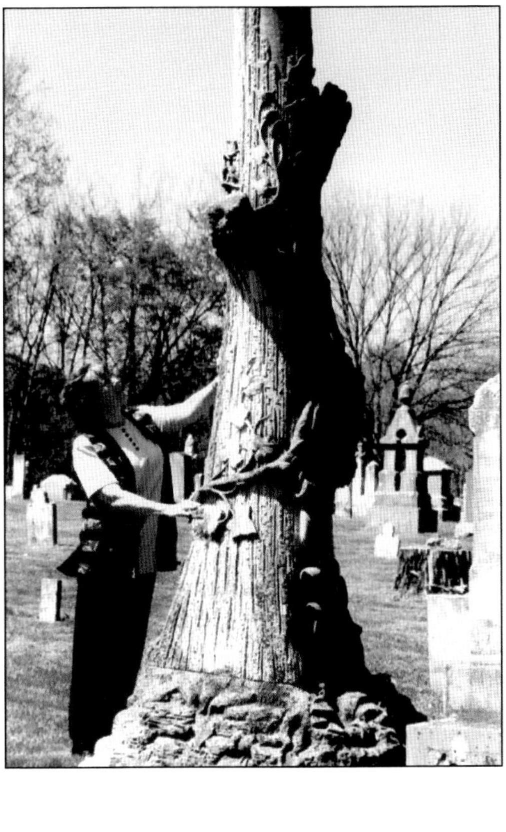

Edy Craig is admiring the tomb of a bachelor who had a love for hunting. This tree trunk carving is one of the three tallest in the county. Vines with grapes are carved around the trunk, two hounds chase a fox around the base, and a muzzleloader and powder horn are on the other side of the tree.

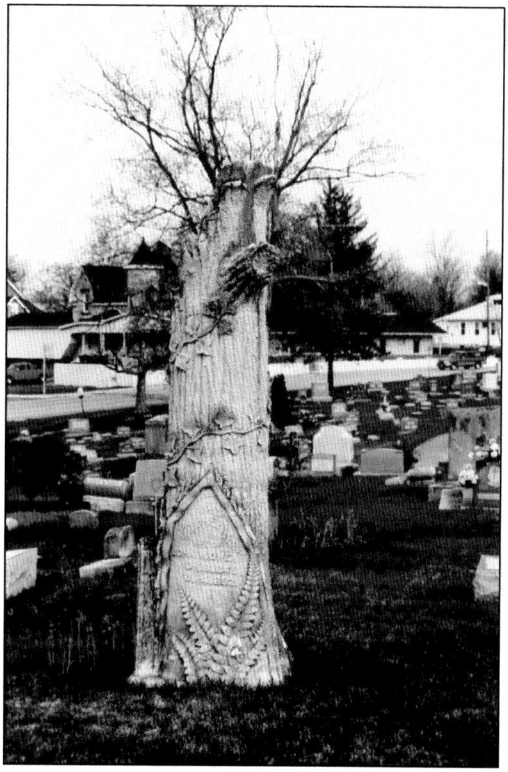

Sometimes the severed limbs of the tree trunk carving mean the loss of children in the family. Flowers, doves, vines, and other artwork can be found around the rustic tree trunk. The carving is in Green Hill Cemetery.

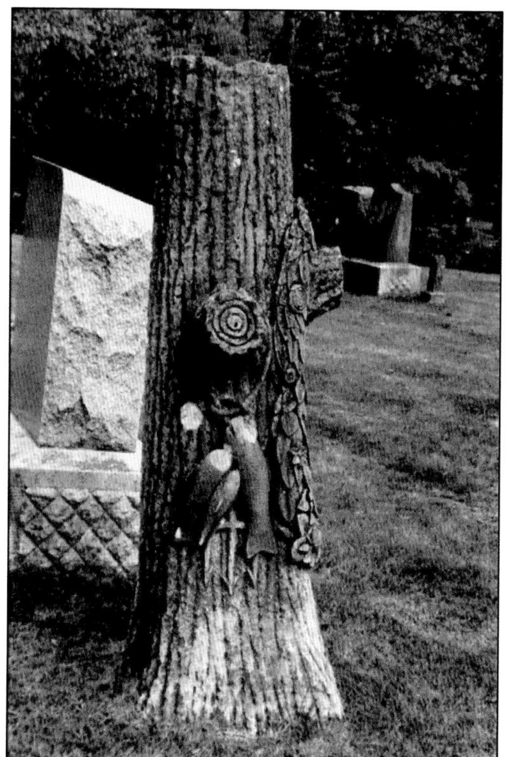

This tombstone marks the resting place of a fisherman. Notice the fine string of fish that hang from a limb that has been cropped.

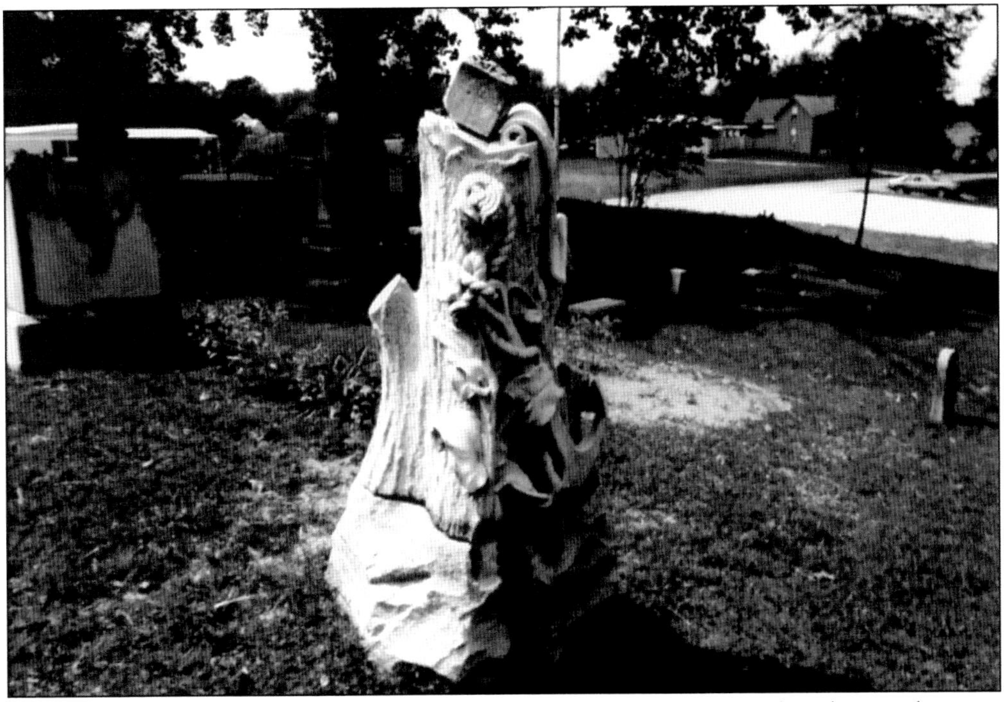

The carver of this tombstone is unknown. Notice the anchor that is tied to the rope hanging from a limb. This marker can be found in the Breckinridge Cemetery in Bedford.

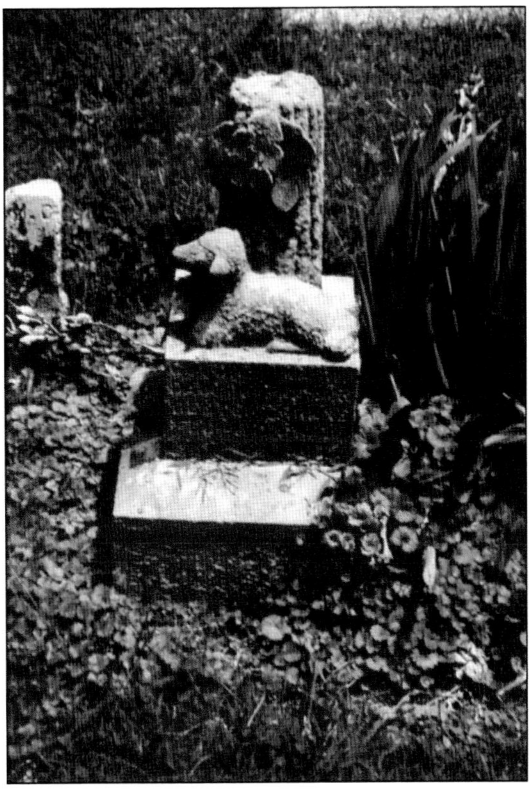

Limestone lambs were quite popular as markers for deceased children. This little lamb rests beside a tree trunk carving.

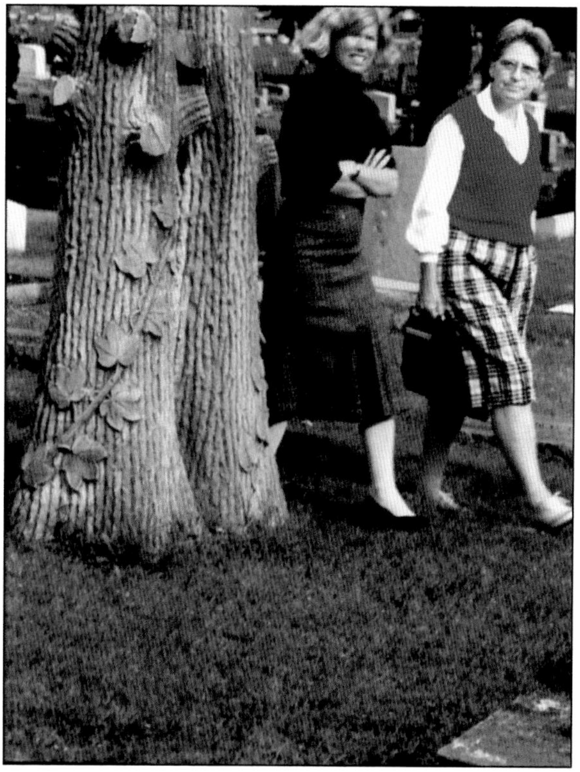

This double-tree trunk carving is located in Green Hill Cemetery. The two women passing by are Marjorie Hunt from the Smithsonian and Mary Margaret Stipp.

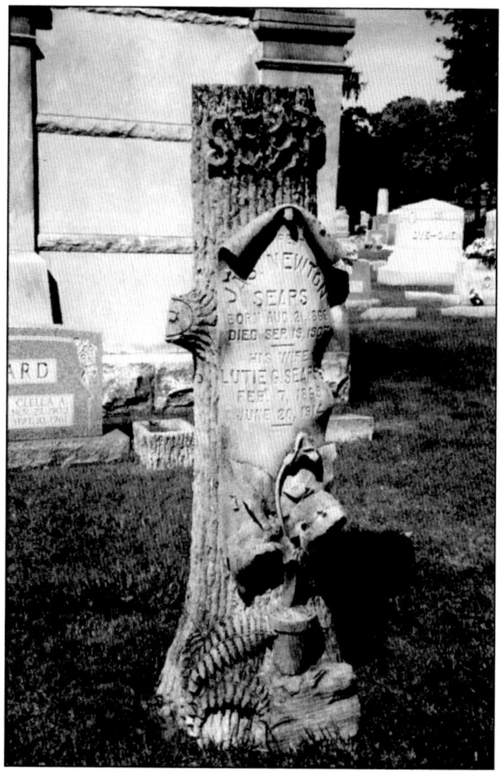

People stroll in Green Hill Cemetery to see the fine rustic tree trunk carvings that represent the simple life. There are many of these throughout the county. Some of the early stone carvers chose this type of monument and carved their own tombstones.

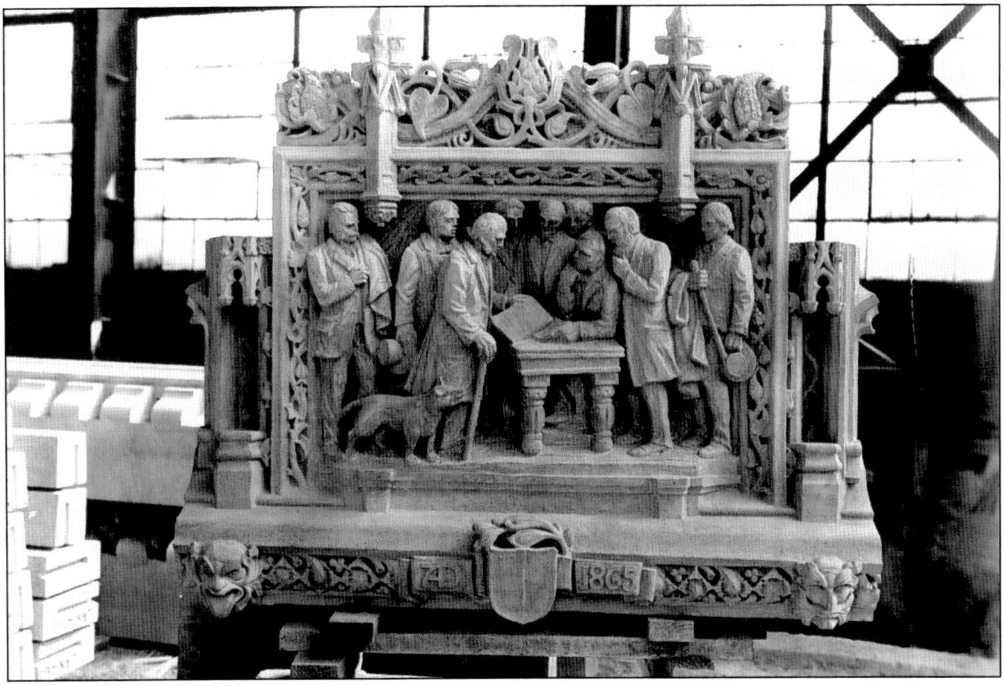

Indiana limestone is known for its ability to retain fine detail. Decorative carving and sculpturing, like in this picture, can be found all across America. It is not known who carved this beautiful masterpiece or where it will be shipped.

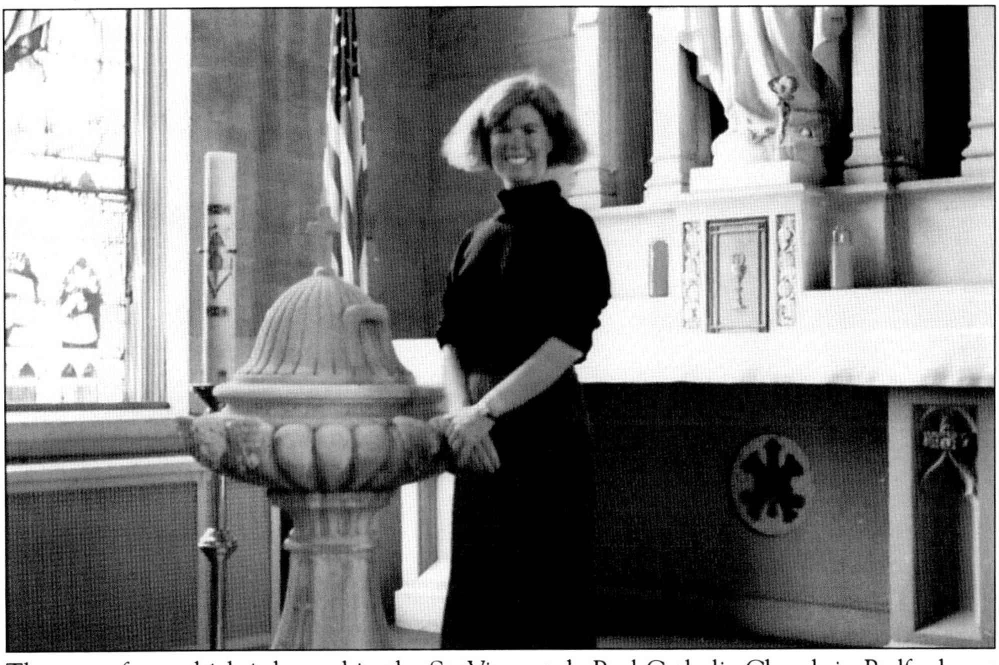

The stone font, which is housed in the St. Vincent de Paul Catholic Church in Bedford, was carved by master stone carver John O'Brien. His work can be seen throughout the country. After World War II, he was commissioned to repair the broken arm of a statue in London that had been damaged during the war.

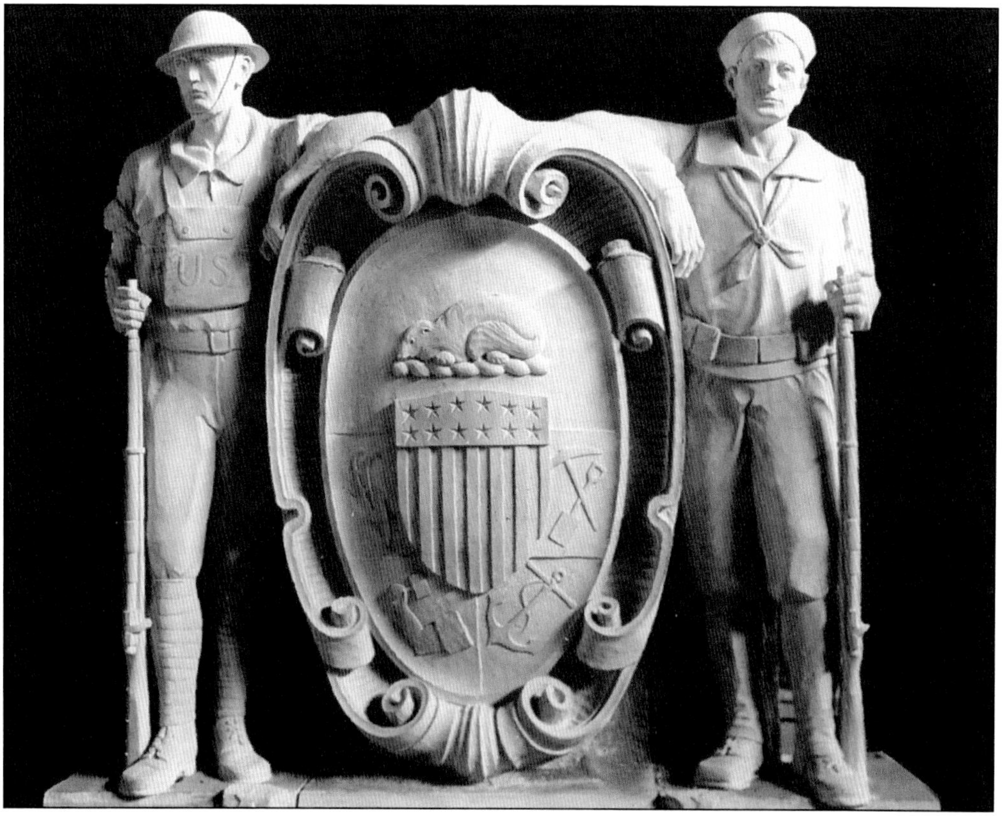

In 1927, Atlee Osborn of Bedford completed this carving of a soldier and sailor. It was for a war memorial in Milwaukee, Wisconsin.

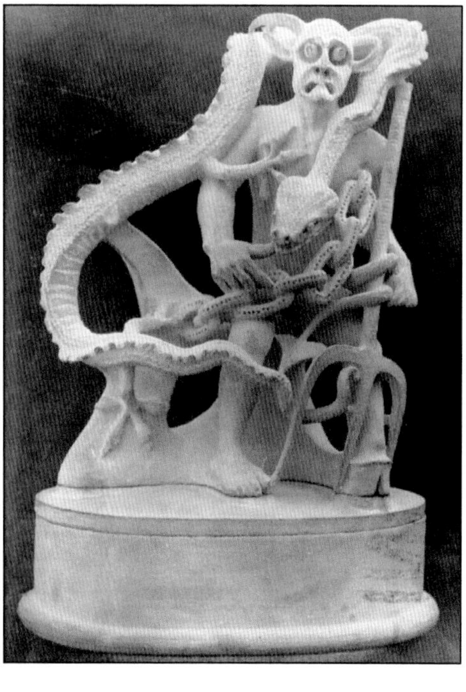

This carving was the work of Elmer Jordan of Bedford. The gargoyle is wrapped in chains with a serpent around his neck.

Six

Sports and Recreation

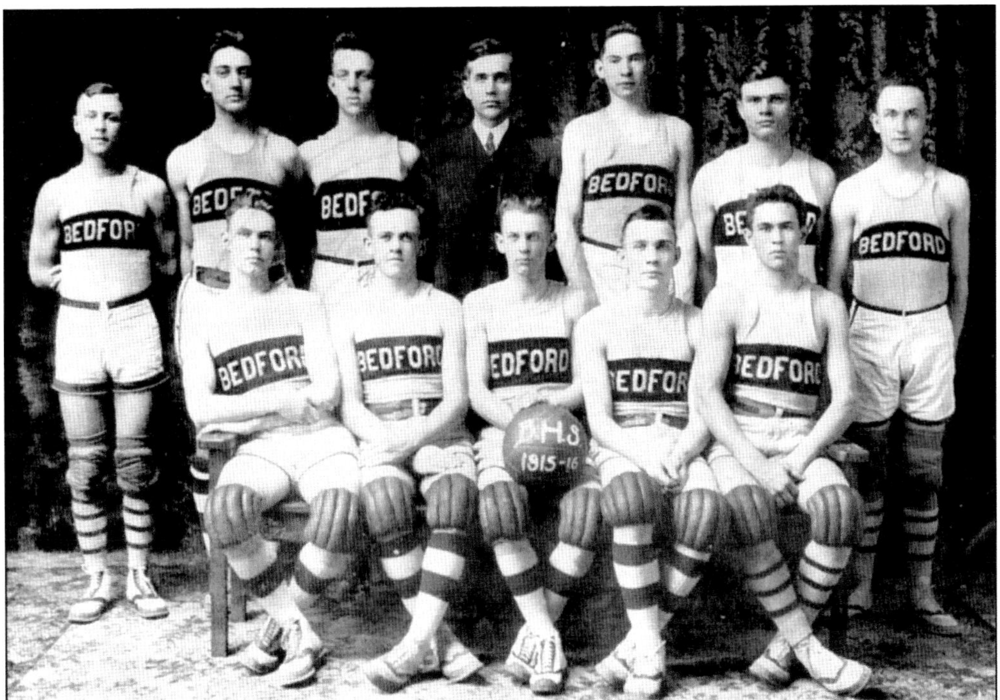

Indiana, the "Hoosier State," has always been known for its love of basketball. Bedford's first team is pictured here in the 1915–1916 year. Names of players have been lost through the years.

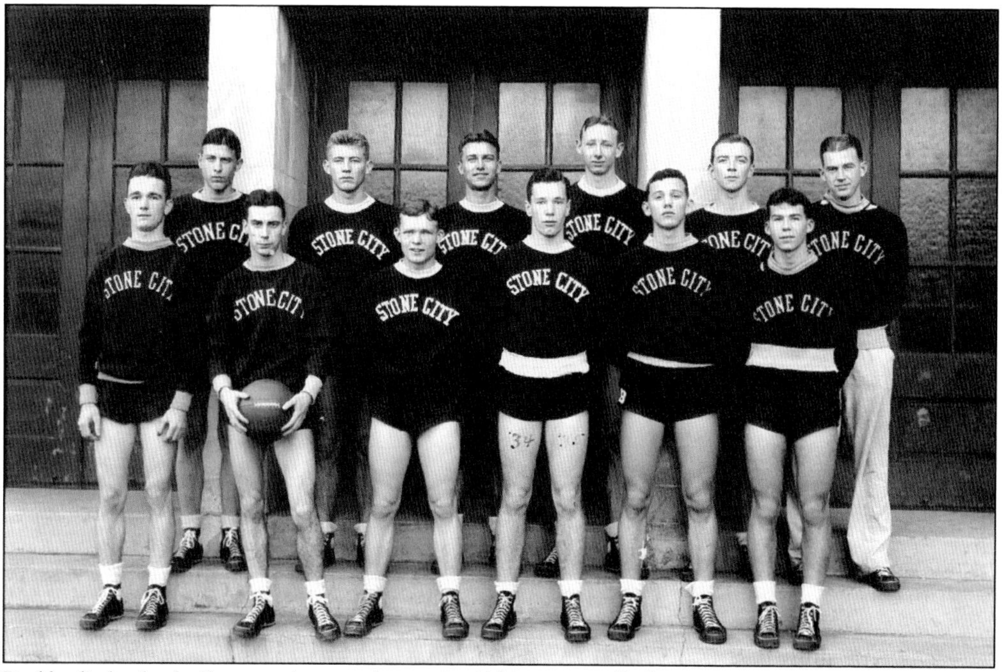

Bedford's basketball team during the early 1930s was called Stone City. Known players on this 1934–1935 team were Amel Murray, Jim Bruce, Don Webster, Wayne "Tick" Terry, and Fred Beretta.

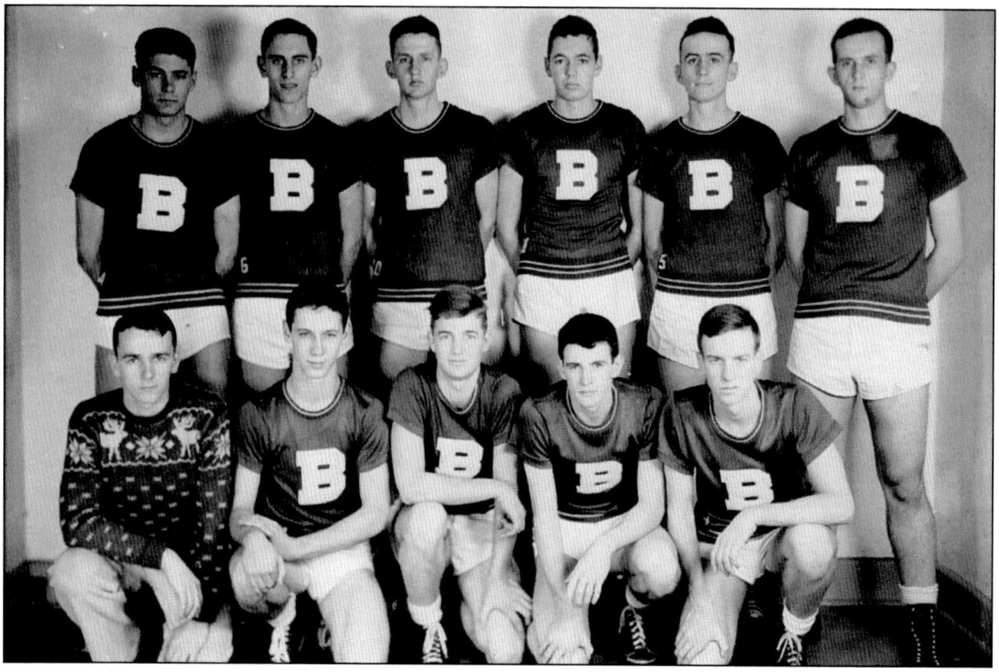

By 1946, the Bedford basketball team was known as the Stonecutters. Team members pictured from left to right are (first row) Jim Keotter (student manager), Jack Allen, Morris Root, Joe True, and Jim Flick; (second row) Bob Corbin, Jack Turner, Dick Pace, John Condiff, Wayne Girdley, and Bob Sohn. Flick became a well-known golfing authority.

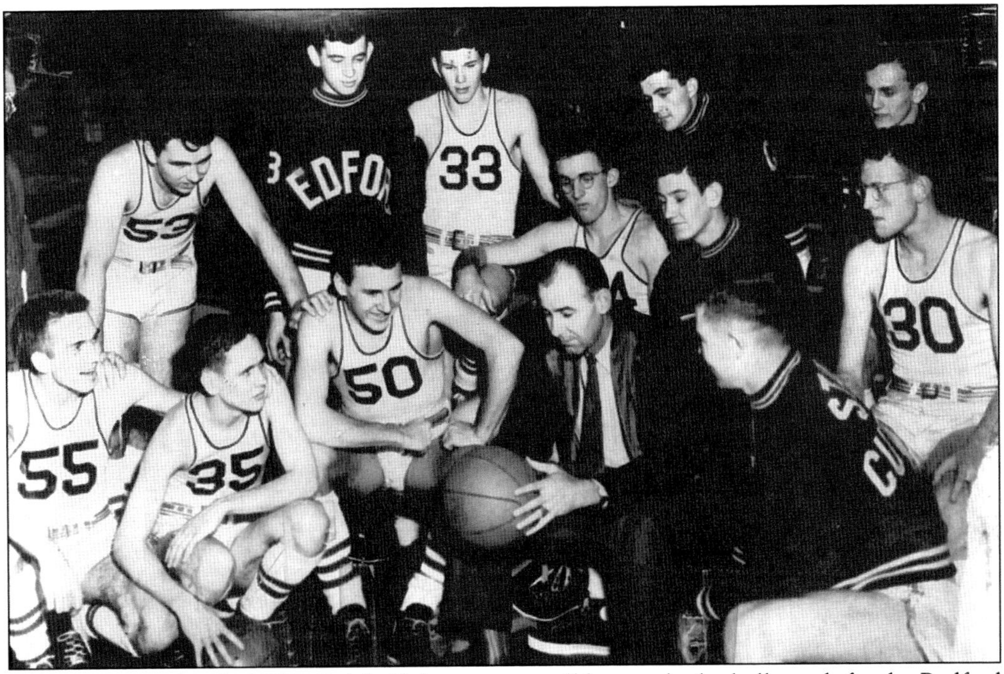

In the 1940s and early 1950s, Ralph Holmes was a well-known basketball coach for the Bedford Stonecutters. Basketball was the number one sport for the Hoosier State. Before consolidation of the Lawrence County schools, sectional and regional tournaments were held in one of the largest and finest gyms in southern Indiana.

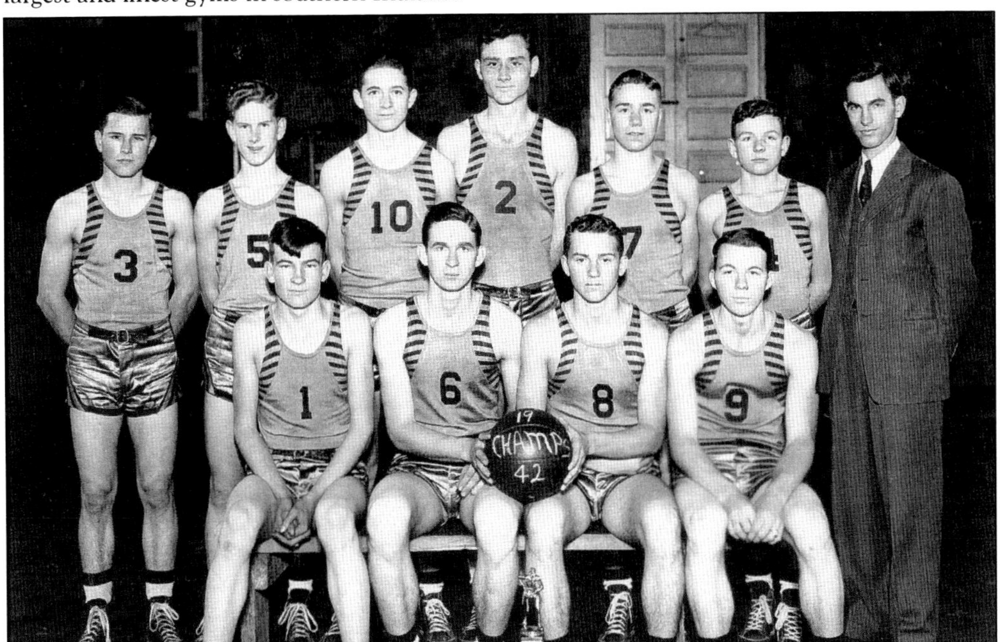

Springville High School in 1942 was the Lawrence County Basketball Champion. Team players are Bob Gardner, Fred Byers, Ralph Bolton, Buster Kern, Gerald Wagoner, Bob Hayes, Morton Jean Puk, Bob Giles, Paul Clark, and Farrell Hayes.

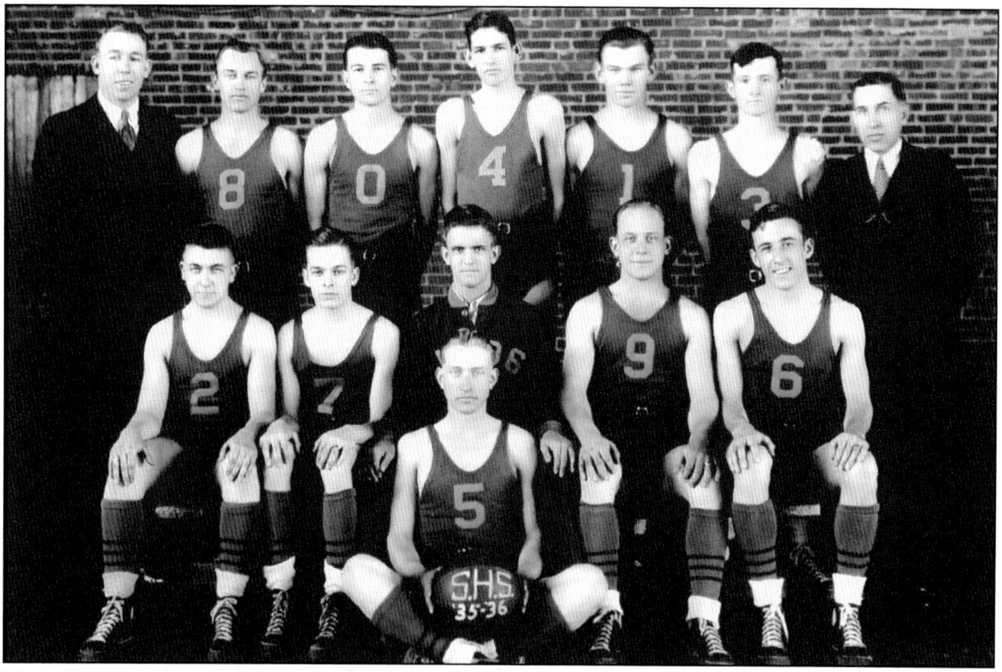

This photograph is the Shawswick High School basketball team in 1935–1936. Team members include, from left to right, (first row) Ralph Beavers, with the ball; (second row) Gordon Keck, Robert Cupps, manager James Baumgarden, Robert Inman, and Edward Pudd; (third row) coach Ed Cuddy, Harold Guthrie, Morris Jackson, Ernest Mathews, Everett Younger, Leon Gardner, and principal Loren Raines.

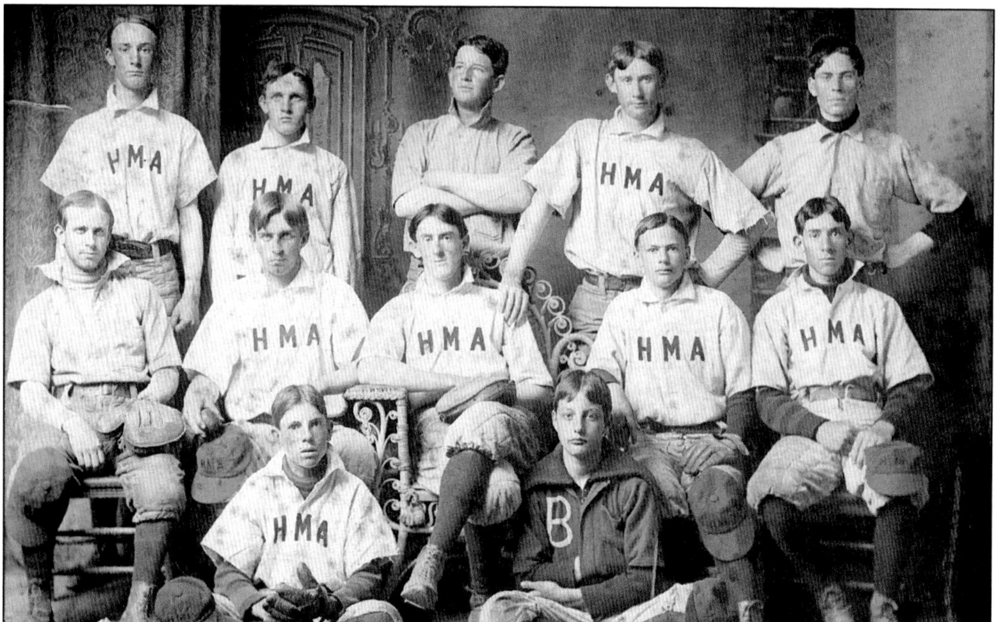

This is a 1900 photograph of Hogsett's baseball team. Known players are C. F. Wilson, C. Manninni, E. F. Raine, P. Grinstead, Hopkinson (substitute), Swanson (substitute), Mustaine (manager), Terrill (second base), Walker (captain), Caie (left field), and Hopkinson (third base).

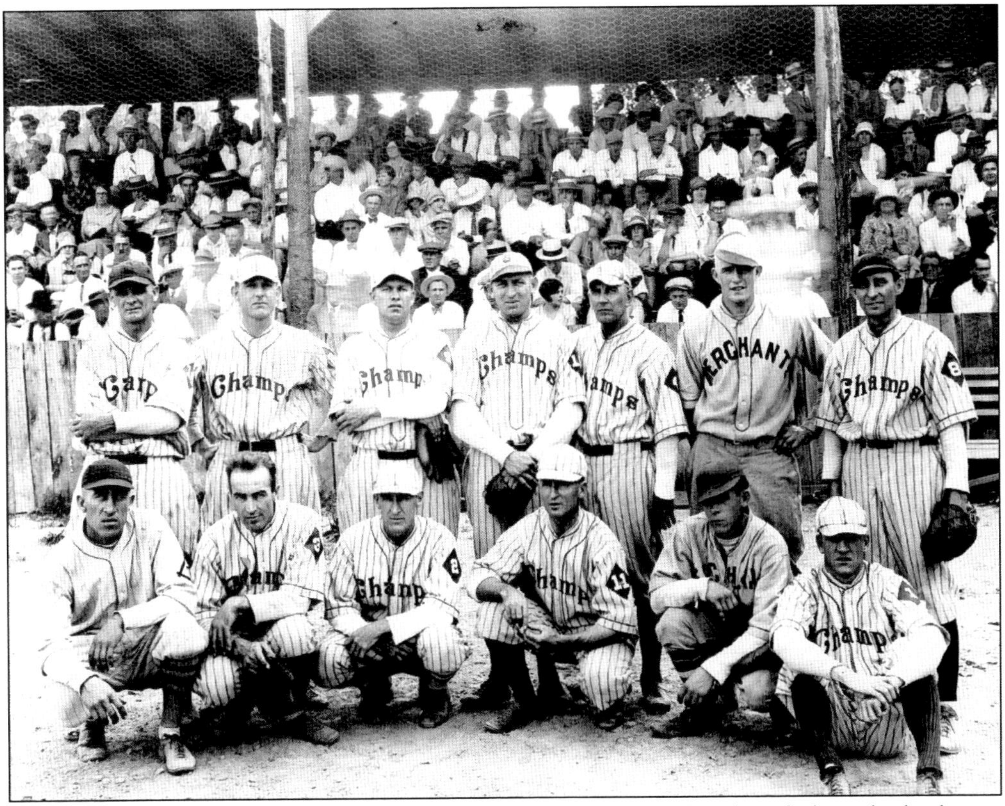

This is a baseball team in the late 1930s. Only two players can be identified: in the back row, second from right is Morrell Beasley and far right is Gus Bivins.

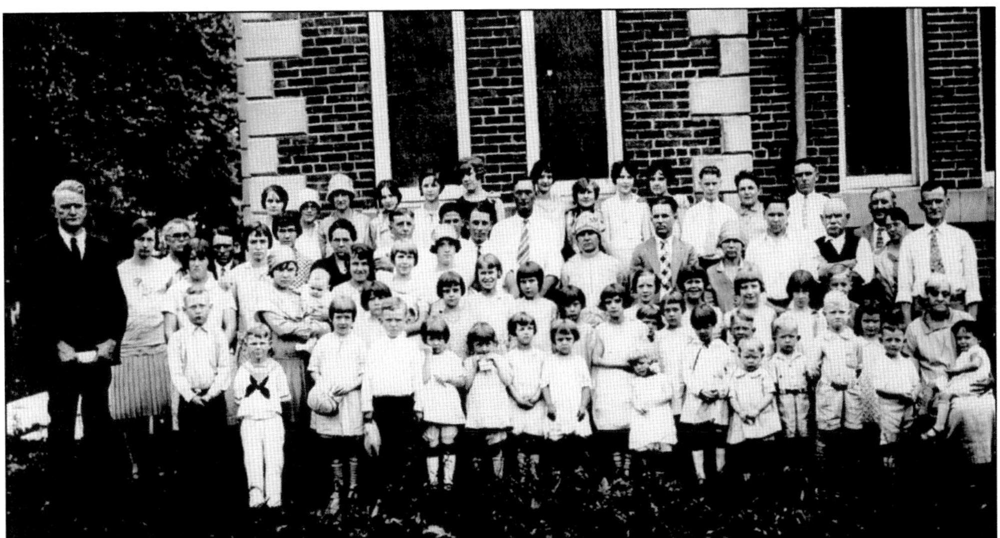

In 1928, this photograph was taken of the Tunnelton Methodist Church Sunday school class. Some of the family names in the picture are; Payton, Wright, Lee, Weaver, Crane, Cecil, True, and others.

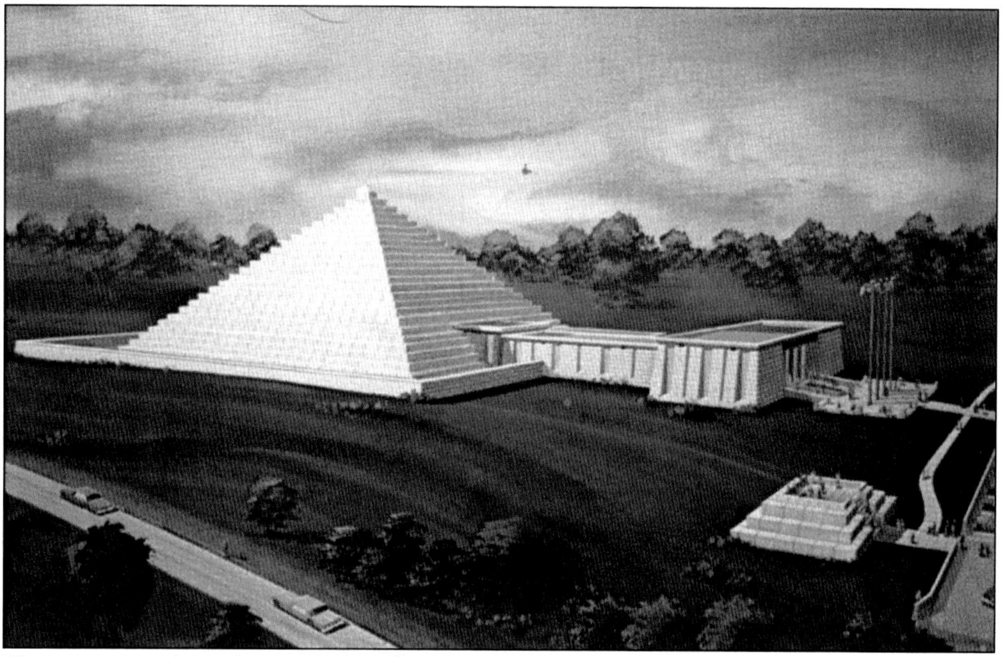

This is an artist's rendering of the administration building museum and pyramid, which was planned for the Indiana Limestone Tourist and Demonstration Center, just north of Bedford. This project began around 1978, but was never completed due to lack of funds.

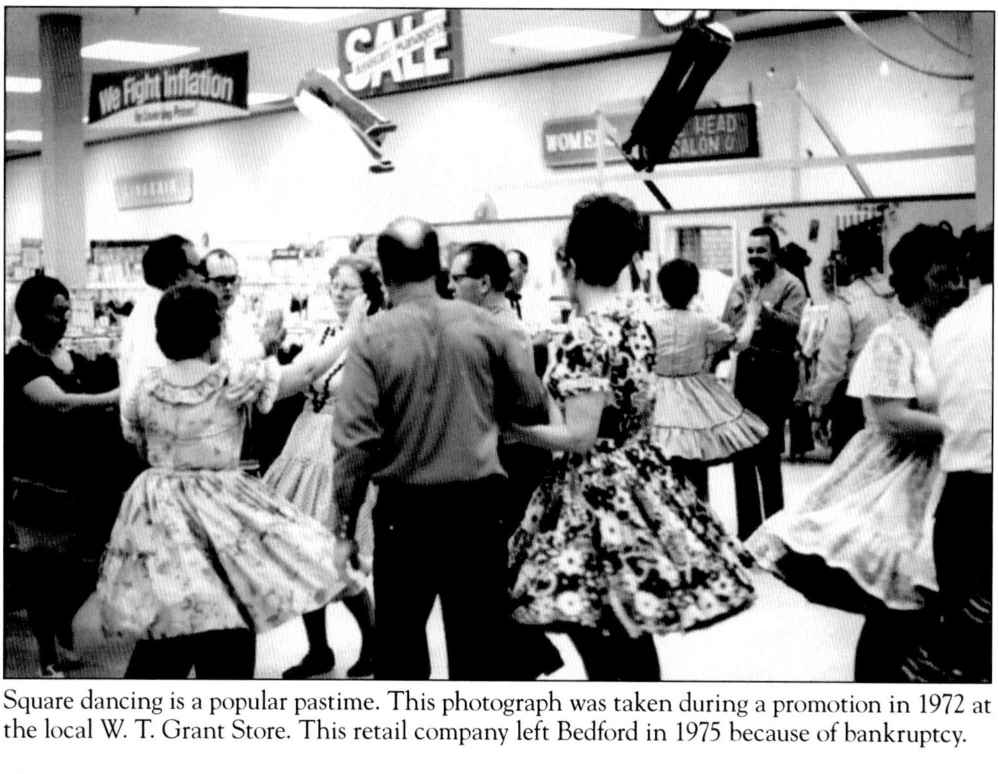

Square dancing is a popular pastime. This photograph was taken during a promotion in 1972 at the local W. T. Grant Store. This retail company left Bedford in 1975 because of bankruptcy.

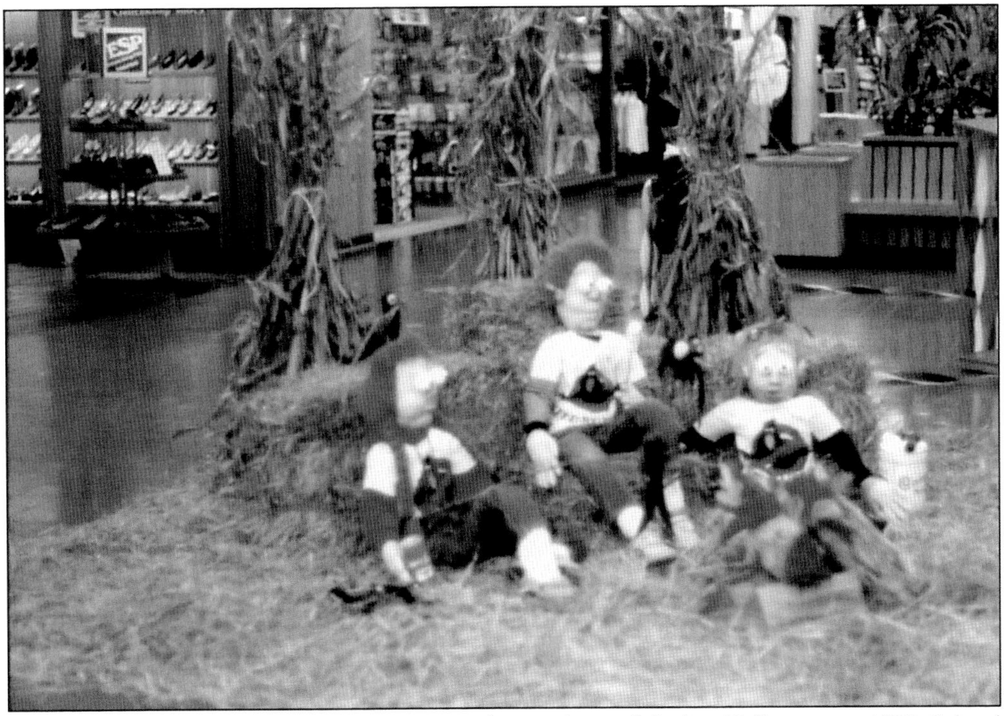

Stone City Mall had a scarecrow competition during the week before Halloween in 1984. School organizations and individuals were invited to enter. This was the first-prize winner of the sum of $100.

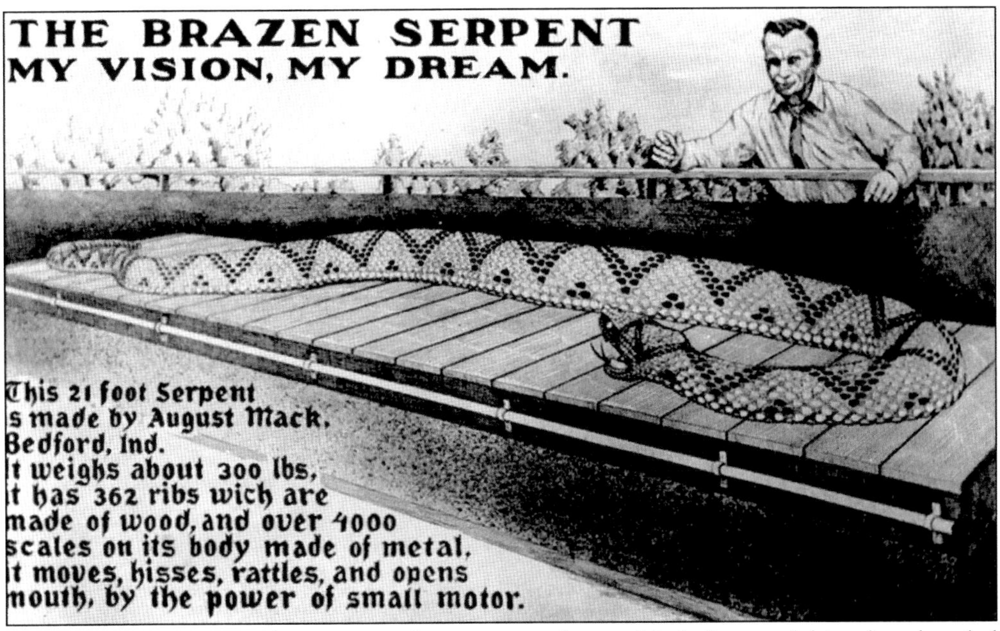

The Brazen Serpent was the creation of stone carver August Mack. It moved, hissed, and rattled by means of a small motor. The snake was on display for visitors to view just north of Bedford off Indiana Highway 37.

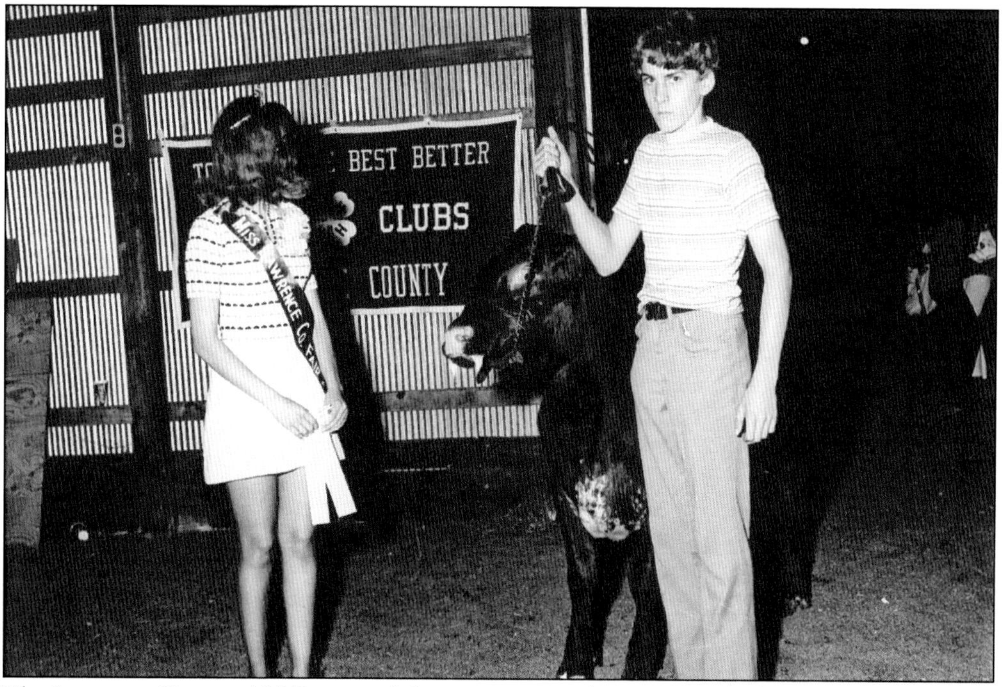

The Lawrence County 4-H Fair is in July every year, and young people show their animals and compete for showmanship and prizes. This young man on the right is showing his steer and the young girl at the left has been chosen as Miss Lawrence County Fair Queen.

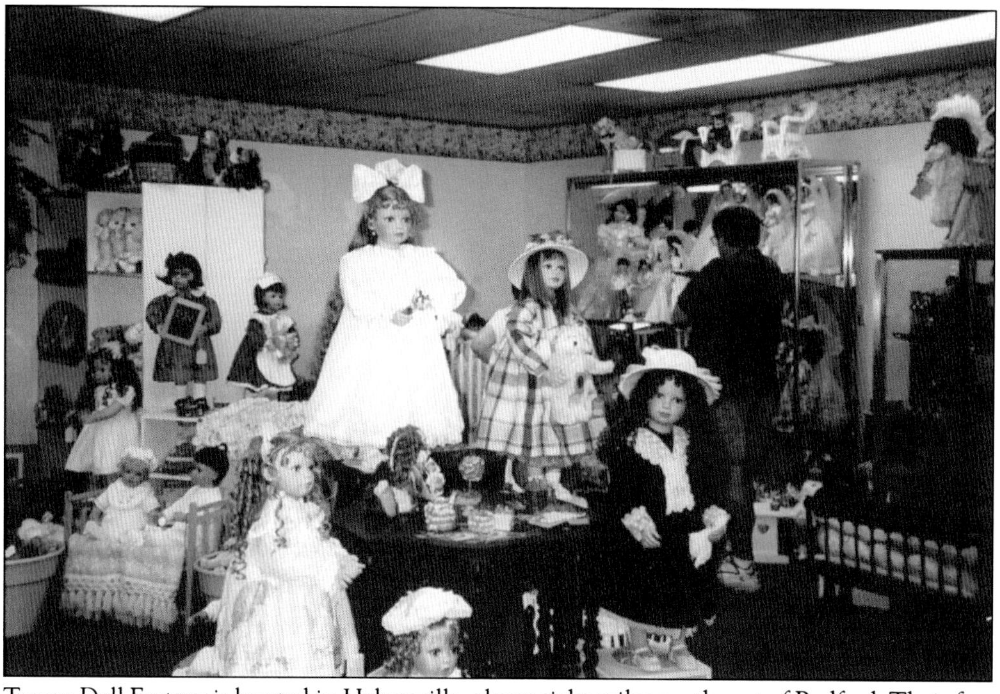

Turner Doll Factory is located in Heltonville, about eight miles northwest of Bedford. Their fine collectable dolls are nationally known. Visitors enjoy their unique gifts and a pleasant interlude at the tea room.

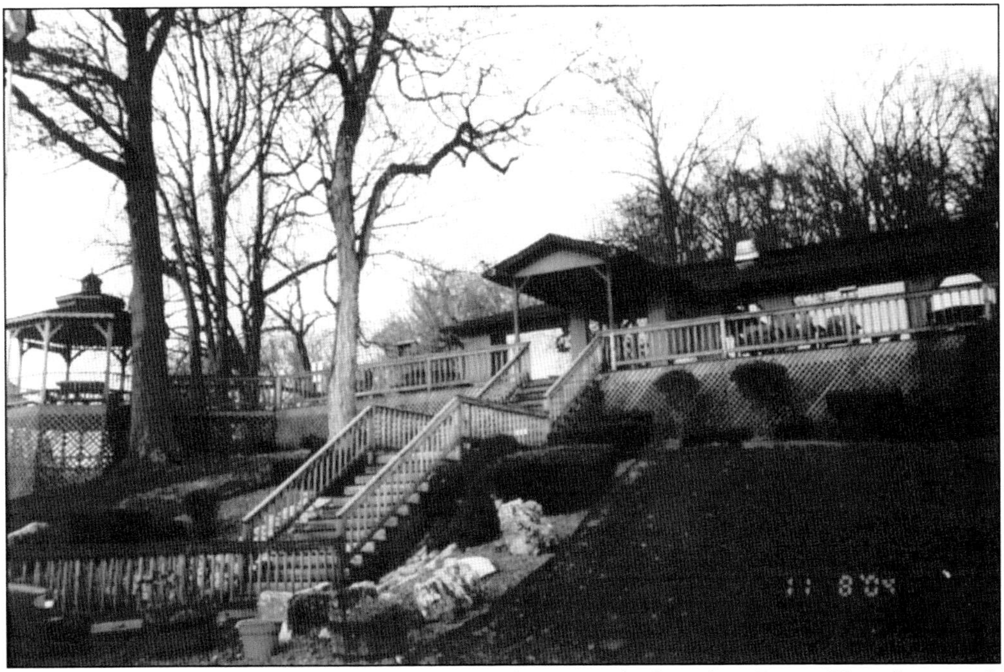

The Bedford Boat and Sportsman's Club, high above, overlooks White River. This photograph was taken from the bottom of the hill and shows the scenic view. Many activities are carried on every year such as dances and dinners as well as shooting matches and boating events. (Courtesy of Wilma Wildman Tirmenstier.)

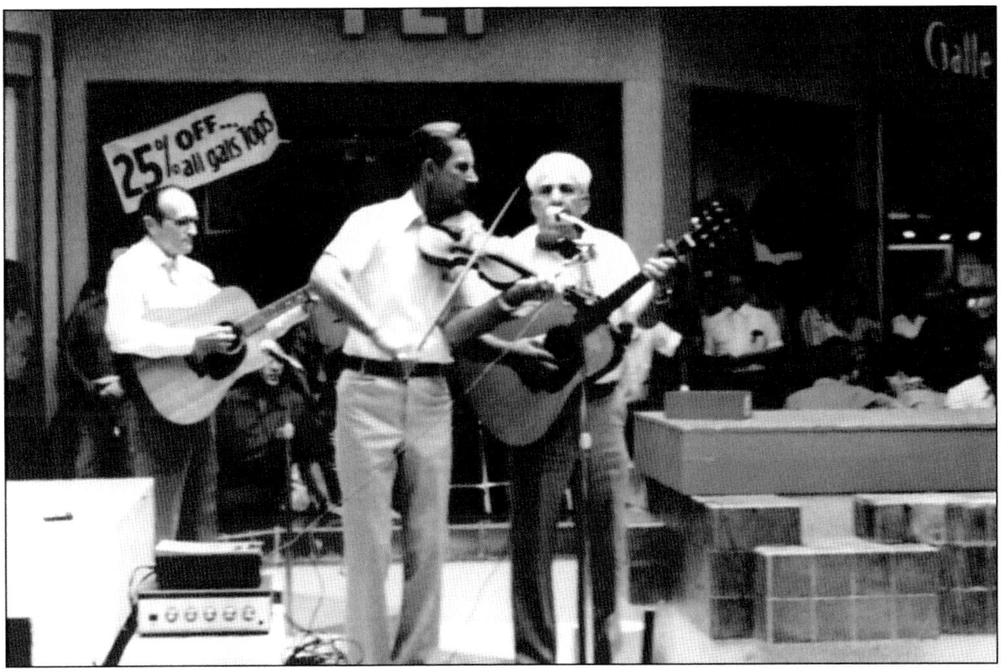

An old-time fiddler's contest in 1985 was one of the promotions at Stone City Mall. First prize was $200, second prize was $100, and third prize of $50. This proved to be quite a success and for several years this was a yearly event. The audience did the judging.

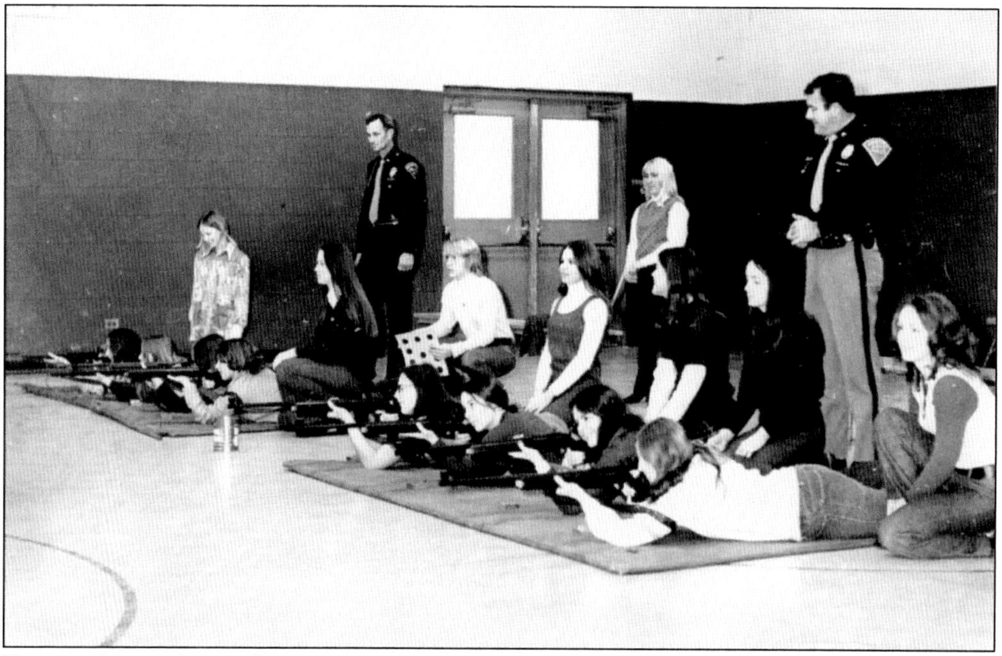

Young girls are taking rifle training at the local Boy's Club. Dean Blackwell (left) and Sam Kruse (right) are the instructors.

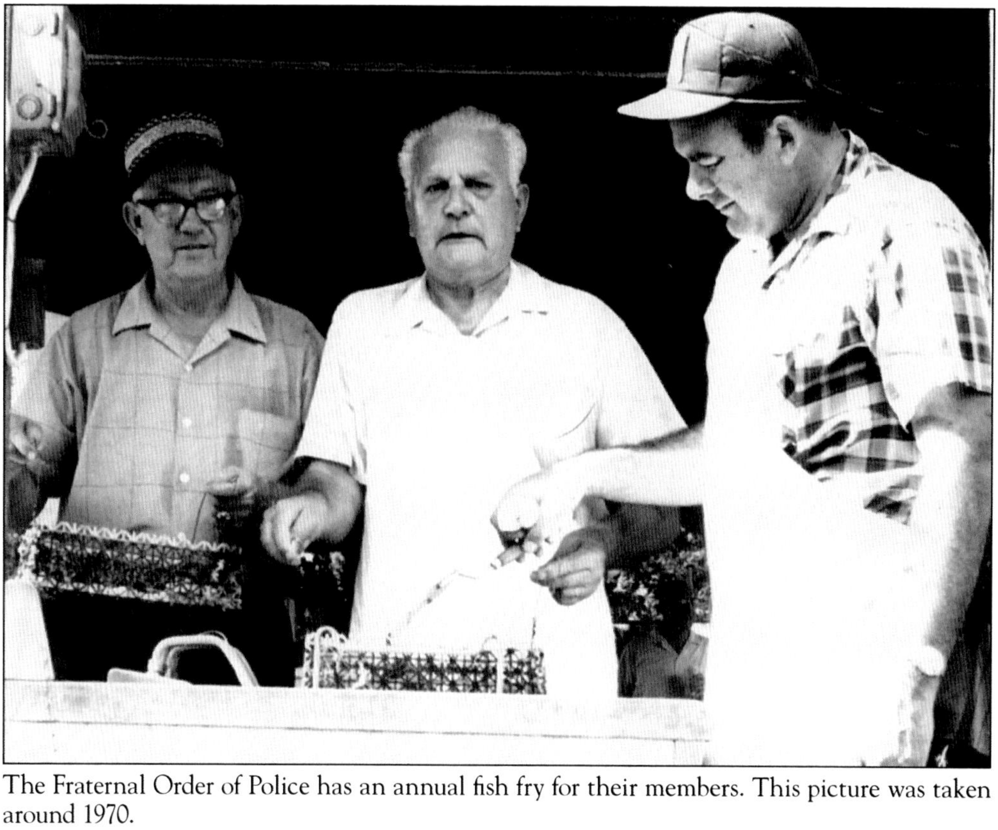

The Fraternal Order of Police has an annual fish fry for their members. This picture was taken around 1970.

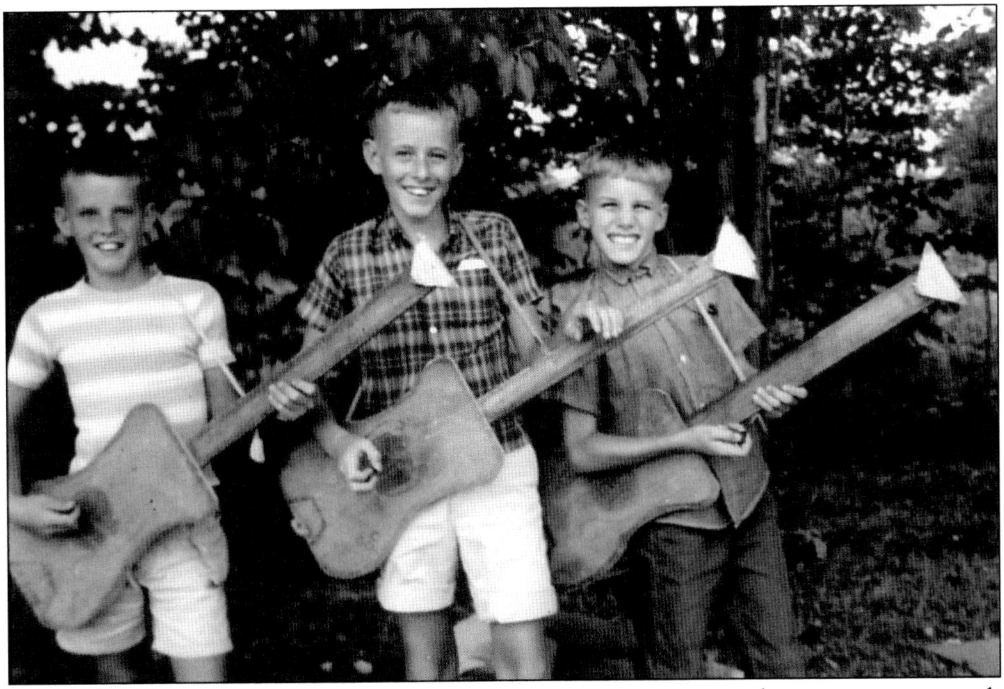

Three young boys from Sunny Acres Drive in Bedford are practicing to become musicians with their fake wooden guitars.

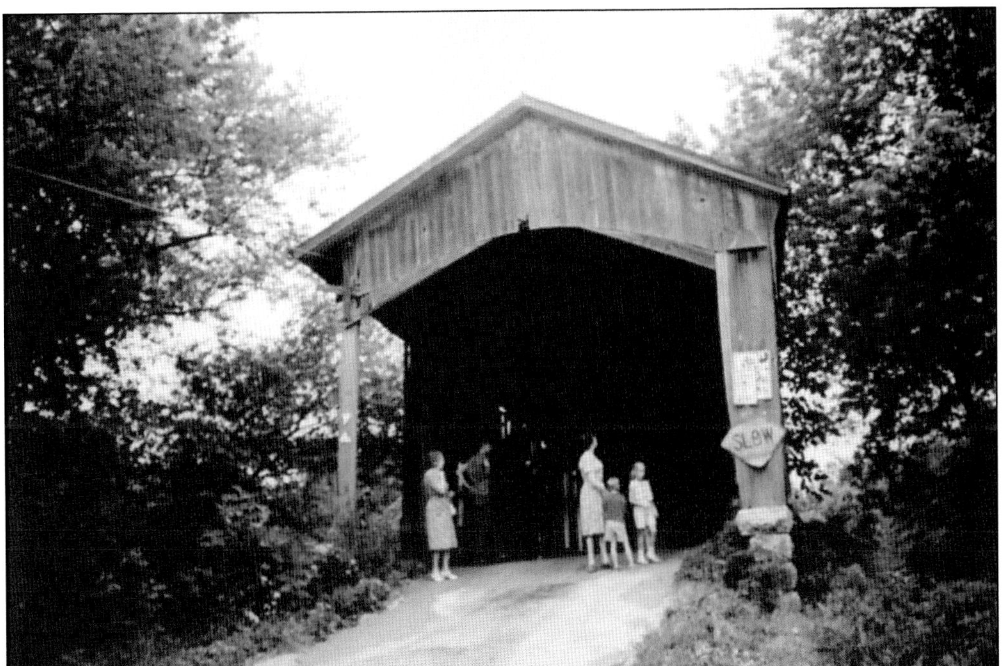

The Tunnelton covered bridge is no longer in existence. At one time, Lawrence County had five covered bridges, and now only one remains, the Williams covered bridge. It was a Sunday afternoon treat for young people to walk through the bridges.

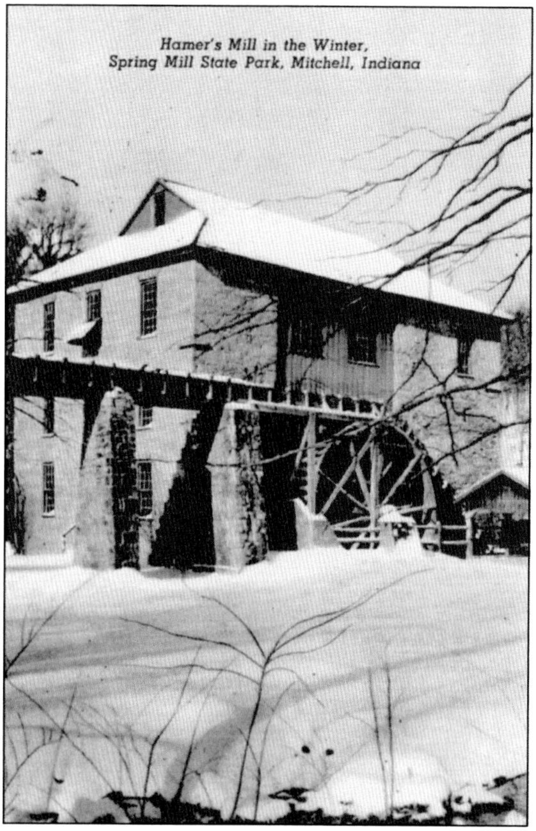

Hamer's Mill is located in Spring Mill State Park, south of Bedford near Mitchell. The mill now houses a museum and working gristmill.

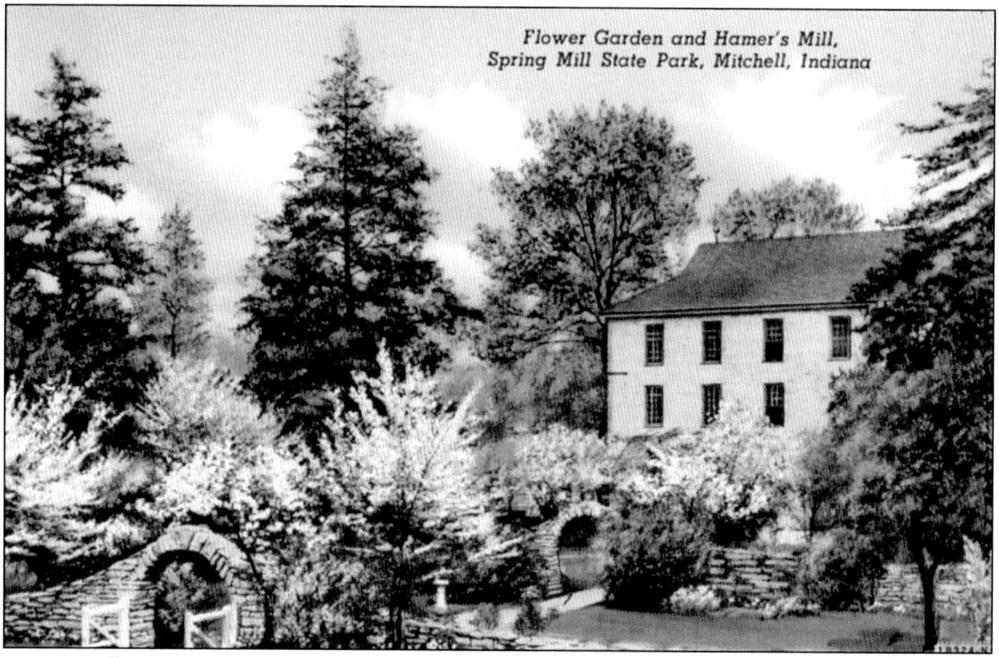

Spring Mill State Park is one of the best state parks in Indiana. It has an 1800s pioneer village, a gristmill, and beautiful flower gardens. It is the number one tourist attraction in the area.

In the early days, Spring Mill State Park had a beach, which was quite popular with young people. This unidentified visiting young man is enjoying the sun on the beach, which was closed to swimming years ago.

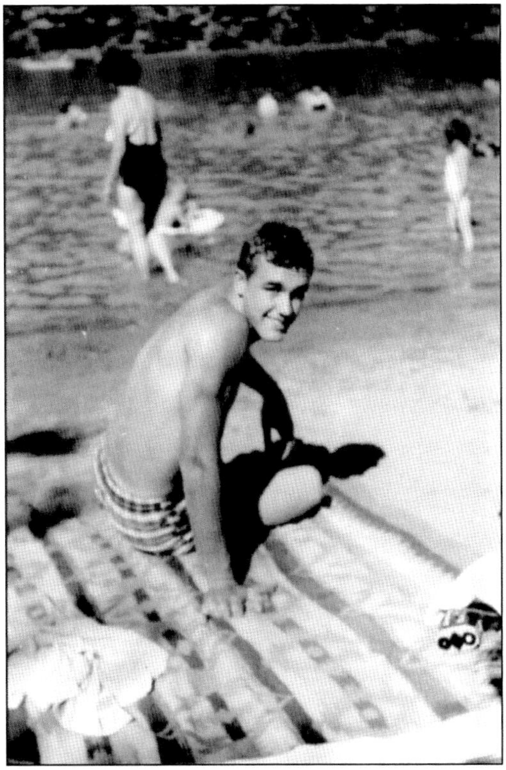

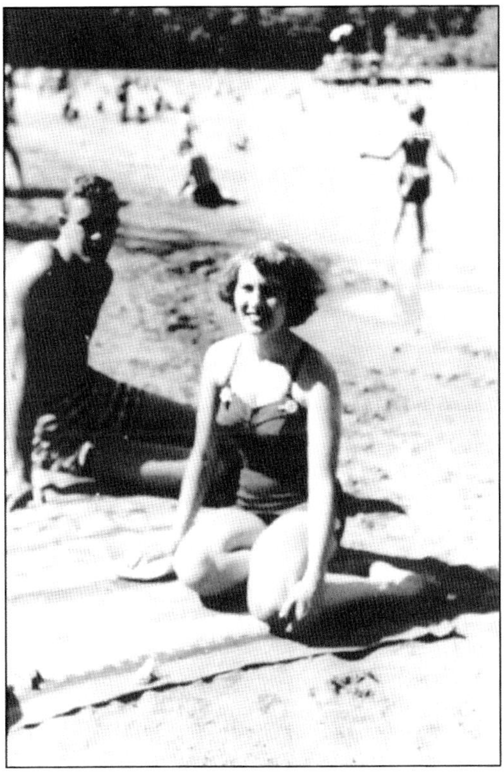

Visitors enjoy the beach at Spring Mill State Park in the 1940s and 1950s. It was nearly always full of sun bathers on the weekends and Wednesday afternoon when most businesses were closed.

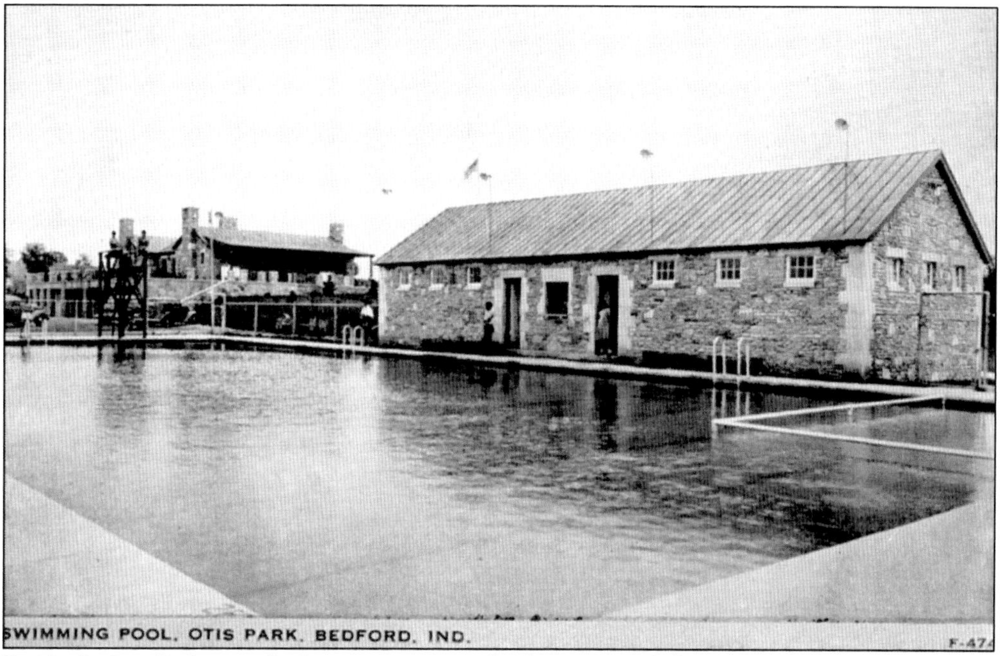

Bedford's Otis Park once had a swimming pool. This postcard shows the pool and bathhouse. The pool was replaced with a parking lot for golfers.

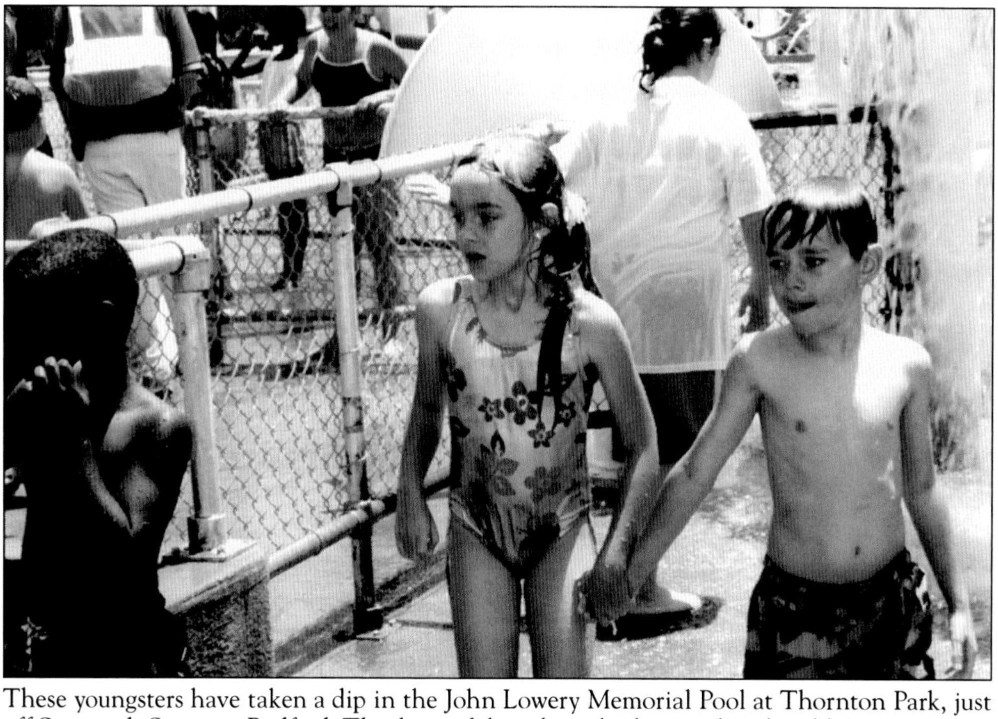

These youngsters have taken a dip in the John Lowery Memorial Pool at Thornton Park, just off Sixteenth Street in Bedford. This beautiful pool was built just after the old Otis Park pool was demolished.

During the summer when children are out of school, the pool is a favorite spot. Bedford has several parks for the enjoyment of all.

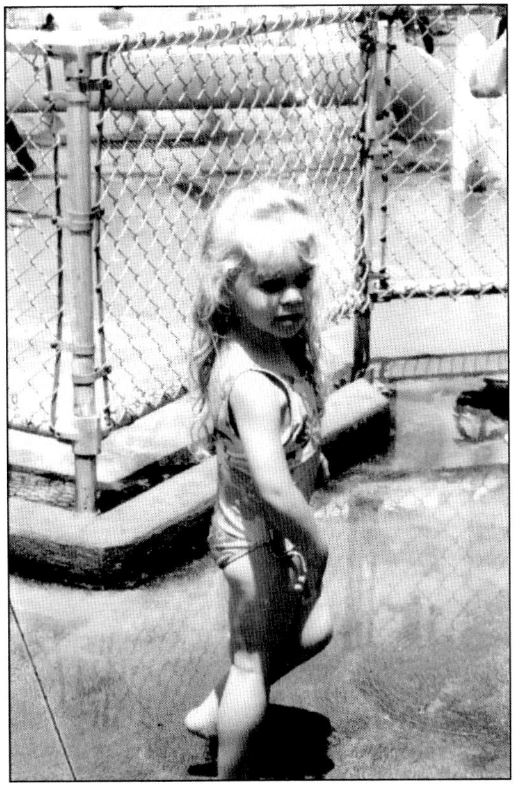

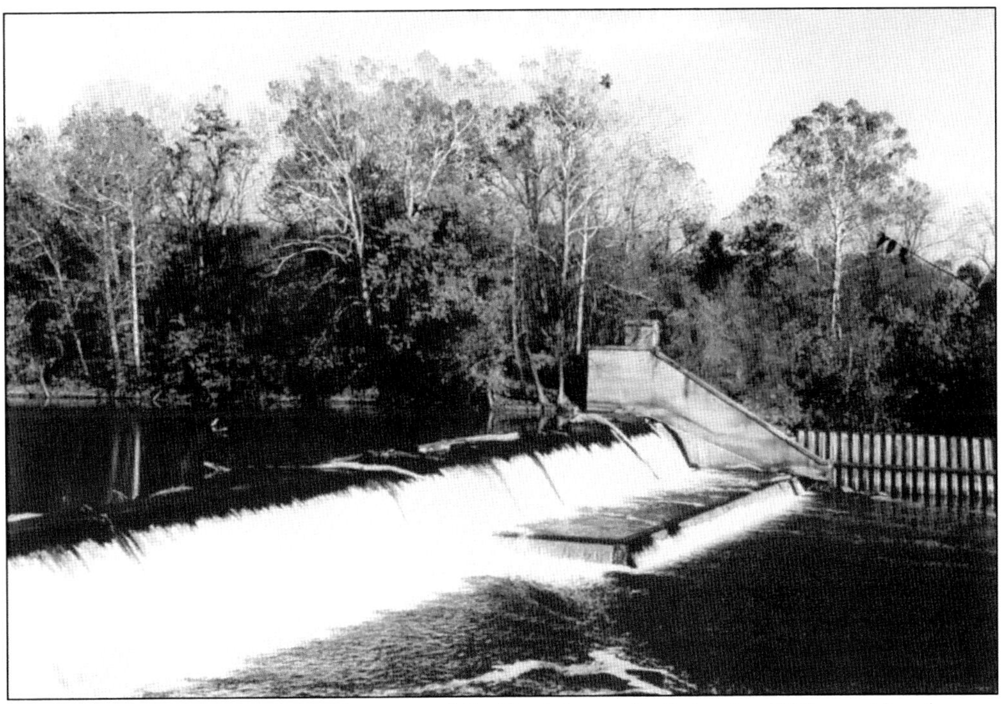

The Williams Dam is a few miles west of Bedford. It was built in the 1920s and has been a favorite spot for fishermen.

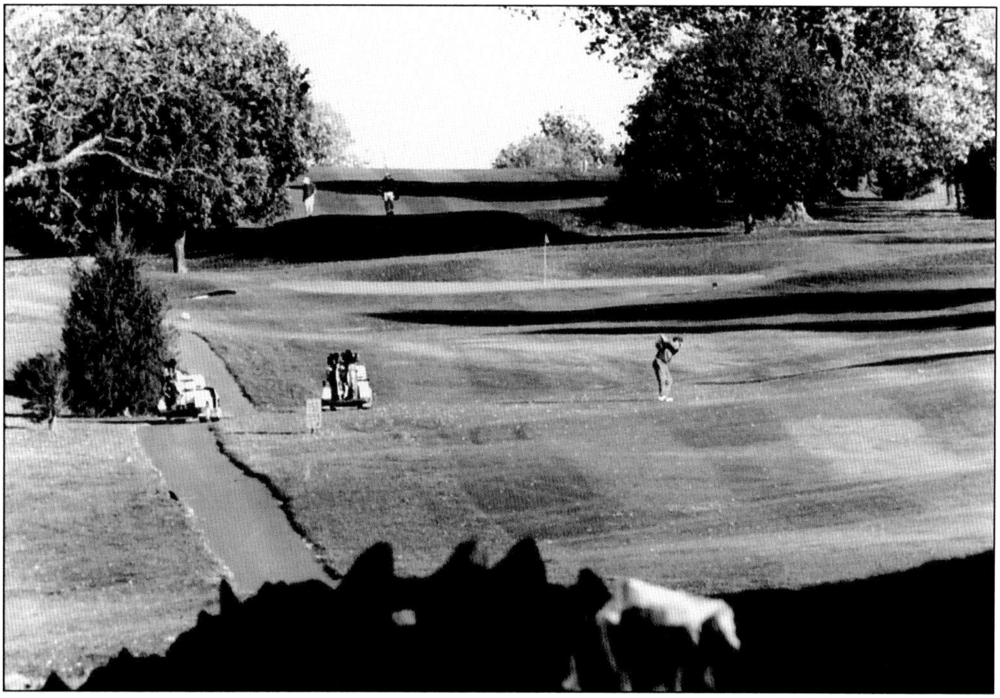

Otis Golf Course was once advertised as the finest in southern Indiana. There are now several more golf courses in the area.

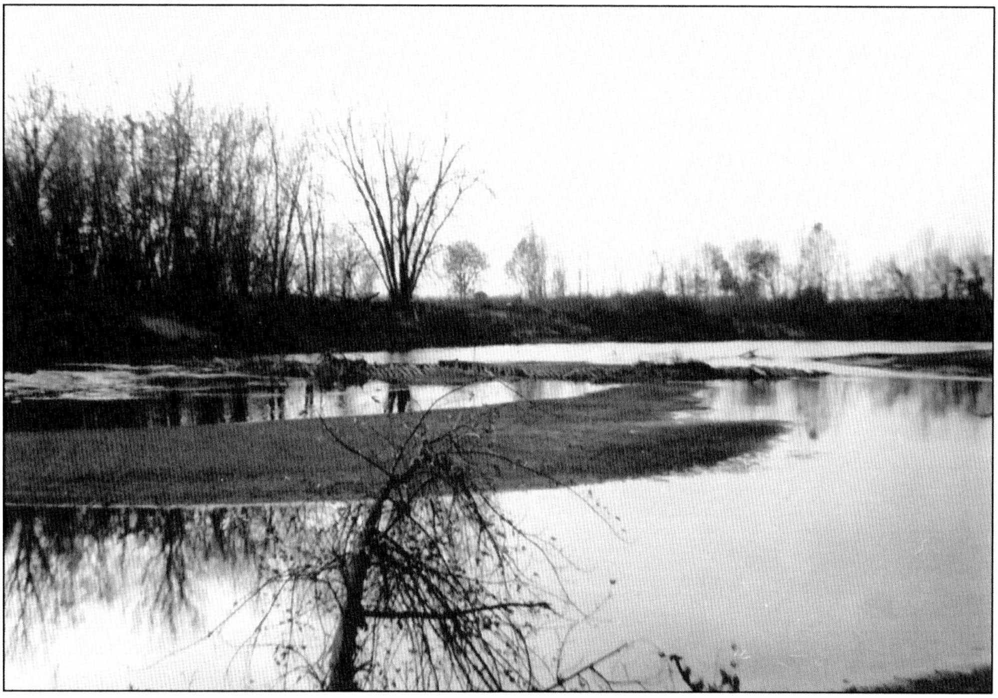

An early dam across White River, southeast of Bedford, can be seen when the river is so low. At one time there was a ferry near the area. The rural roads throughout the county are very scenic and many people spend a Sunday afternoon driving.

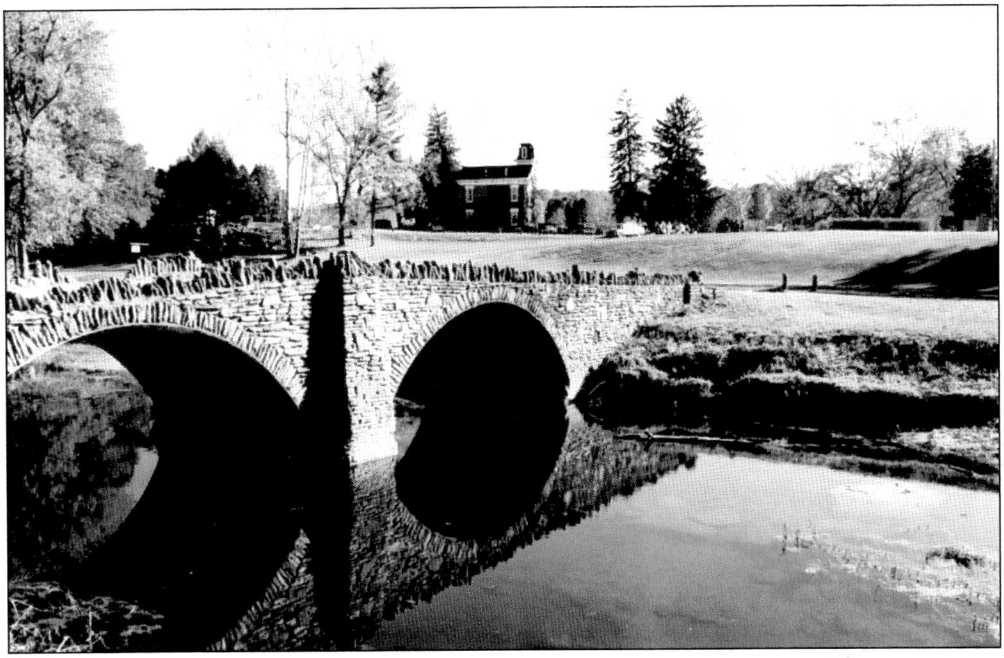

Otis Park is located on land given to the city by Fred Otis, a newspaper man. This scenic view shows the section of the park where an 18-hole golf course is located. The course has been hailed as the best in southern Indiana. Each September, the Bedford Area Chamber of Commerce hosts the Claude Akins Golf Tournament, honoring the actor who came from Bedford.

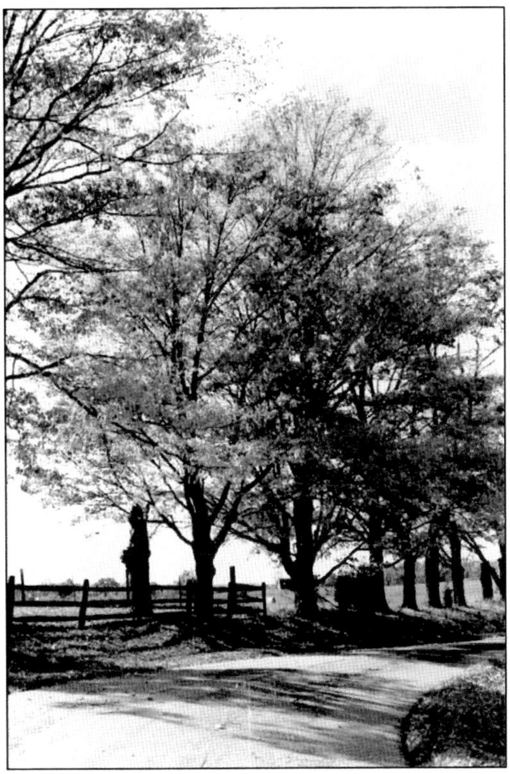

Autumn colors are everywhere during the fall, as this image, along one of the county roads east of town, whould show in color. The early spring is filled with the color of redbud and dogwood.

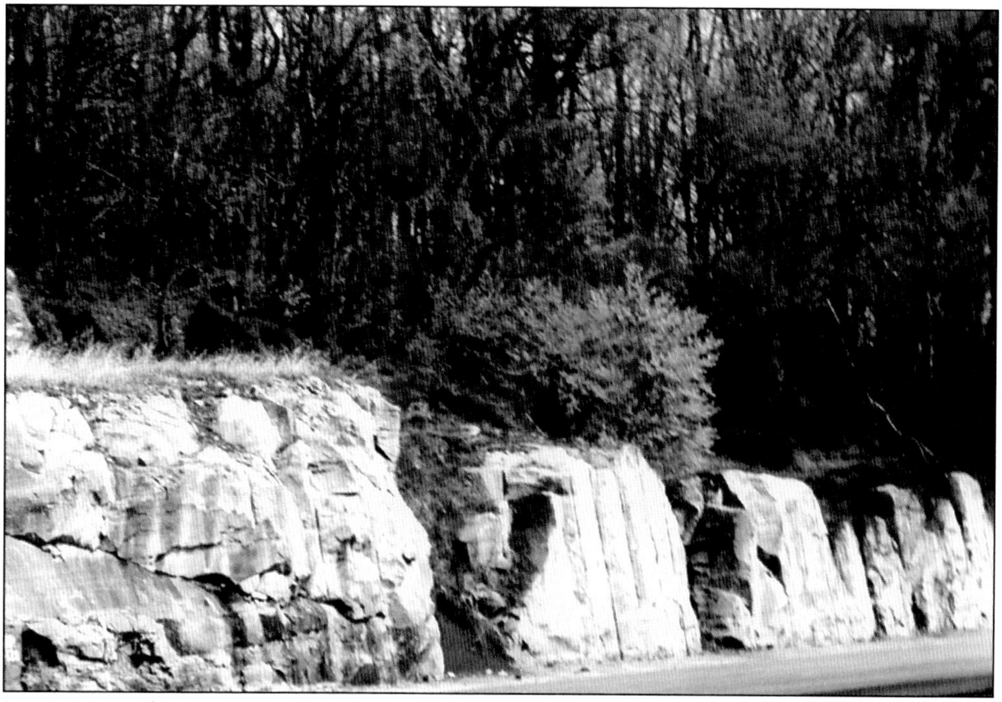

Limestone is always a part of the scenery in this part of the country. This photograph was taken in the spring along Indiana Highway 37, south of Bedford. Redbud can be seen along the top of the limestone out cropping.

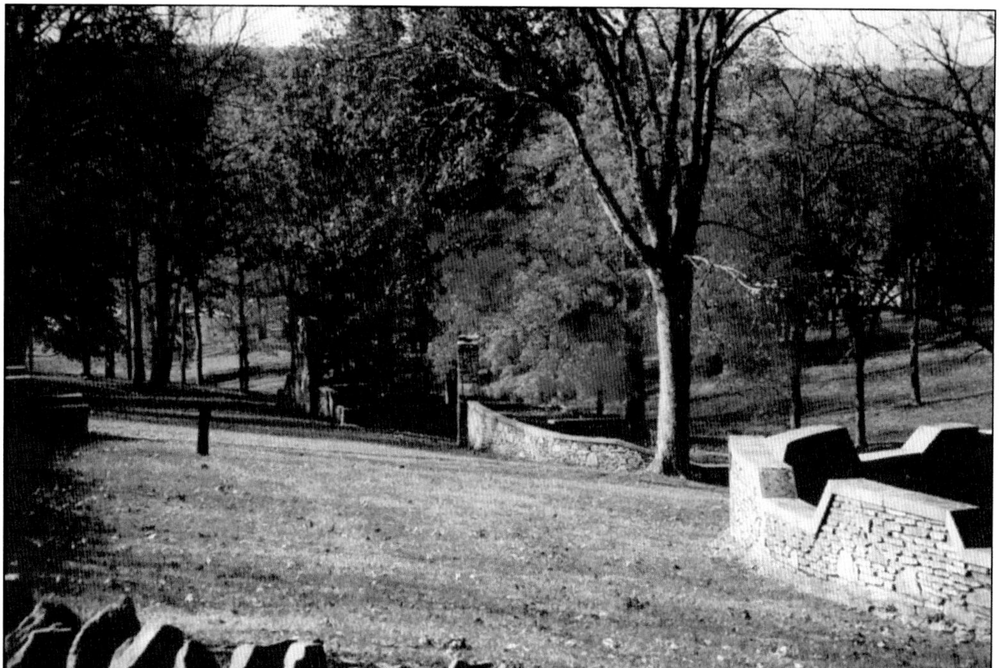

This is beautiful Otis Park as seen in the fall. The winding roads and stone fences enhance the view. Picnic areas on the right feature grills and local limestone tables.

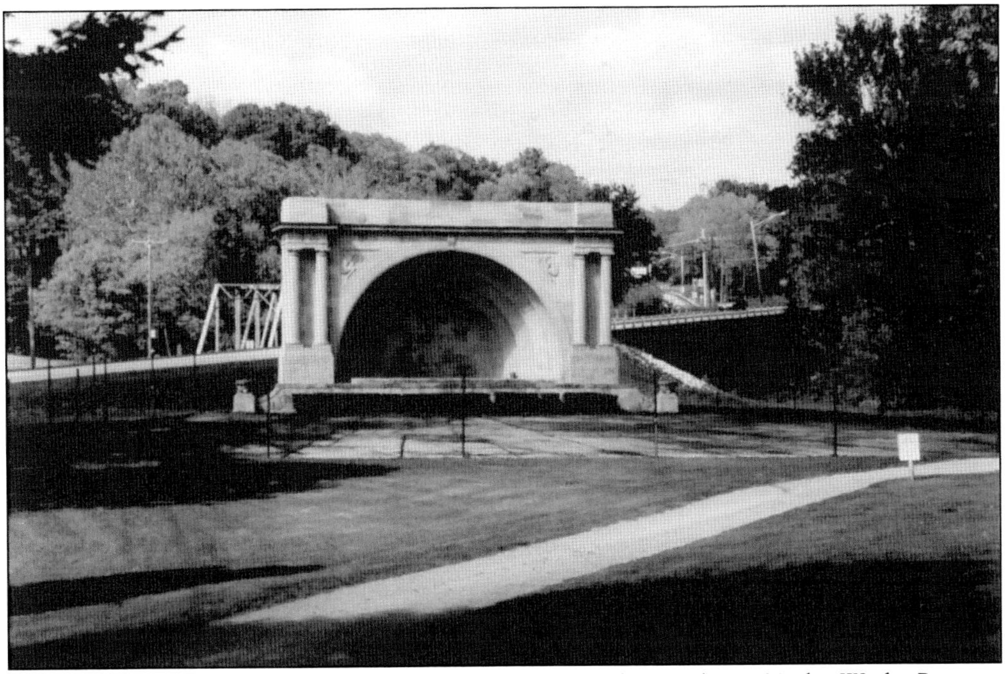

The band shell, located in Otis Park, was constructed during the 1930s by Works Progress Administration workers. There are band concerts here every summer and winter. Stone walls encircle the park. The stone in the band shell was quarried in Bedford and cut on the spot.

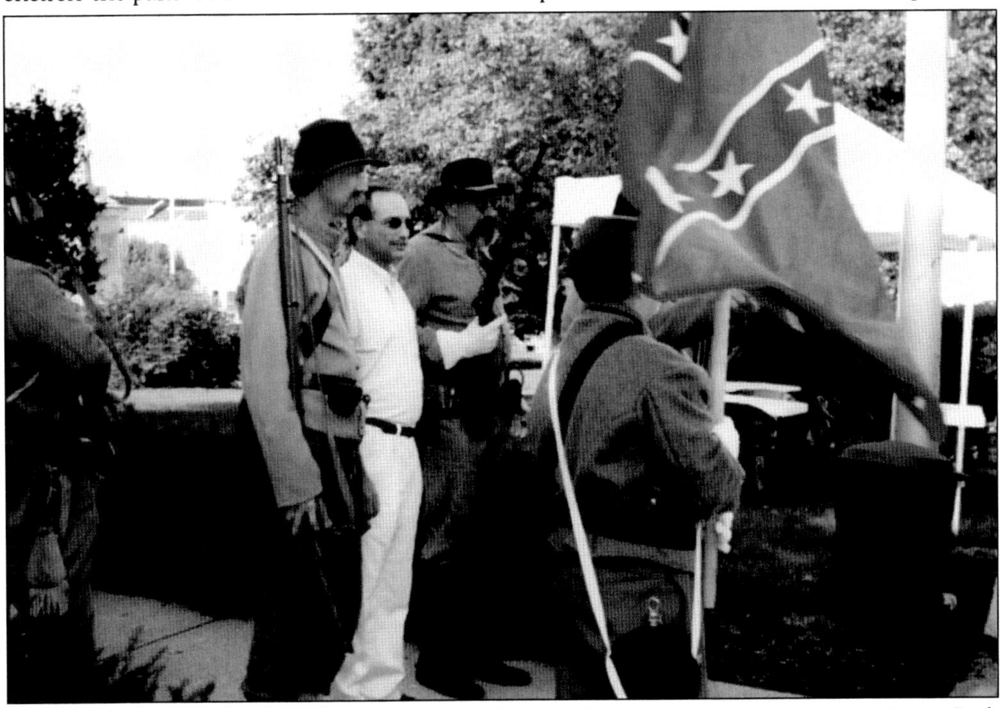

Civil War buffs, in period clothing, appear on the courthouse lawn before going to Murray Park to reenact a battle during the annual celebration of Mums the Word and History Fest. Members of the historical society sponsor such events.

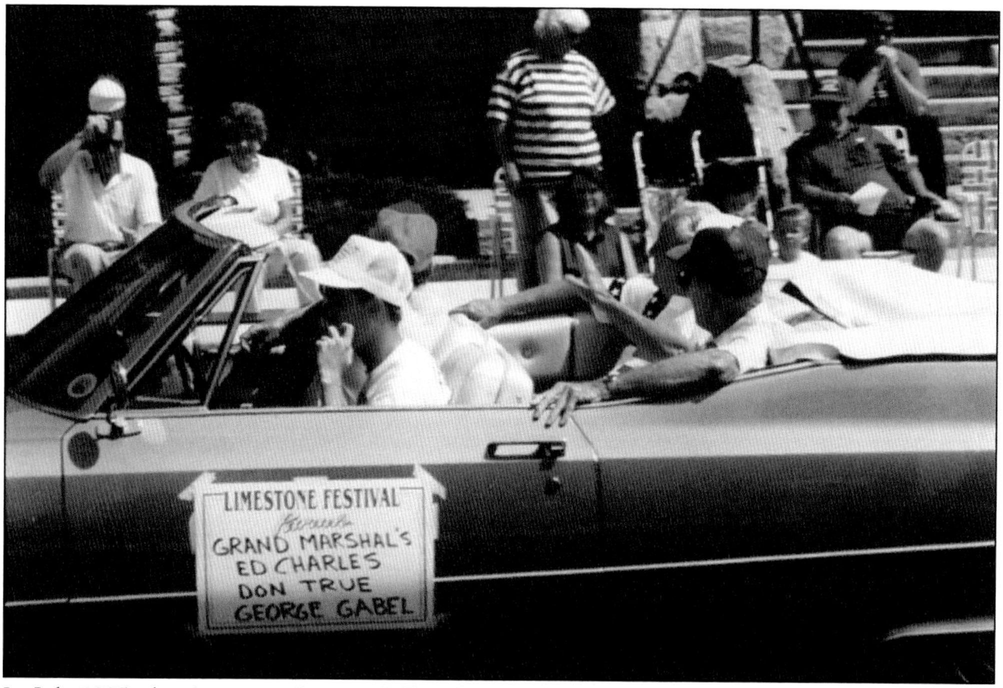

In July 1995, the American Legion Gillen Post No. 33 entered the Limestone Festival parade. Seated in the convertible are World War II veterans Ed Charles, Don True, and George Gabel who were the grand marshals.

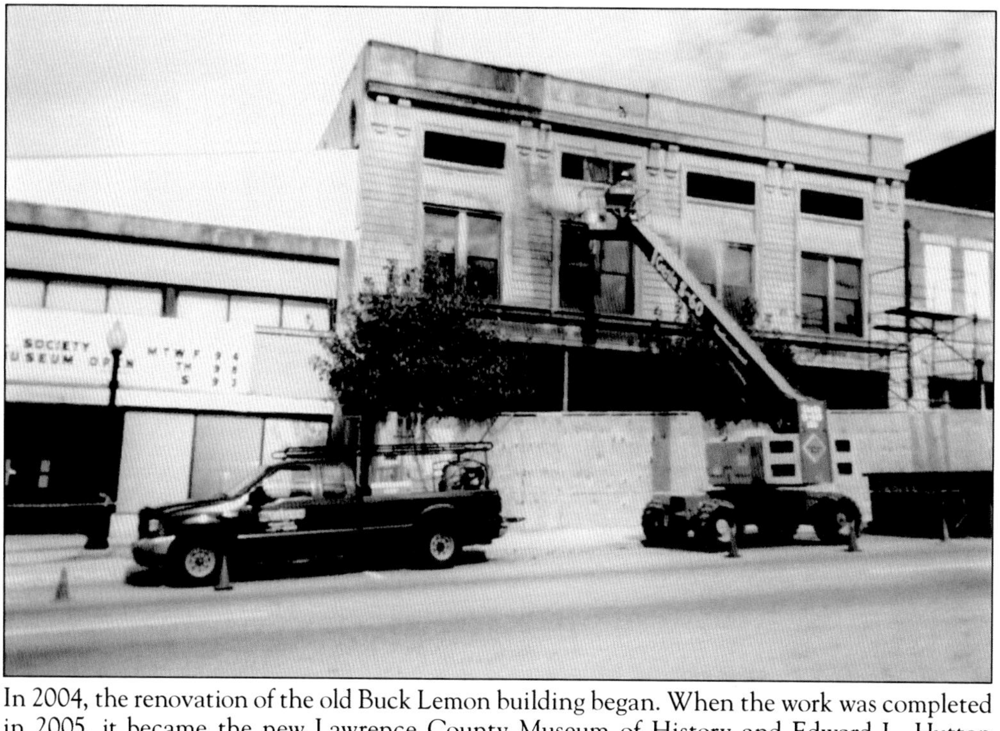

In 2004, the renovation of the old Buck Lemon building began. When the work was completed in 2005, it became the new Lawrence County Museum of History and Edward L. Hutton Research Library.

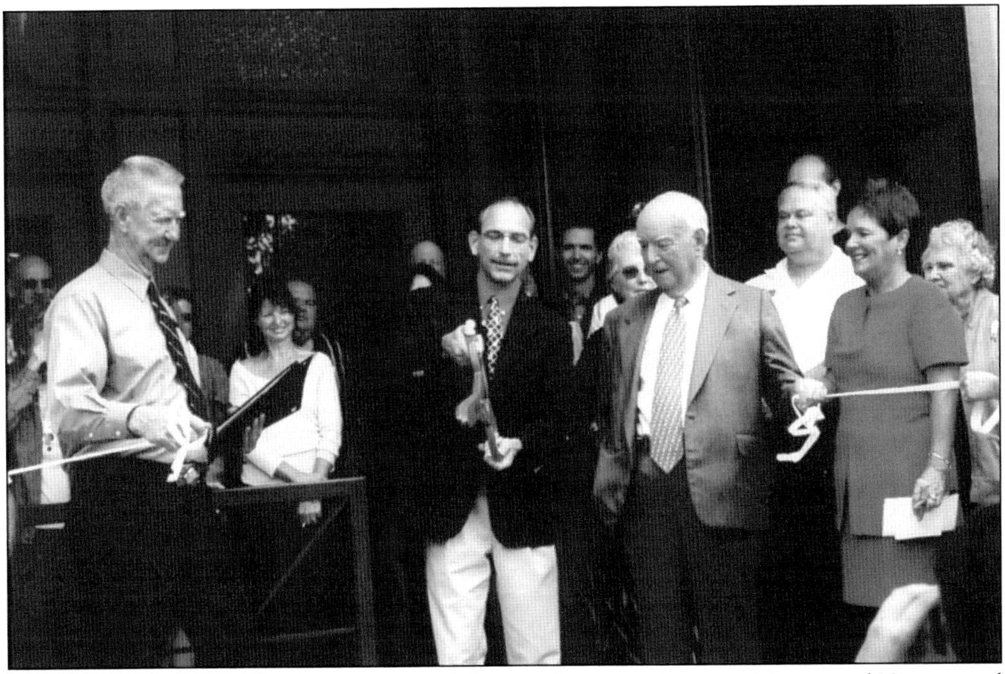

The grand opening and ribbon cutting of the new Lawrence County Museum of History and Edward L. Hutton Research Library was on July 30, 2005. Those pictured in the front from left to right are president Larry King, Bedford mayor Joe Klumpp, and Edward L. Hutton, the major benefactor. Others in the crowd were Greg Taylor, Adele Bowden-Purlee, and Shirley Owen.

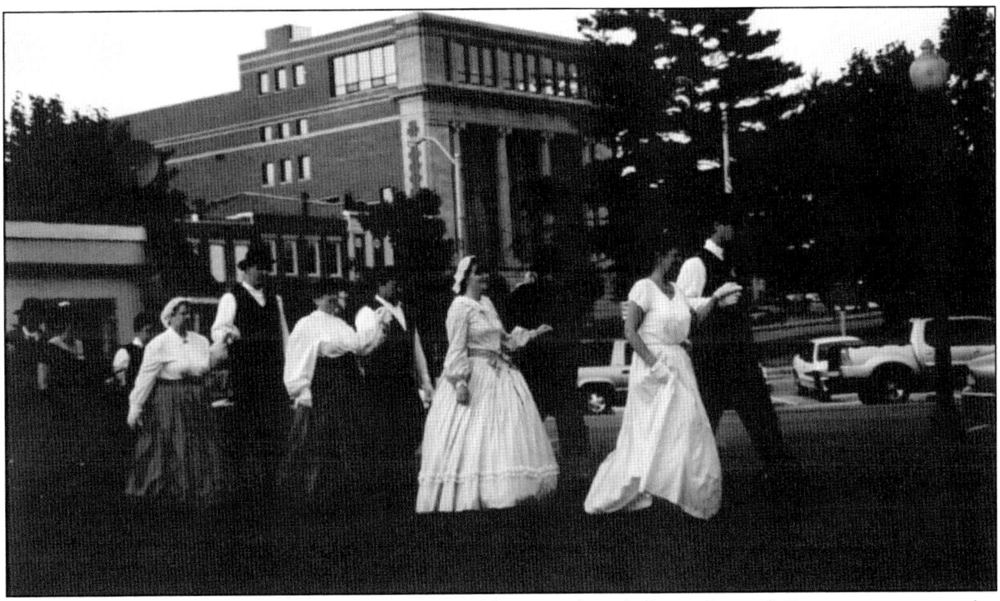

Every year in August, the Lawrence County Historical and Genealogical Society sponsors the History Fest. Pictured in the courthouse yard, dressed in period attire, are society members during this event.

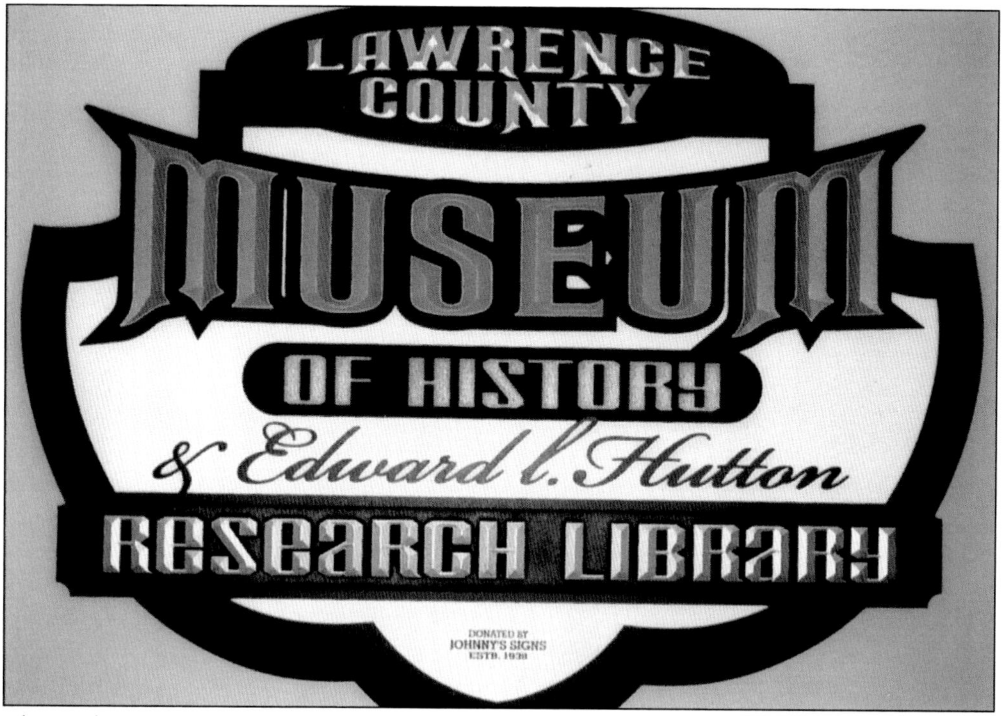

This is the sign that identifies the new Lawrence County Museum of History and Edward L. Hutton Research Library in downtown Bedford.

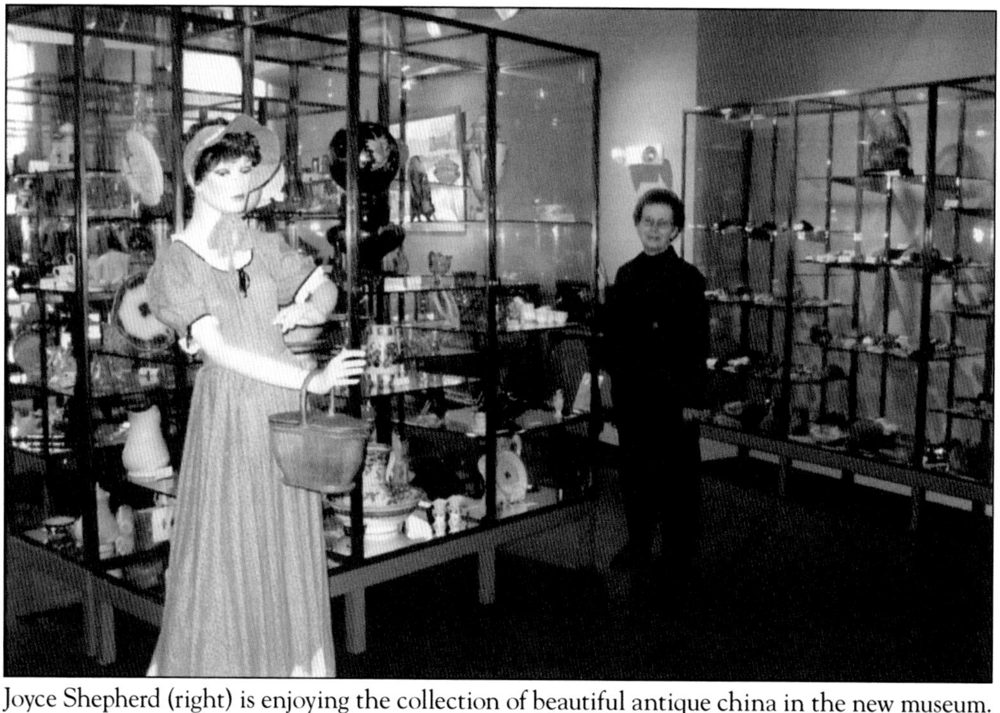

Joyce Shepherd (right) is enjoying the collection of beautiful antique china in the new museum. The brass frame cases were purchased in the 1920s for the first museum located in the basement of the courthouse.

Seven

HOMES AND BUILDINGS

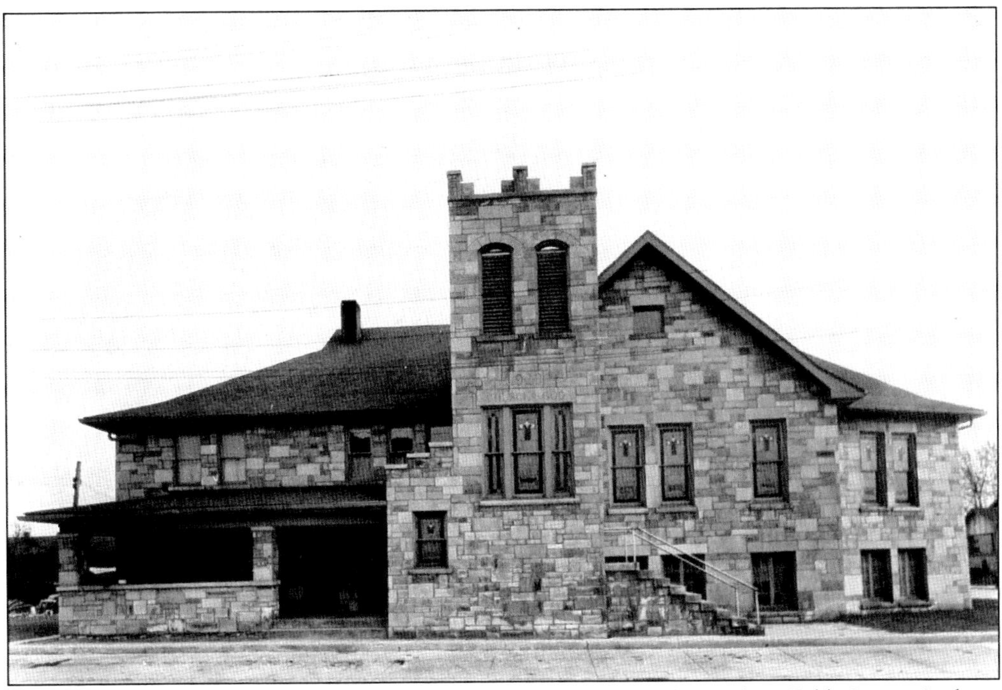

One of the early churches in Bedford was the Church of God, located on Fifth Street. In later years, the congregation built a new church on Sixteenth Street, west of the downtown.

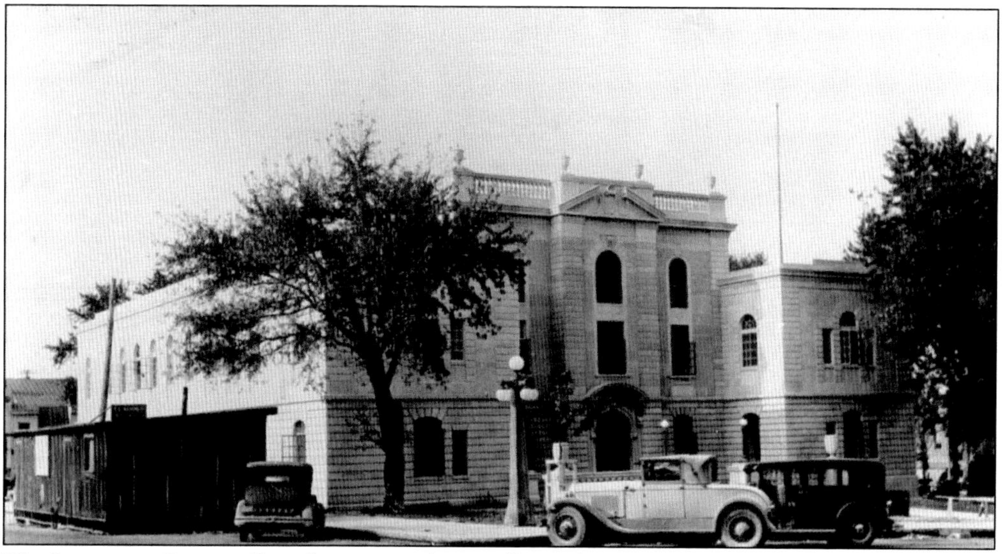

The Lawrence County Courthouse stands proudly in the center of the downtown square. The center section of the building is the original part built in the 1870s.

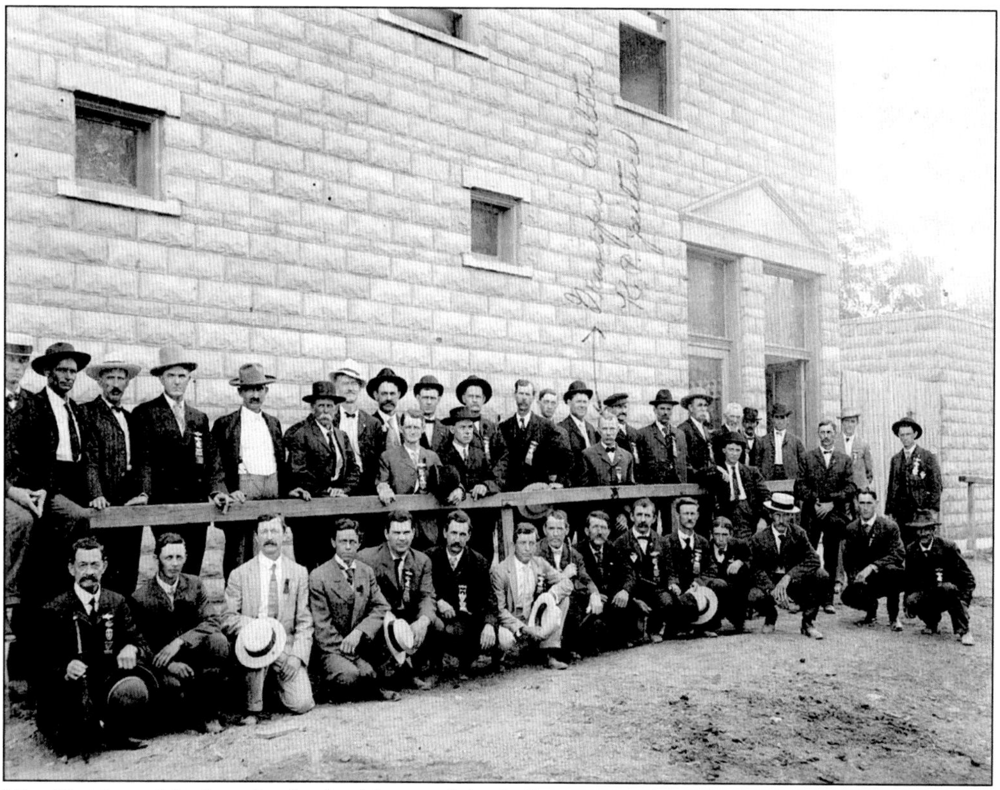

The Knights of Pythias Lodge building in Mitchell is pictured in the background. A group of members poses for this photograph.

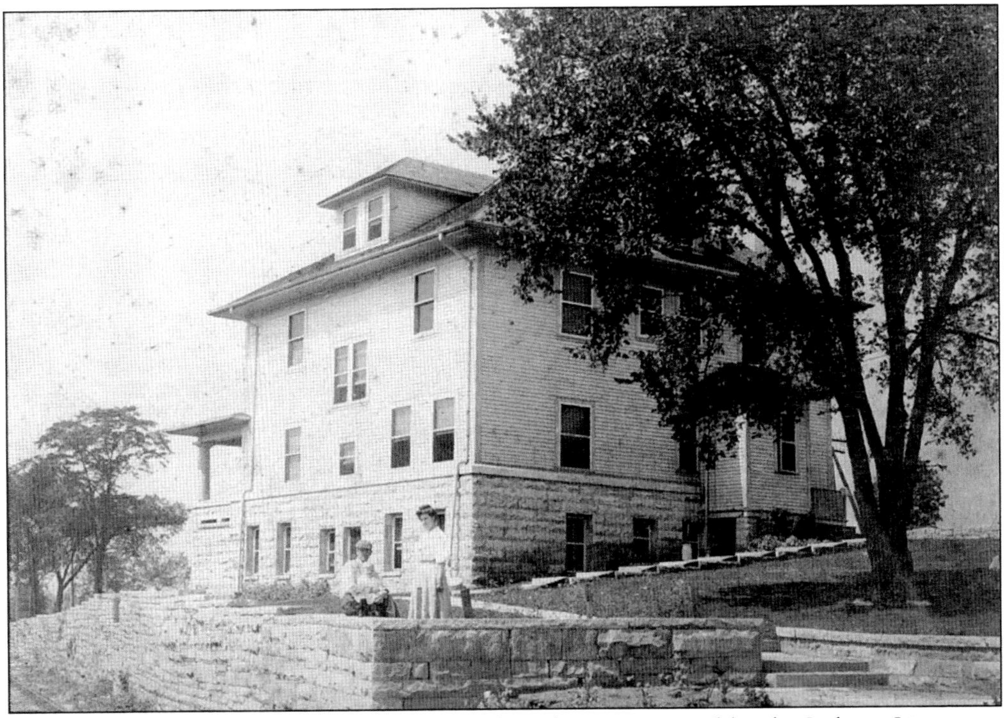

This house is among a group of houses in Oolitic that were owned by the Indiana Limestone Company. It is believed that the houses were built through the authority of John R. Walsh and that executives of the limestone company lived in the homes.

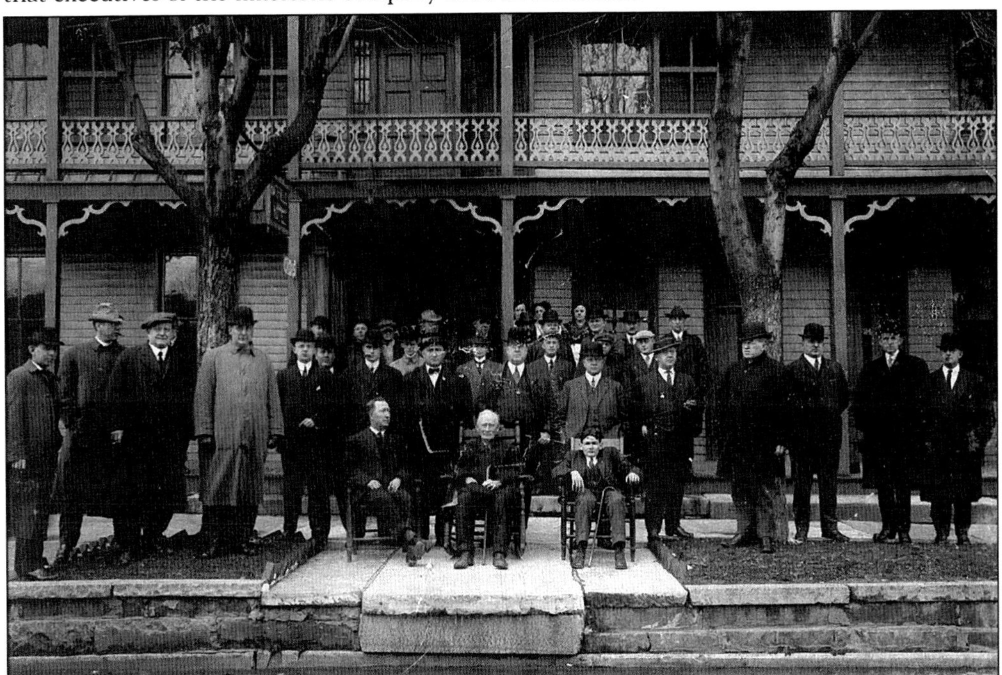

The Hatfield Hotel was located on the west side of the public square in the 1800s. Ruby Pitman and Ruby Tincher are pictured in the back row.

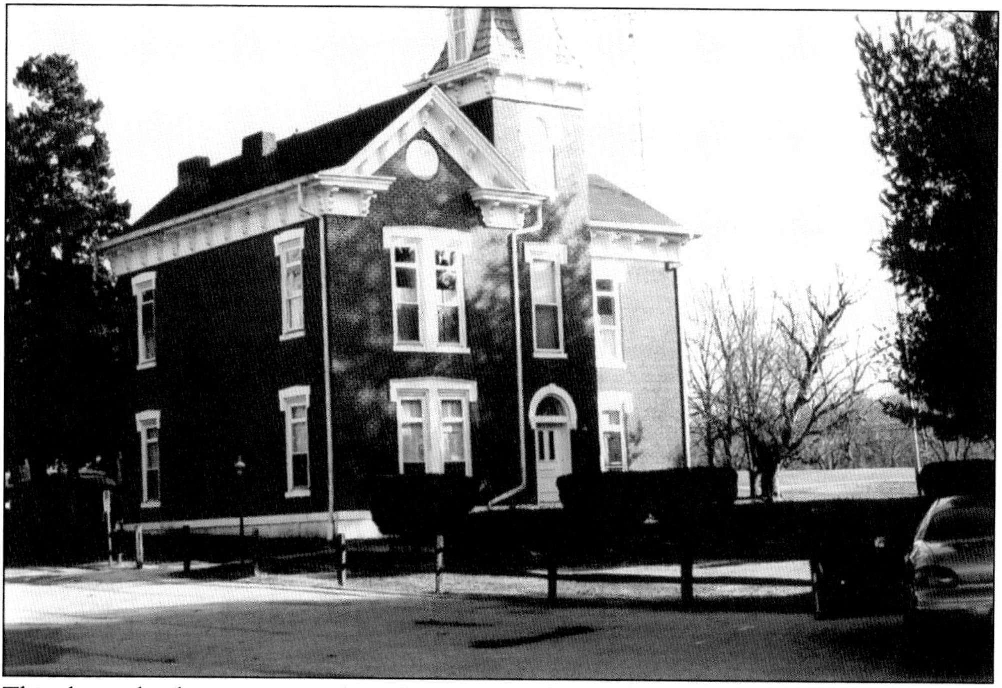

This elegant brick mansion stands at the entrance of Otis Park and is known as Pine Hall. The Ragsdale family built it in the mid-1800s. Today it is used for receptions and special events.

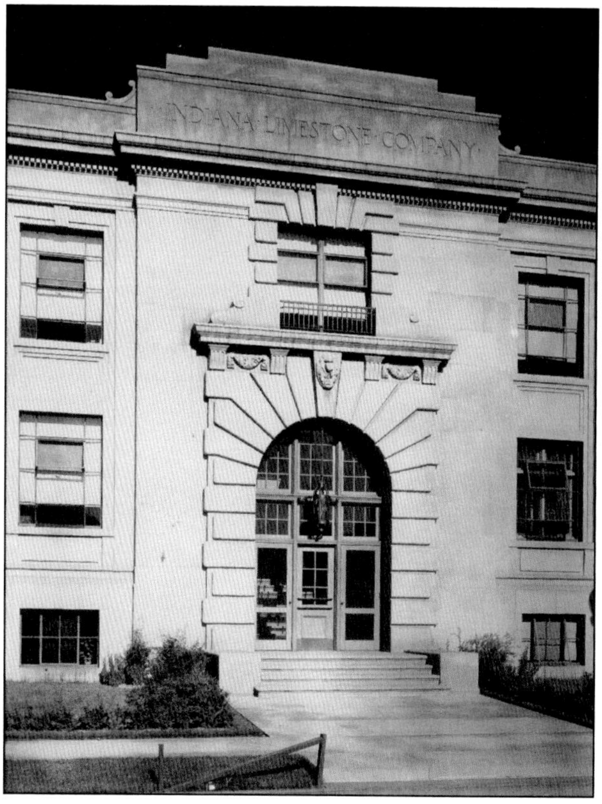

This is the entrance to the Indiana Limestone Company offices. The carvings above the door are of tools used by stone carvers.

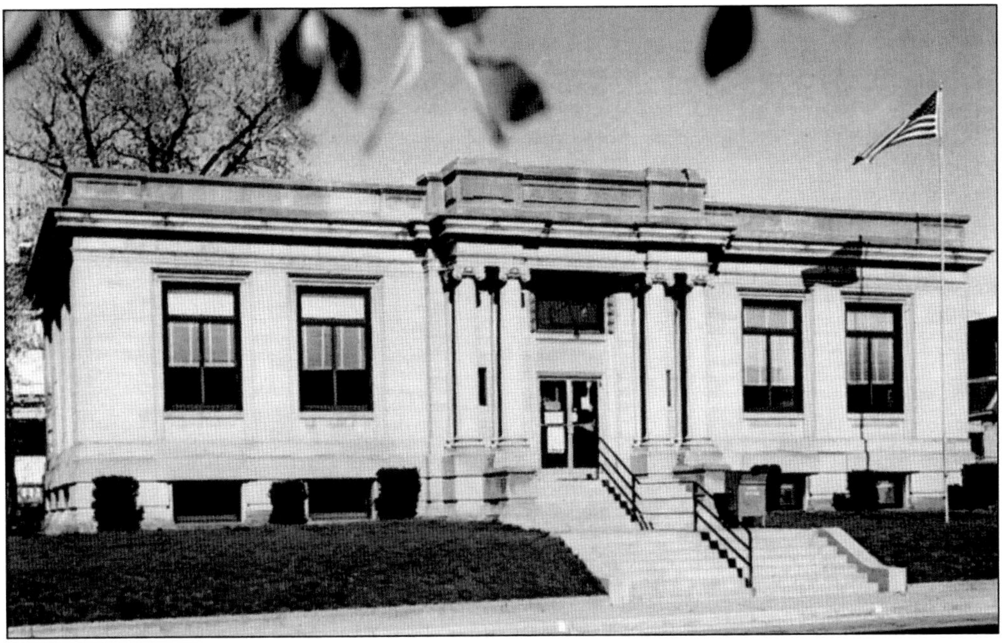

This Greek Ionic architectural building is the Bedford Public Library. In recent years, an addition has been added to the library.

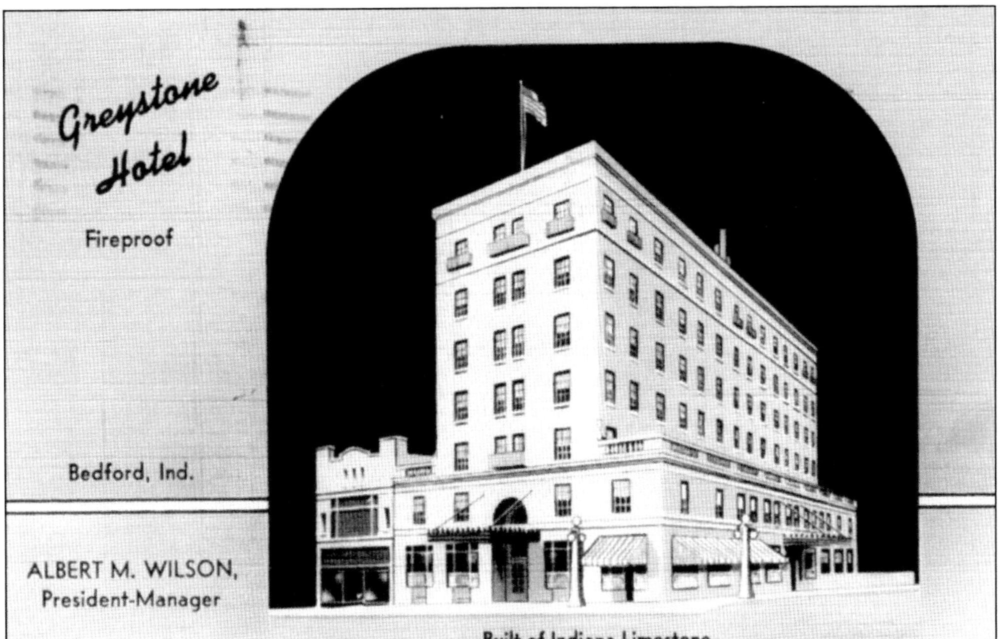

The Greystone Hotel, built of Indiana limestone in the 1920s, was advertised as fireproof. It was located on the northeast corner of the public square. Al Wilson was the president and manager. The building burned and was torn down. A new brick and stone building stands in its place.

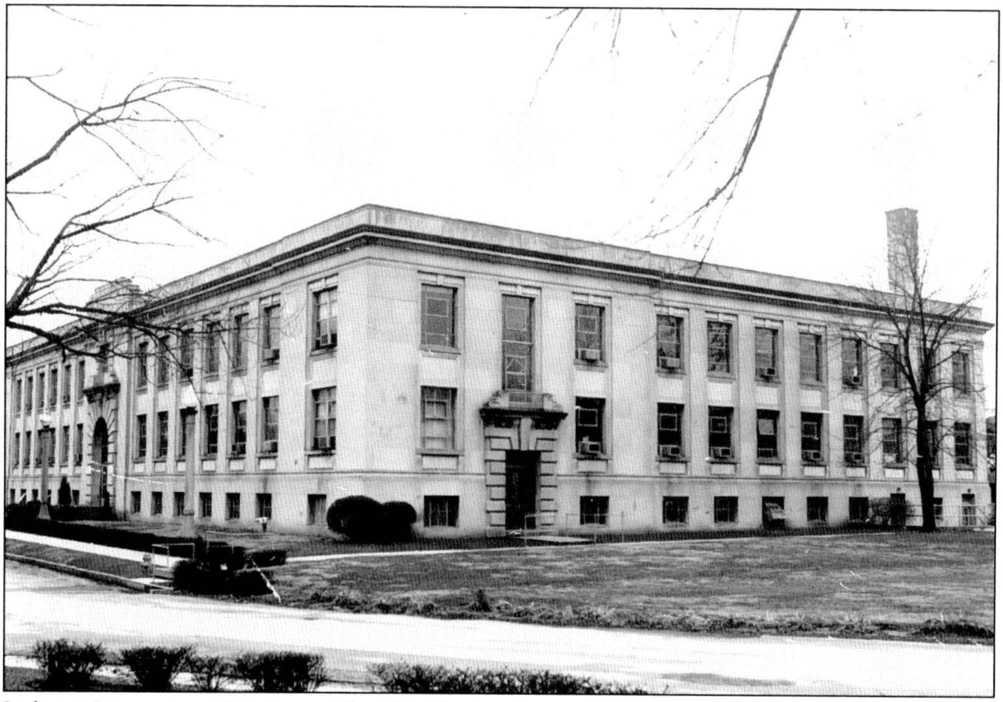

Indiana Limestone Company office building is located in the northern part of Bedford on I Street. The building is now the home of Oakland City University–Bedford.

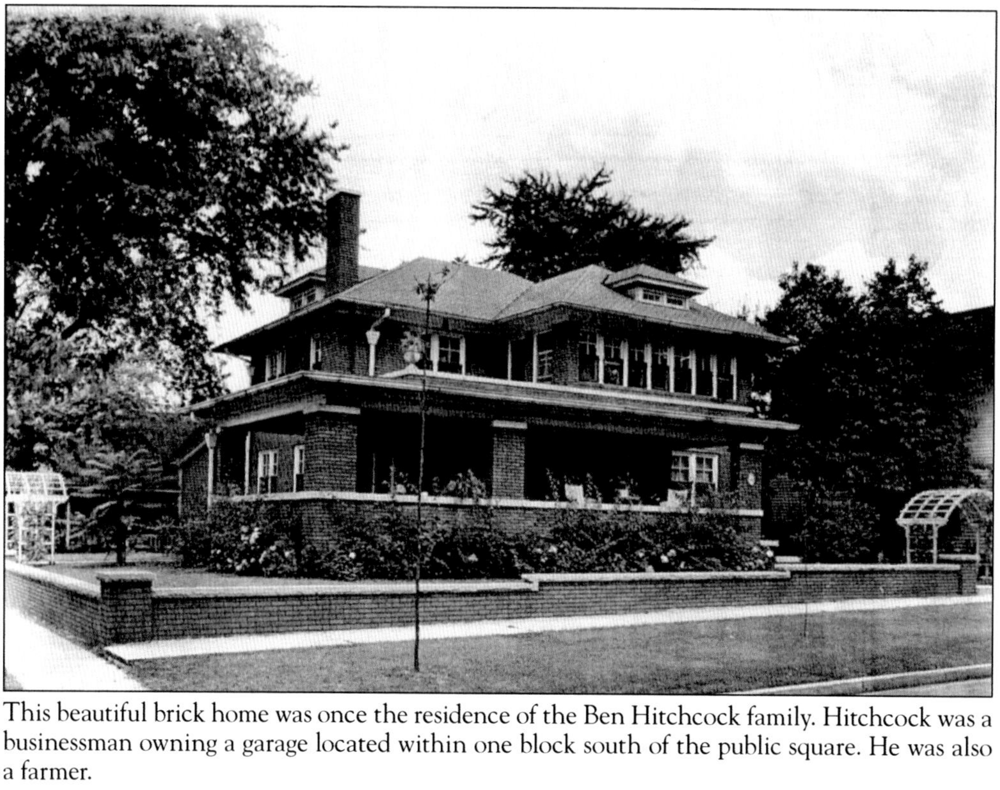

This beautiful brick home was once the residence of the Ben Hitchcock family. Hitchcock was a businessman owning a garage located within one block south of the public square. He was also a farmer.

Eight

IMPORTANT AND FAMOUS PEOPLE

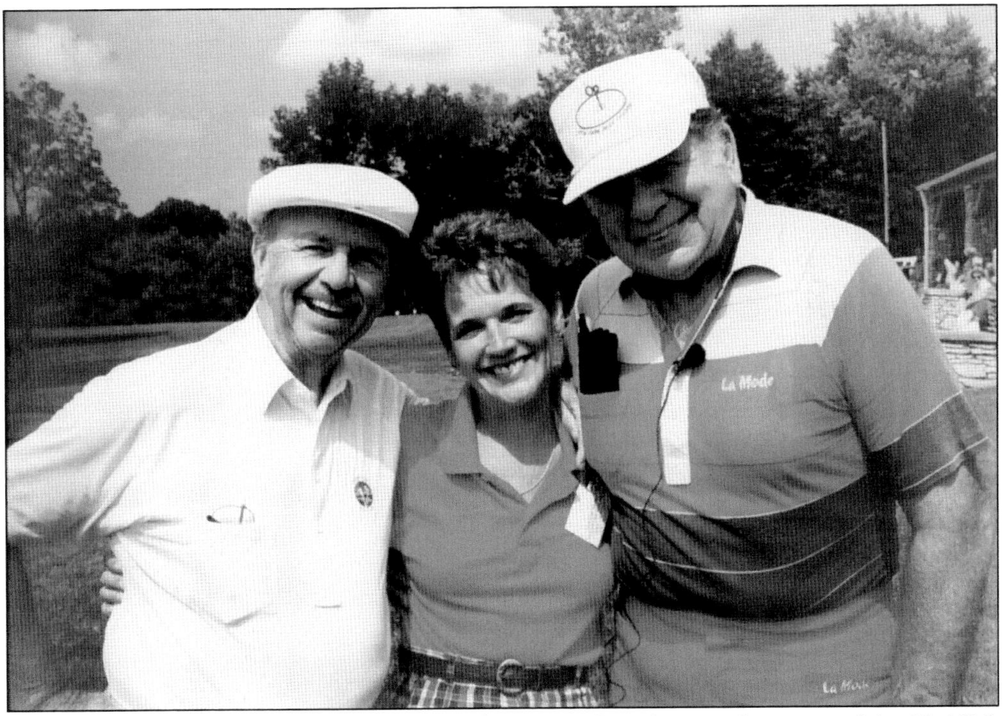

Actor Claude Akins, pictured at far right, was born in Nelson County, Georgia, on May 25, 1926. The family moved to Bedford soon after and Akins graduated from Bedford High School. He is best known for his many movies and his role as Sheriff Lobo in the television series *Misadventures of Sheriff Lobo* (1979–1981). Standing with Akins is Alvey Moore and Adele Bowden-Purlee. (Courtesy of Adele Bowden-Purlee.)

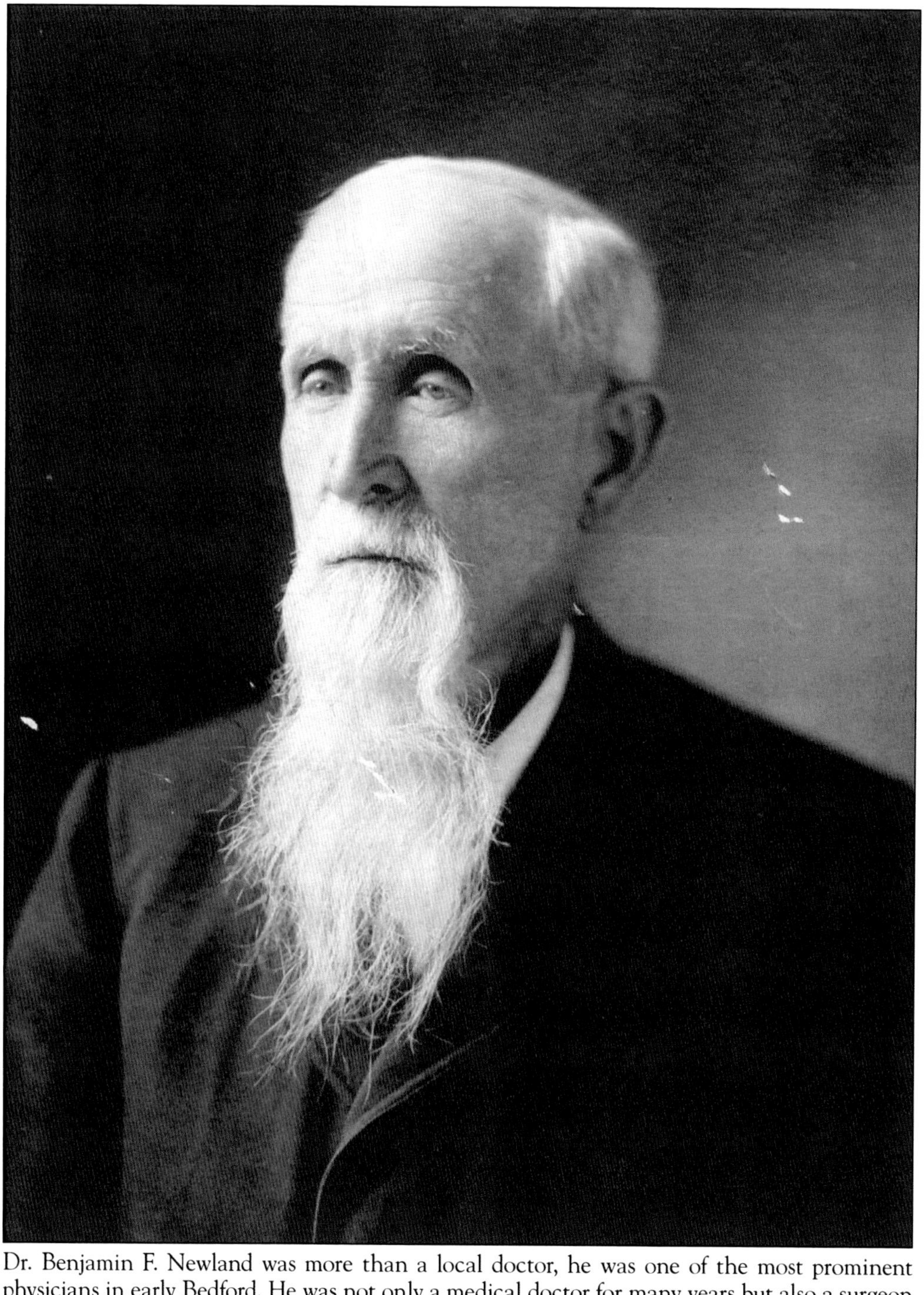

Dr. Benjamin F. Newland was more than a local doctor, he was one of the most prominent physicians in early Bedford. He was not only a medical doctor for many years but also a surgeon general in the Civil War and a state senator. As a youngster of 12, he carried mail by horseback and he became a rail splitter. Newland also taught school part-time. He was born in 1821 and died in 1889. His funeral was the largest ever held in Bedford.

Dr. Joseph Gardner and his wife, Enola Lee, were members of the American National Red Cross. This photograph of Joseph was taken around 1980 at Rogers Studio. The Gardners were friends of Clara Barton of Red Cross fame.

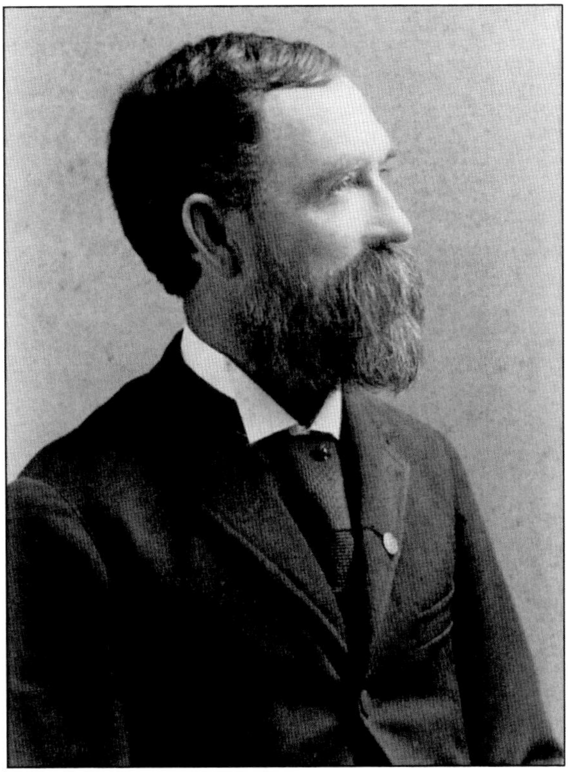

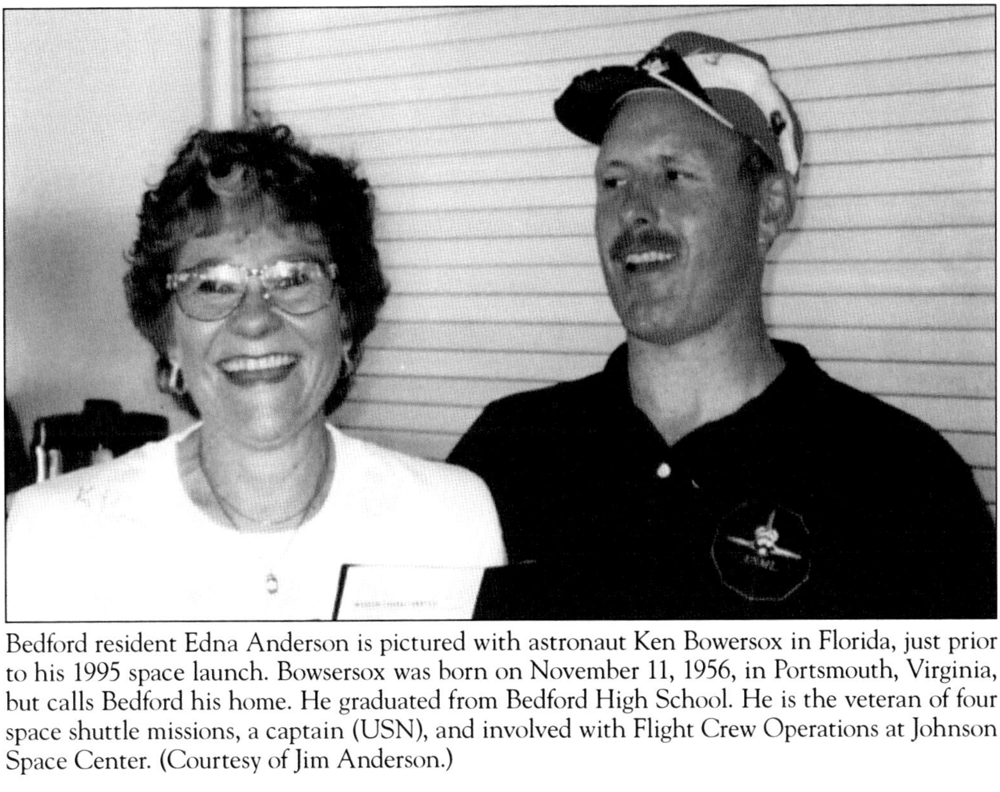

Bedford resident Edna Anderson is pictured with astronaut Ken Bowersox in Florida, just prior to his 1995 space launch. Bowsersox was born on November 11, 1956, in Portsmouth, Virginia, but calls Bedford his home. He graduated from Bedford High School. He is the veteran of four space shuttle missions, a captain (USN), and involved with Flight Crew Operations at Johnson Space Center. (Courtesy of Jim Anderson.)

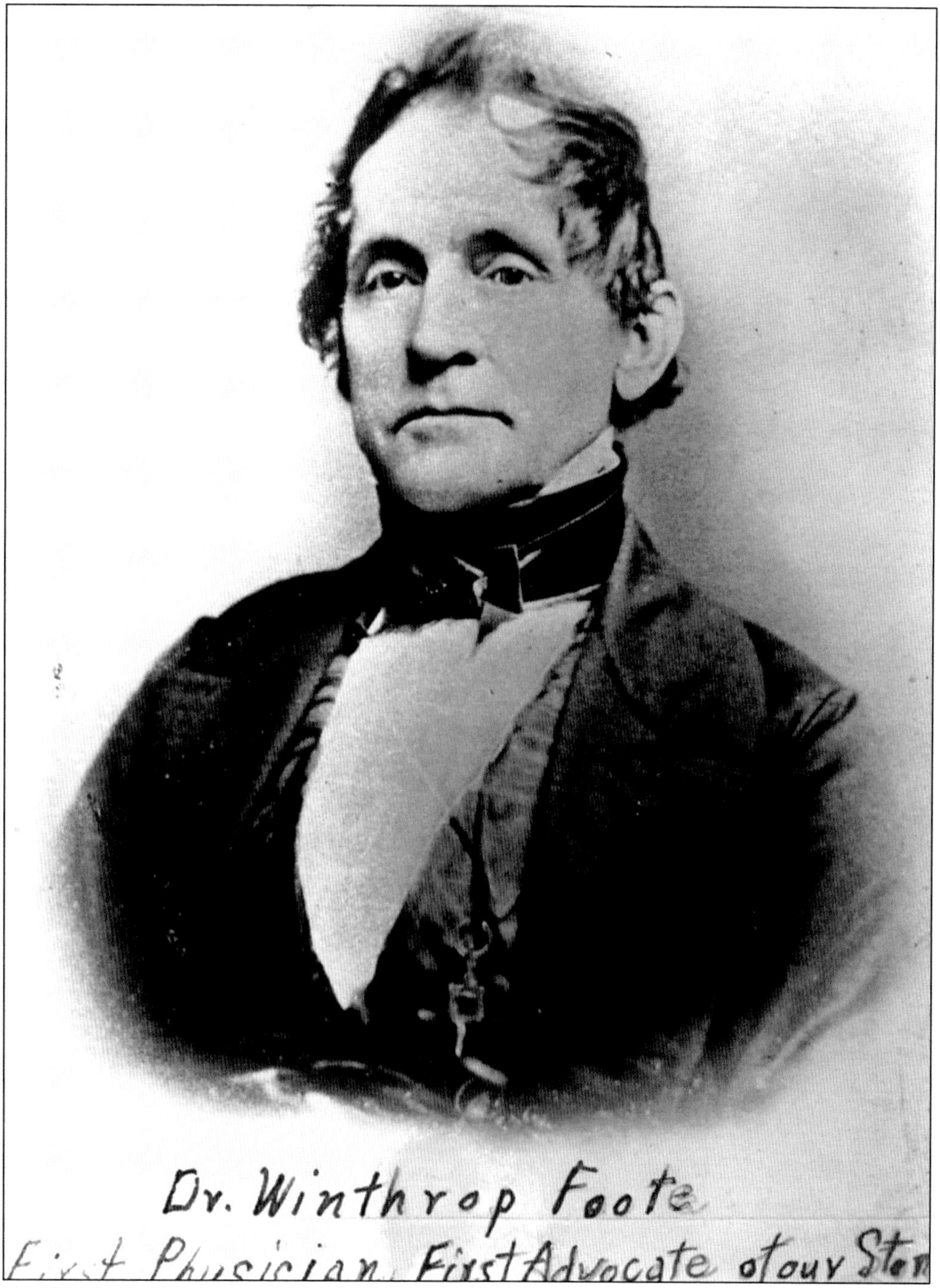

Dr. Winthrop Foote is considered the father of the limestone industry. Although the first limestone quarry was not in Lawrence County, Foote owned Blue Hole Quarry around 1830, and predicted that the market would be in the East. The coming of the railroads around 1858 made it possible to ship the limestone to various destinations. The major market today is still in the East. Foote is buried in a limestone boulder near the site of his quarry.

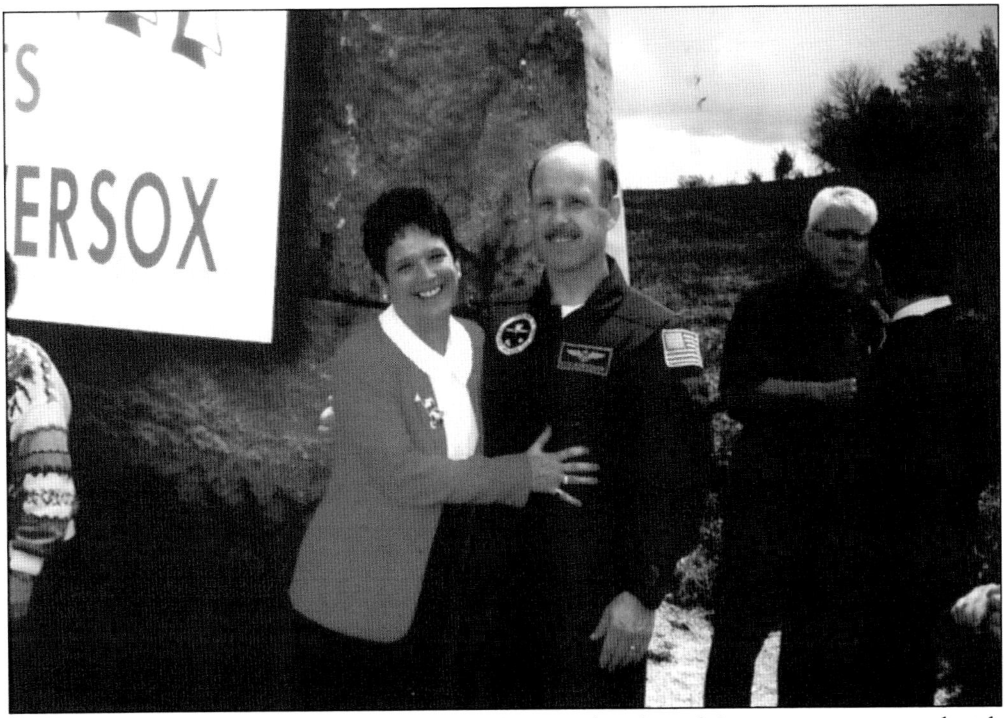

Adele Bowden-Purlee, president of the Bedford Area Chamber of Commerce, is pictured with astronaut Ken Bowersox. This photograph was taken on one of his visits back home. (Courtesy of Adele Bowden-Purlee.)

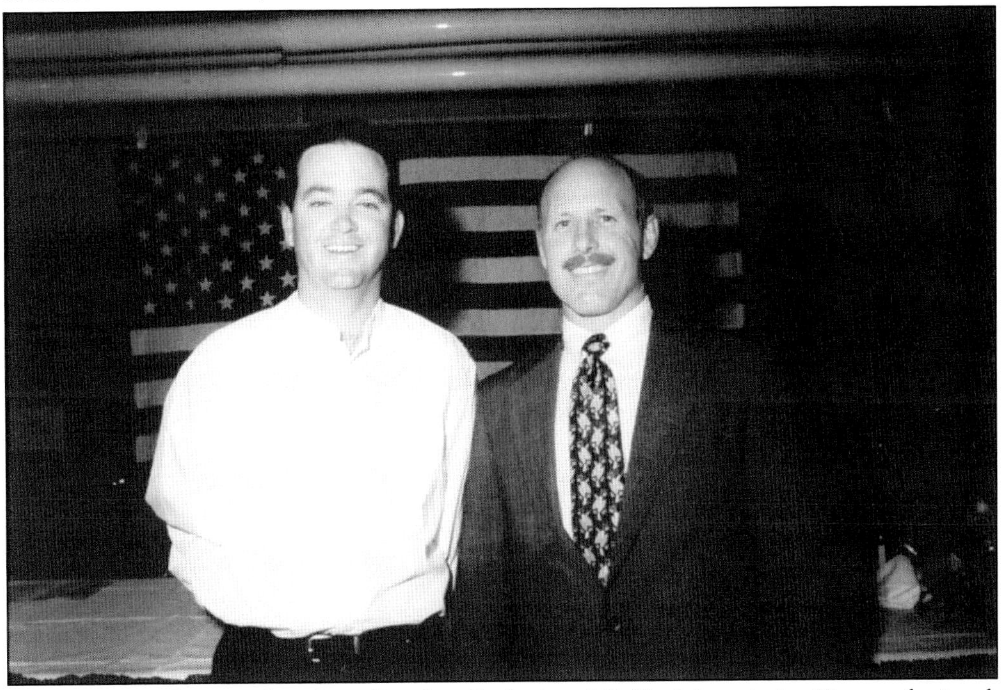

Shown in this photograph is Craig Bowden, Professional Golfers' Association Tour professional, and astronaut Ken Bowersox (right). Bowden has been involved in professional golf since 1989.

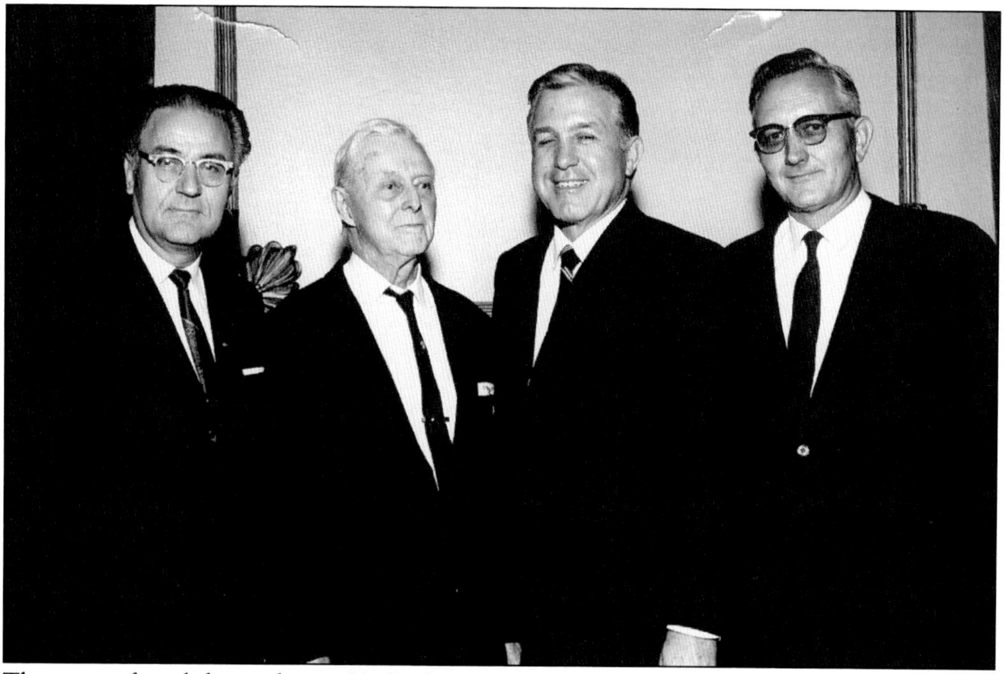

These men, from left to right, are H. Cook, congressman Eugene B. Crowe, Indiana governor Ed Whitcomb, and historian Jim Guthrie. Crowe and Guthrie, now deceased, were from Bedford. Whitcomb was from Seymour.

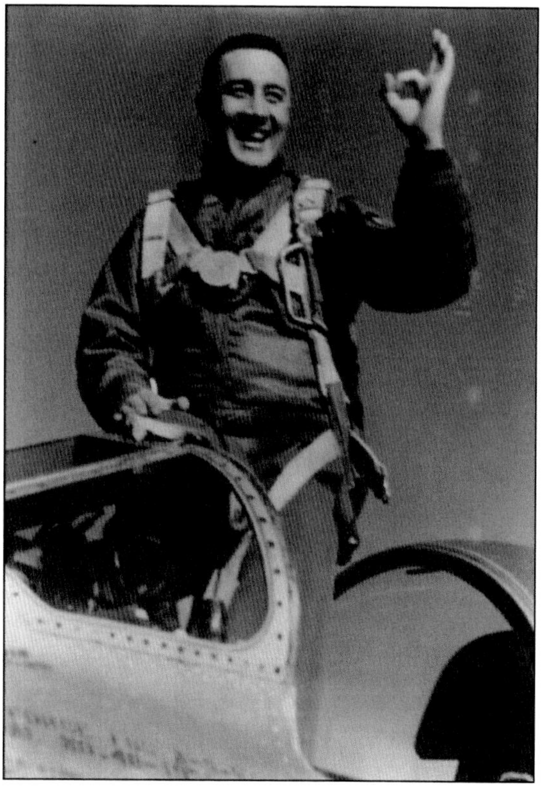

Lawrence County has produced three astronauts, Virgil "Gus" Grissom from Mitchell and Charles Walker and Ken Bowersox from Bedford. Bowersox is still in the space program. Grissom, seen here, was killed in 1967 when the Apollo went up in flames. Relatives of Grissom still live in the area. His birthplace has been purchased to be made into a museum in the future.

Nine

MILITARY

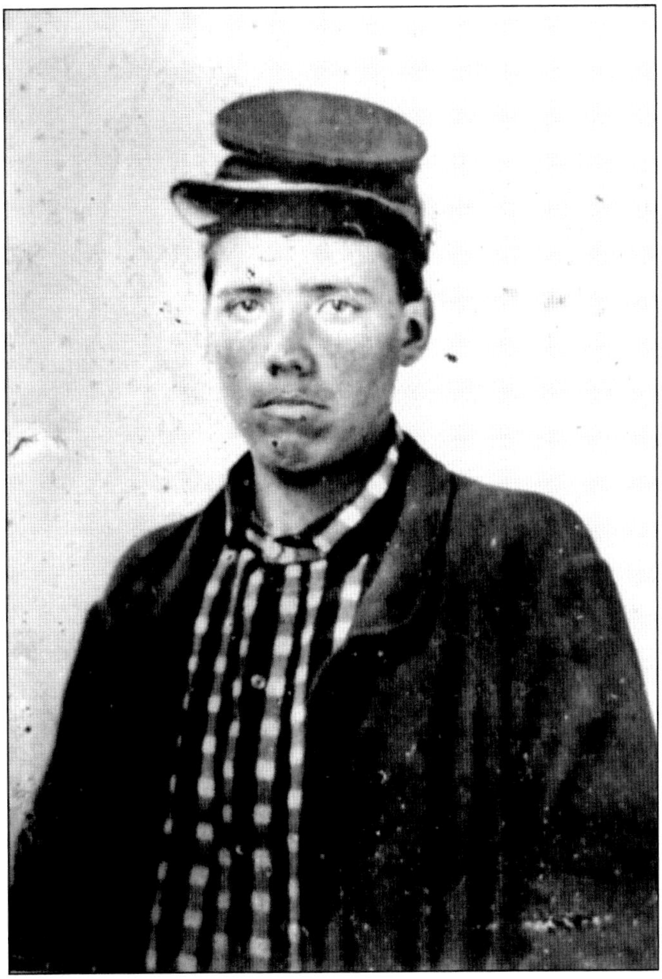

This tired, worn out, union soldier has been photographed probably during a furlough home. He is unidentified, but found in the collection of the pictures belonging to the Lawrence County Historical and Genealogical Society.

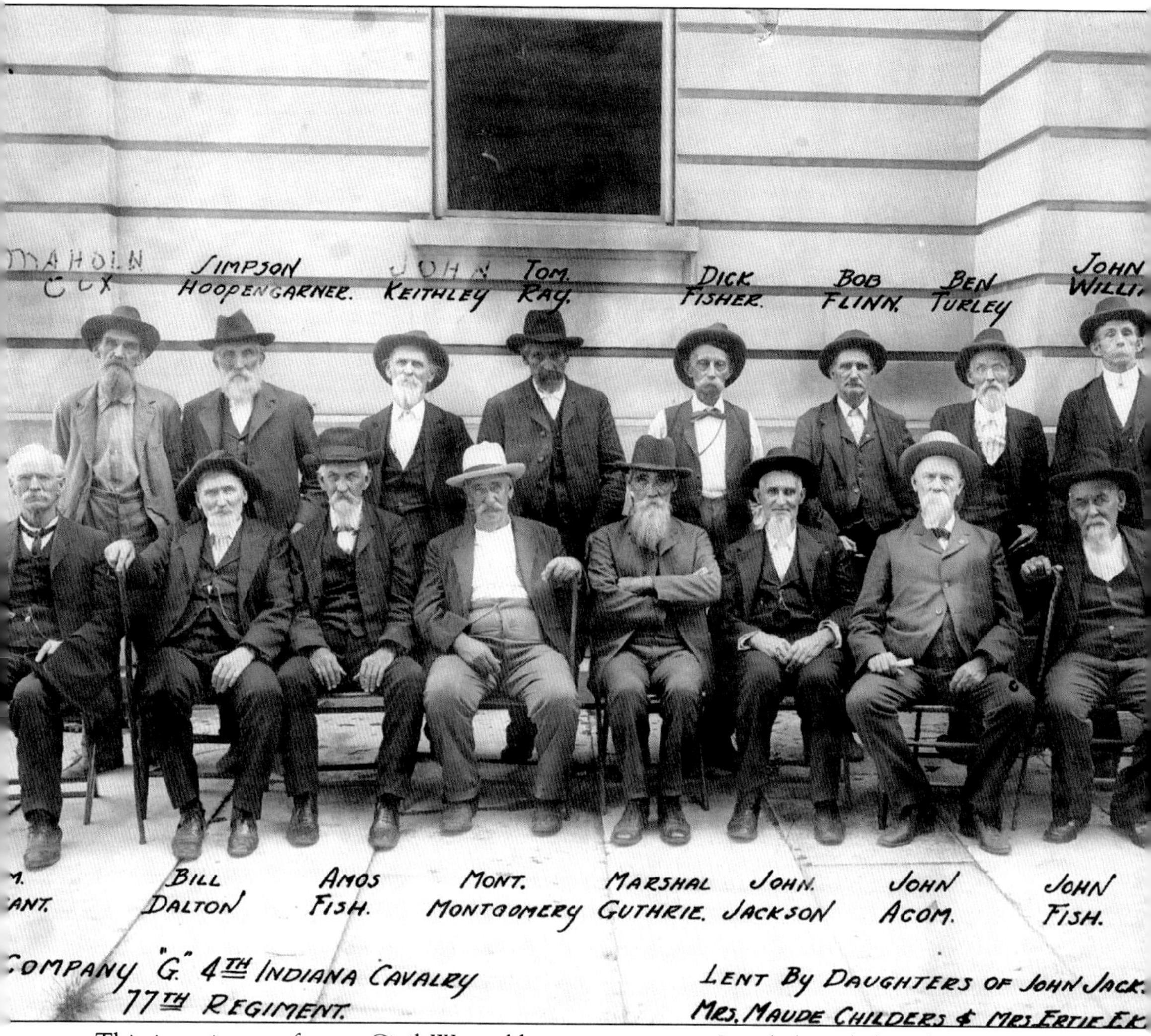

This is a picture of some Civil War soldiers at a reunion. It is believed that the picture was taken beside the Lawrence County Courthouse, in the center of the public square, around 1900. (Courtesy of the Lawrence County Historical and Genealogical Society.)

Fielding Sterling served in World War I. There are no World War I veterans living in Lawrence County. The Great War ended in 1918.

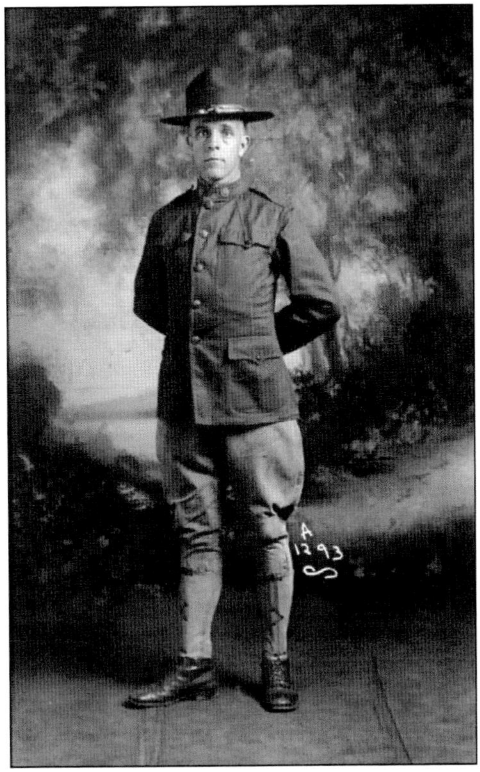

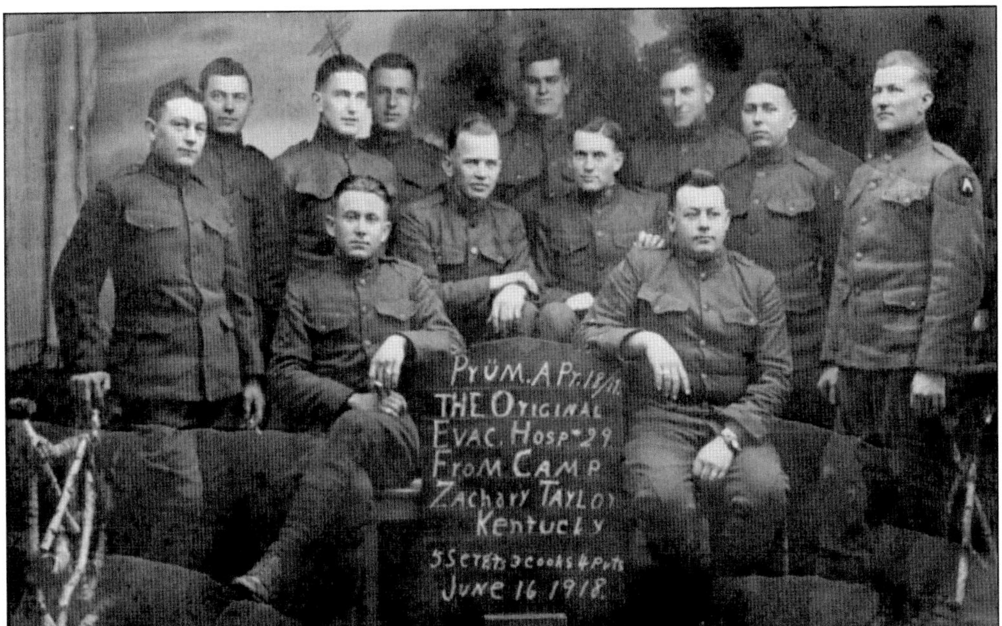

This pleasant looking group of doughboys arrived on foreign soil in time to join the Armistice celebration. They were hospital corpsmen during World War I and did not see much action because the war ended in 1918. While they are unidentified, some are known to have been from Lawrence County.

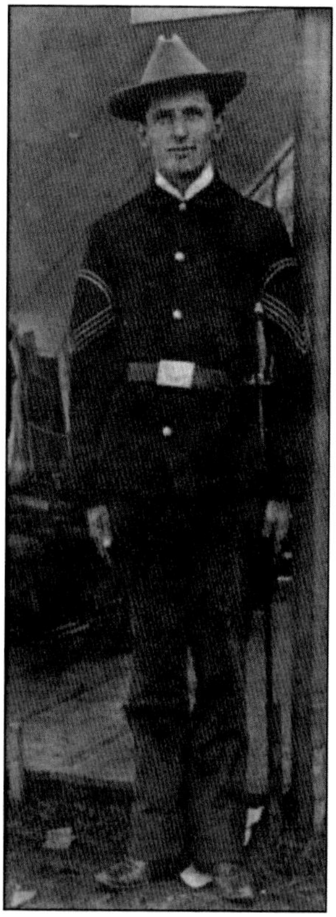

This unidentified soldier is believed to have served around the time of the Spanish American War. The picture was taken around 1900.

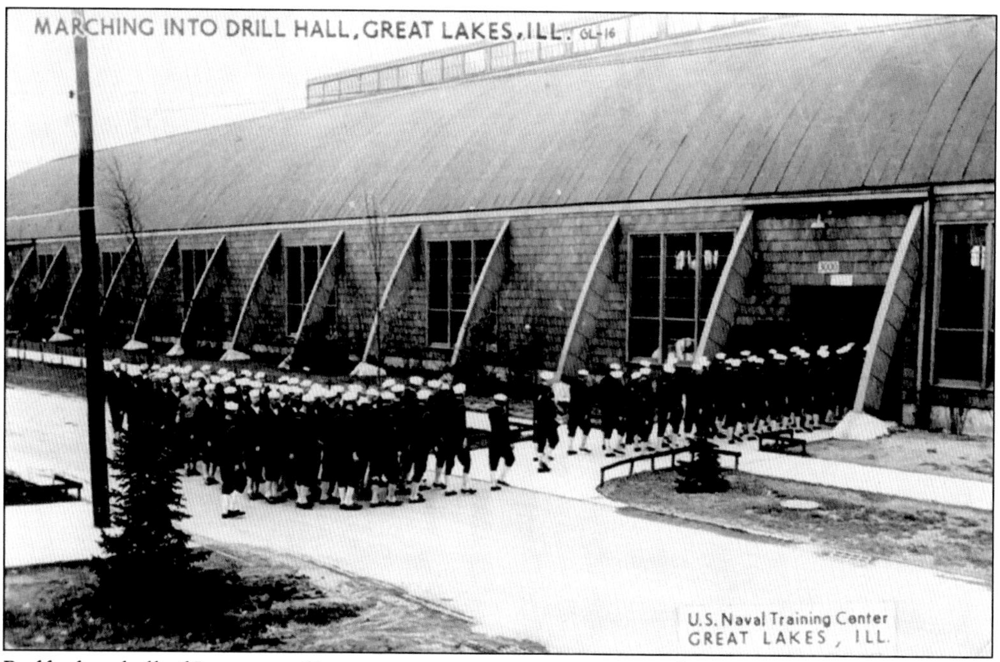

Bedford and all of Lawrence County sent many men to serve in the Navy during World War II. This postcard was sent to family back home from the U.S. Naval Training Center at Great Lakes, Illinois, where most recruits in the area had their training.

Ralph V. Ritchey was in Hawaii in 1941 when the Japanese attacked Pearl Harbor in World War II. He survived and made the navy his career until retirement.

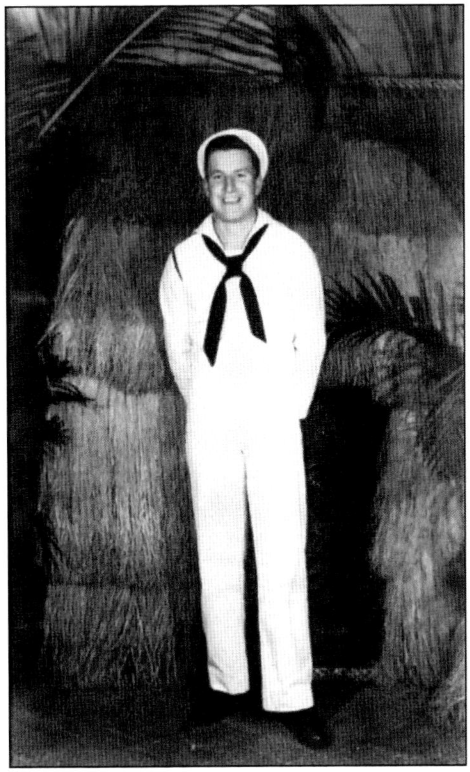

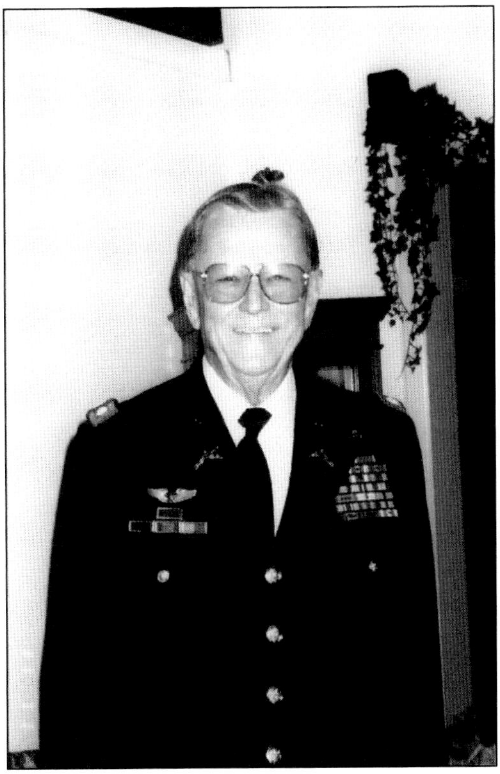

This photograph is of Lt. Col. Kenneth Hodges who is a native of Bedford. He is now retired and lives with his wife Sue Hodges (née Edington). (Courtesy of Ken Hodges.)

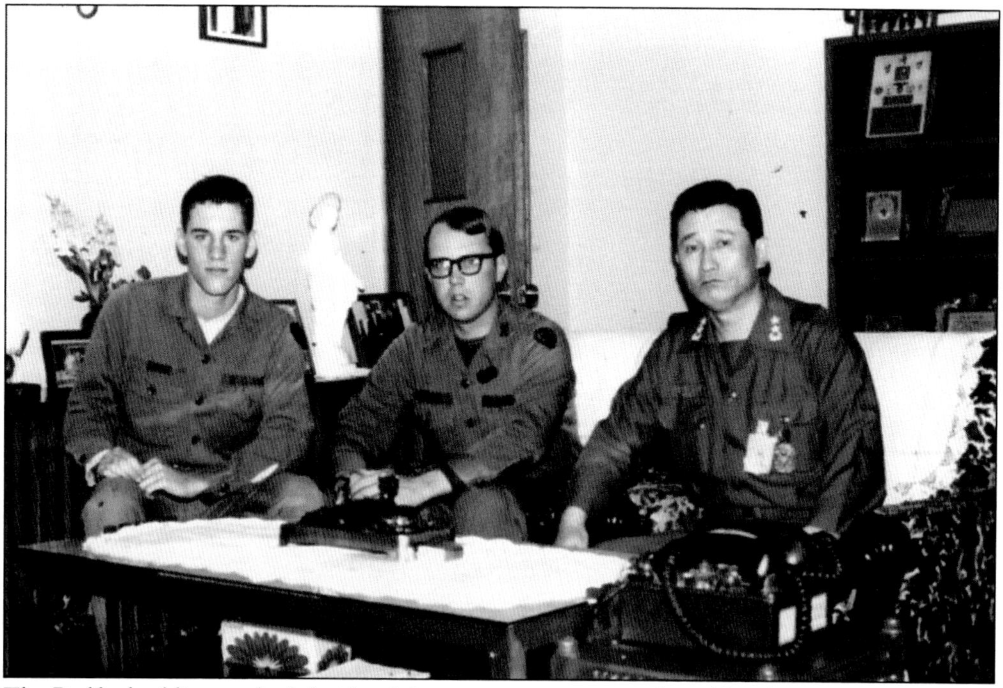

The Bedford soldier on the left side of this picture is sitting at the table of Korean commanding major general Chung Soon Hyon with the 27th Infantry Division. This photograph was taken in Korea.

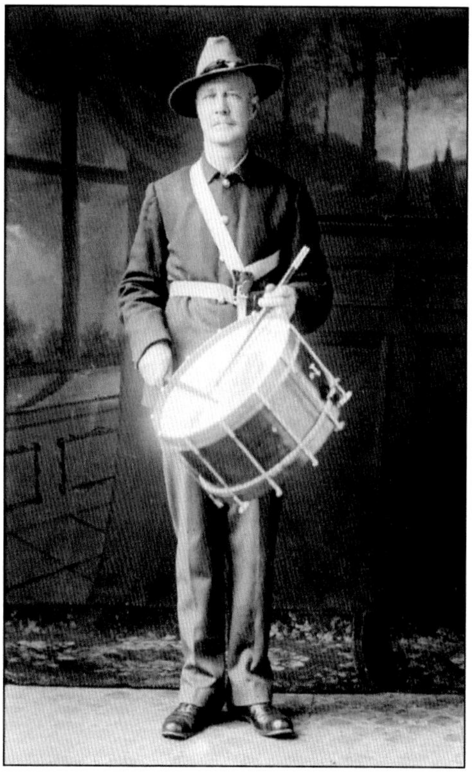

Capt. Buddy Cook was a drummer during the Spanish American War. This photograph was taken in the 1890s. Cook was also the cab driver who found the body of Sarah Schaffer, the school teacher who was murdered in 1904.

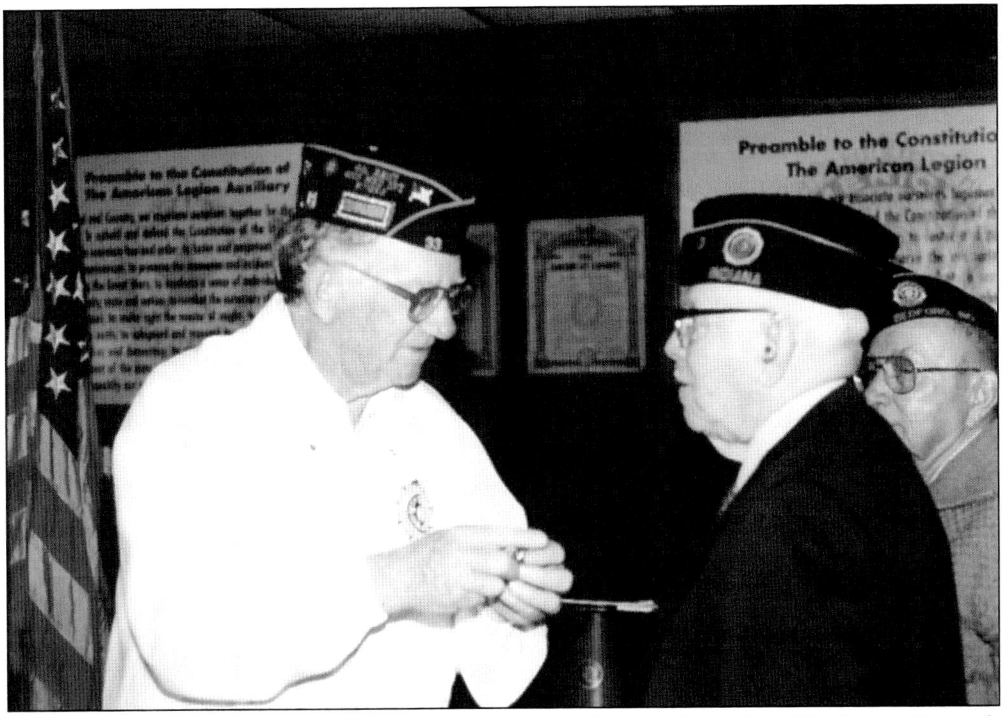

These World War II veterans, members of the American Legion Gillen Post No. 33, are Kenneth Plummer (left) and Wayne Anderson.

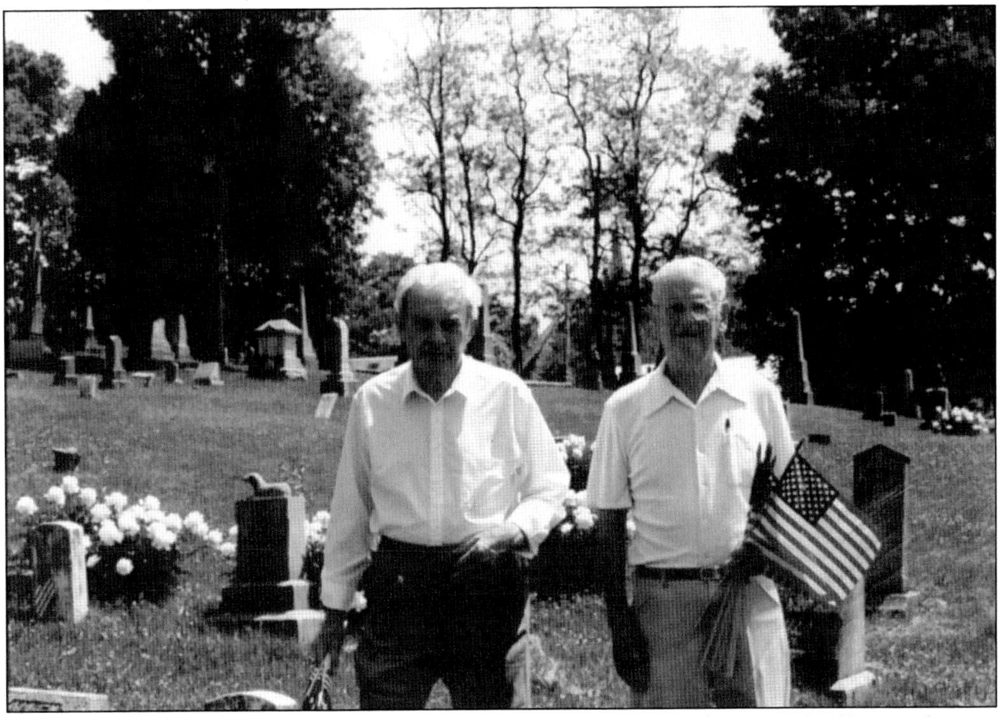

Every Memorial Day, American Legion members Bill Browning and Homer Girdley put flags on the graves of deceased soldiers in Green Hill Cemetery, until they also passed.